SPIRIT

VERSUS

SCALPEL

SPIRIT

VERSUS

SCALPEL

Traditional Healing and Modern Psychotherapy

Edited by Leonore Loeb Adler and B. Runi Mukherji

Forewords by Albert Pepitone and Uwe P. Gielen

BERGIN & GARVEY
Westport, Connecticut • London

Library of Congress Cataloging-in-Publication Data

Spirit verus scalpel : traditional healing and modern psychotherapy /
  edited by Leonore Loeb Adler and B. Runi Mukherji ; forewords by
  Albert Pepitone and Uwe P. Gielen.
      p.   cm.
    Includes bibliographical references and index.
    ISBN 0-89789-406-5 (alk. paper)
    1. Parapsychology and medicine. 2. Mental healing. 3. Holistic
  medicine. 4. Mind and body—Miscellanea.   I. Adler, Leonore Loeb.
  II. Mukherji, B. Runi.
  BF1045.M44S68   1995
  615.8'52—dc20   94-29715

British Library Cataloguing in Publication Data is available.

Library of Congress Catalog Card Number: 94-29715

ISBN: 0-89789-406-5

First published in 1995

Bergin & Garvey, 88 Post Road West, Westport, CT 06881
An imprint of Greenwood Publishing Group Inc.

Printed in the United States of America

The paper used in this book complies with the
Permanent Paper Standard issued by the National
Information Standards Organization (Z39.48-1984).

10 9 8 7 6 5 4 3 2 1

This book is dedicated to our future, to our pride and joy:
Romola and Basudev,
Beth, Derek, Lynnette, Annette, Harrison & Taylor.

Contents

Foreword

Albert Pepitone

Beliefs about health and illness have occupied the human mind and have driven behavior since our species evolved a consciousness of self and the capacity to communicate about life experiences. From such raw precultural beginnings, beliefs of remarkable variety have become a seminal part of world cultures (Murdock, 1980). In the last century and a half, much of this folk medicine has become transformed into modern, scientifically certified clinical practice, surgery, pharmaceuticals, and rules of health. Monthly, so it seems, we are informed about rediscoveries of ancient pro-health wonders among plants, fruits, trees, and vegetables. Thus, Queen Anne's lace and the pomegranate, believed by the Greeks to prevent pregnancy and abort fetuses, may turn out to do just what was claimed for them.[1] Garlic, cauliflower, and broccoli, long believed to be health promoters, are now impressing nutrition scientists who have isolated some of the beneficial ingredients. Indeed, broccoli contains *Sulphoraphane*, which has been shown to block the growth of the tumors induced in mice.[2] It is a mistake, however, to suppose that all such kinds of culturally constructed beliefs, discovered in ancient pharmacopoeia or orally passed down by generations of grandmothers, can, even in refined form, help with the diagnosis, prevention, or cure of disease. Probabilistically, if they were rigorously tested, most would not be found to be practically useful at all. Further, it should not be taken for granted that those beliefs that fail to make it are being replaced by useful ones as knowledge expands and defines what is legitimate medicine. Even in this celebrated age of science and technology, it cannot escape notice that numerous beliefs about fitness, disease prevention, treatments, and longevity make what can at best be judged as exaggerated claims. For every belief that lung cancer is caused by tobacco smoke, and that saturated fat is not good for the arteries, there are hundreds of beliefs about the curative powers of sulfur baths, copper bracelets, ginseng tea, apricot pits, ground rhino horns, Lydia Pinkham's tonic, and megavitamin therapies. Some of these false beliefs undoubtedly flourish where there is ignorance of modern medicine, due not only to cultural insularity, but to the inaccessibility of modern medicine, which is seen as a technoscience guild of expensive and priestly practitioners wholly removed from the illnesses of people. Nevertheless, despite their ubiquity and tenacity, cultural beliefs that falsely attribute illness and health to trees, weeds, metals, insects, poisons, and the like—in essence, to material things and processes—are potentially open to empirical analysis, and their effectiveness in respect to what is claimed for them can be assessed. If material beliefs refer to the tangible, the palpable, and the objectively identifiable, they can be validated against scientific and practical criteria. Moreover, there is a strong incentive to make such rigorous assessments; to verify, refine, and market the prescriptions of material beliefs about health and illness is a handsomely profitable enterprise. In the long term, then, as medical knowledge is diffused, a selection process will leave the world with fewer and fewer false material beliefs and be the healthier for it.

NONMATERIAL BELIEFS

Beliefs about health and illness that implicate the unseen, insubstantive, and inpalpable are quite another story.[3] Perhaps predating beliefs that material things and processes cause, prevent, and cure illnesses are beliefs that spiritual, metaphysical, transcendental, paranormal, and extraordinary powers, processes, agents, places, events, emanations, and energies do so, distally or proximately, exclusively or in combination with material factors. The objective existence of such nonmaterial variables is not ascertainable in the material terms by which science is understood; science, after all, denies nonmaterial reality and rules out of bounds such subject matter for scientific investigation. But, undeniably, people hold nonmaterial beliefs, and for many they are of central importance in defining the realities of their lives. It is a social scientific fact that far more people believe in some God or gods and some form of afterlife than do not. Most people, in fact, hold a variety of nonmaterial beliefs about health and illness, as well as those of the material kind, without any dissonance—they may believe that the evil eye has made the baby sick and believe that worms cause intestinal disease, that a guardian angel protects their health and that a vaccine prevents polio. The general question for analysis and research is: How do nonmaterial beliefs affect health and health-relevant behavior?

Common observation recognizes that the following beliefs in the nonmaterial class profoundly affect how the world, life events, and states of being are perceived and interpreted: the belief in God or gods and other spiritual beings, the belief in an impersonal power of fate, the belief in an extraordinary power of luck, the belief in chance (nonmaterial because typically the belief implies an abstract model of randomly interacting hypothetical elements), the belief in witchcraft and the evil eye, the belief in the power of personal will, and the belief in a transcendental moral law of justice.

The purpose in what follows is to indicate some familiar and not so familiar relations between a sample of these nonmaterial beliefs and health. The reader will notice many points of correspondence between these preliminary and programmatic comments and the more detailed chapters in this book.

SPIRITUAL BELIEFS

First and most obvious, the belief in God and other spiritual powers becomes salient when health and life are endangered by illness or injury. In such threatening circumstances, the belief in spiritual beings is expressed and communicated by prayer (to deities, saints, angels), and by acts of devotion, sacrifice, atonement, obedience to holy laws, good works, fasting, or vows of chastity, in the hope or expectation that health will be restored, illness prevented, and dangers to body and mind removed. "There are no atheists in foxholes" is the insightful observation of World War II GIs. The "activation" of religious beliefs in times of real danger was shown in a controlled field experiment by Broota and Shrimali (1988), who found that clinic patients awaiting major surgery (as medically classified) rated themselves as more religious and, specifically, stronger believers in God, than patients awaiting minor surgery and nonhospitalized comparable adults. However, the general question of whether and how faith—the hope and expectation of help from a spiritual agent—affects the susceptibility, course, and outcome of various illnesses is not now verifiably answerable despite the vast anecdotal and subjective testimony about the power of faith.

There is a more focused hope and expectation about spiritual assistance—indeed God's personal intervention—that may be influential in the restoration of health. Every year tens of thousands of the sick and physically disabled travel to sacred shrines, bathe in holy waters, touch holy objects, keep a vigil at sites where the Virgin has appeared—all seeking miracle relief and cures for their afflictions. To many believers, all cases of medically unexplained remission of tumors are indisputable markers of God's personal and hands-on involvement. Most claims to miracles, of course, are not authenticated by church authorities, but whatever their official status, the *belief* in miracles is as real as rain for many. The long- and short-term effects of the belief on health, however, are difficult to evaluate without controls—for example, those with the same affliction who believe in miracles but have not visited holy sites, those who do not believe in miracles—and without pre- and postmedical records with which to measure original conditions and change. Moreover, the detection of change—an improvement or deterioration in the particular medical condition for which relief was sought or in general health—wants further information on the mediating psychological and physiological processes.

It is a realistic estimate that, in the world at large, more people seek help more often from faith healers, shamans, and other varieties of holy men or women than from medical doctors. For one example, from everywhere else in the world, tens of thousands a year come to the Philippines for faith-based, sometimes knifeless, "psychic" surgery (Valentine, 1973). Here, the typical believer expects cures from the psychic energies from God to the surgeon and the organs being cut open. In another engagement of belief, evangelical preachers from certain sects confidently pronounce cures and bestow health on the crippled and otherwise afflicted people who come forth and affirm their faith in Jesus. In both examples, it is faith in a human agent who is believed to be a conduit of God's energies that underlies the expectation of a cure. However, the objective medical and psychological effects of the beliefs in healers and of the involvement in surgery and born-again experiences are not very well known.

For some believers, illness is not a physical condition at all but the symptom of a spiritual malaise. Restoration of health, therefore, is not a matter for physicians, but believed to require spiritual insight and repair. It is not surprising that such believers make few if any visits to doctors and hospitals, nor that, in general, members of certain religious sects and communities live healthier and longer lives. But is this a function of beliefs (e.g., in the spiritual nature of illness) or is it the healthful lifestyle, occupation, salubrious environment, or, perhaps, genetic selection?

What complicates matters is that the physical or psychological health effects of believing in God may depend on the kind of God believed in. In the population of believers, there are strikingly varied images. For some, God is believed to be wrathful and punitive against those who disobey His laws. Where the moral righteousness of God is the salient feature, the individual's self-evaluation is critical in health effects. In the simplest of cases, a sinner who has offended God cannot expect help or only help. How frequently and openly expressed is the belief that AIDS is God's punishment for the sin of homosexuality! The effects of guilt on the cure, prevention, and course of illness are thus rooted in the belief of God, but are highly contingent upon whether God in the particular instance is punitive or forgiving. We may note in passing that guilt or guilt anxiety was once a major dynamic underlying psychosomatic illness, to some degree documented in the case histories constructed in psychotherapy. However, in the past decade or more, perhaps due to changing societal norms, the role of guilt has been displaced by the almost monolithic focus on depression. From the point of view of isolating the psychological causes of illness, the subsumption of guilt, anxiety, and other distinctly identifiable emotions under the one rubric of depression is probably an obfuscation.

A special problem for the believer arises when the sufferer from illness or injury is led to contemplate the meaning of the experience—when, for example, he or she is the only victim among others perceived to have equal vulnerability, or when the illness or injury is symbolically related to the victim's past experience. The "Why me?" question is asked when the victim cannot blame self: "I was driving slowly and carefully," "I have taken excellent care of my health." Even God, who moves in mysterious ways and always has a purpose, cannot always be held responsible. "The Lord would never punish me like that; I am devoted to God and a good (Christian, Jew, Muslim, etc.)." If chance or bad luck are not tenable because what has happened seems so personally intended, the belief that the devil or other evil spirit emerges as the dominant cognition.

The beliefs in devil or spirit possession, corruption of the soul, and kindred processes are often directly manifested in alterations of bodily states in the form of trances, paralysis, skin disorders, blindness, and such, and thus have manifestly bad effects on health. One can raise here the reverse question: What are the effects on physical health of what the bedeviled individual believes to be exorcism or other mode of purging the devil's corruption of the soul?

SECULAR NONMATERIAL BELIEFS

The separation between spiritual and secular nonmaterial beliefs is not hard and fast, but is useful in putting light on an area that is relatively uncharted by contrast with religious beliefs, especially in modern societies.

Not at all unusual in our modern society and common in traditional, peasant, and tribal societies is the belief that an impersonal power, often connected with the transit of the stars, preordains one's destiny in life, including illnesses, injuries, escapes from life-threatening situations, and the manner and time of death. One health implication is immediately obvious: individuals who believe disease and death are prearranged are less likely to live healthier lives by modifying harmful lifestyle habits, and to seek medical attention when health problems arise. A frequent accompaniment to the belief in fate is resignation. "If I am to come down with a disease and to die only when my number is up, why bother with health practices and doctors?" or "What will be, will be; no one can do anything about it" are the expressions of those who believe their destiny is controlled by a mystical impersonal power. While some believers in fate tend to be passive about health and illness, others nervously look for signs—auspicious or ominous—to find out what fate has in store. Intuition tells us that there might be a third variation on the resignation theme: "Eat, drink, and be merry," presumably because the certainty of having a destiny already decided is psychologically equivalent to setting a date of departure. "It's over."

There are few documented effects on the susceptibility of fate-believers to illness, but a recent study reveals a remarkable disease-specific influence of the belief—more particularly, an influence on the speed with which a fated disease leads to death. In Chinese culture, one finds the belief that the year of one's birth, an indexical sign of astral movement, implies specific organ vulnerability, hence creating in the individual a susceptibility to certain diseases. Philips et al. (1993) examined the California death certificates of more than 28,000 Chinese and sorted them into two groups: those whose death was from a disease fated by their birth year and a sample equated on average age, sex proportion, year of death, and death from the same disease, but who were born in a year that does not preordain death from that disease. Focusing on the 15 leading causes of death, mostly various forms of cancer and cardiovascular diseases, these investigators found that in 12 of the 15 causes, those Chinese whose birth year fated the disease died significantly earlier than those in the control sample. The overall difference between groups (Stouffer test after the Bonferroni correction) is significant. Assuming there are no selective biases, how those fated persons felt or behaved differently from the controls, and how such differences affected their bodies so as to accelerate the disease process, are the next questions on the research agenda. As the authors suggest, the belief in an astrology-based power of fate that affects the course of a variety of lethal diseases strongly implicates general psychological states of resignation, hopelessness, and helplessness.

The belief that there is an extraordinary power of luck—good and bad—that affects life events is so common in so many parts of the world that we may suspect it is a universal belief. In general terms, this special power is beyond what we think of as ability, and its influence is beyond that which can be explained by will power. Further, though the two notions are often confused, the belief that a power of luck has affected an outcome (health or otherwise) means that the outcome is *not* due to chance; indeed, luck is believed to be the cause when the outcome is *against* the odds and thus beyond chance.[4] The belief in luck, good or bad, refers to an extraordinary sense of power within certain individuals that guides decisions and, not wholly predictably, influences outcomes, or to a vaguely identified external agent—the tooth fairy, elves, Lady Luck, which/who under propitious conditions—a lucky ring, hat, pen, sufficient earnestness—influences outcomes. Though luck is an extraordinary power that determines effects, it resembles chance in that the believer can never be certain that in any circumstance when needed the power will be there to help. "This is what gives luck its mystique, though some laboratory data show that luck can be certain enough to influence the riskiness of decisions" (Taylor, 1967). From common anecdotes, we learn that individuals who believe they are lucky tend to believe they lead "charmed" lives, and tend to be risk takers in gambling, work, and play. Consistent with such observations are reports that the belief in luck affects the practice of unsafe sex and hence the HIV infection rate.

On the other hand, because the odds are chronically against them, individuals who believe they are unlucky are likely to be prudent when faced with risks in these areas of life. It is not quite so simple, however. Unlucky types are wont to seek a change in their luck; despite their real or imagined history, many uncharacteristically undertake risks.

The believer in chance essentially has a model in mind in which multiple unrelated factors fortuitously combine to produce an effect. There is a large experimental literature that shows a sensitivity to objective probabilities. That is, if individuals have learned the concept of chance, their response to stimuli whose relative frequencies have been systematically prearranged tend on average to match the probabilities so built into the stimuli. In real-world settings, however, the believer in chance is less able to calculate probabilities and match responses with them. In the area of health, numerically definable probabilities rarely exist for laypersons. What also makes it hard for the chance believer is the essential property that there is nothing behind a chance disease or injury—not God, not bad luck, not the power of fate. Hence there is no sense of predictive control. The believer is often led to perceive that almost anything can happen, and that there is no way of telling when something in particular will happen. In the health domain, then, the believer in chance may more often be dealing with a large mass of uncertainty than with a matrix of calculable risks of illnesses and accidents. When the belief that health-relevant events can occur at random is infused with such uncertainty, it is easy to suppose that believers become chronically wary and hypersensitive to potential symptoms. Call it hypochondriasis, which, in moderation, is healthy!

It is hoped that this brief discussion will convey the strong need for research on belief systems and their effects on health. Since beliefs are items of culture and individual cognitions at the same time, an interdisciplinary approach is the best way to insure that integrative theories are developed on a cross-cultural data base.

Spirit Versus Scalpel provides an amazingly wide range of perspectives on the social psychology of health and illness, and enlarges our insights into the penetration of culture in our thinking and acting about health matters, particularly about the interplay of the material and the spiritual, the medical and the psychological. The reader will enjoy and be generously informed.

NOTES

1. *New York Times*, March 26, 1994.
2. Proceedings of The National Academy of Sciences, April 12, 1994.
3. Murdock's (1980) cross-cultural analysis of illnesses and cures is organized around four primary causal agents and powers: natural (including medical and biological causes; animistic (e.g., Gods and spirits), mystical (e.g., fate, pollution), and magical (witchcraft). There is some obvious overlap between Murdock's classification and our division of beliefs into material and nonmaterial, each of which is broken down further.
4. The psychological transition between luck and chance is elastic; it depends upon the outcome (e.g., the illness, the nature of the accident), and clearly upon the individual's personal experience.

REFERENCES

Broota, Krishan & Shrimali, Swasti (1988). Effects of surgical stress on belief in God and superstition. *Indian Journal of Personality and Clinical Studies, 2,* 135–138.

Murdock, George P. (1980). *Theories of illness: A world survey.* Pittsburgh: University of Pittsburgh Press.

Philips, David, Todd, Ruth & Wagner, Lisa (1993). Psychology and survival. *The Lancet, 342,* 1142–1145.

Taylor, Richard (1967). Habitual short term expectancies and luck. *Journal of General Psychology, 76,* 81–84.

Valentine, Tom (1973). *Psychic surgery.* Chicago: Regnery.

Foreword

Uwe P. Gielen

During the last decades, students of medicine, anthropology, sociology, and psychology have increasingly recognized that health and disease are the long-term outcomes of a complex process of biopsychosocial interactions. Although it is customary to distinguish between physical and mental health, this distinction is artificial in nature; it does not describe what happens to many patients who simultaneously suffer from physical and psychic distress.

In contrast to the modern division between body and mind, traditional notions of healing have always perceived the patient as inhabiting a unitary world of visible and invisible forces. In and around the patient's body, the battle rages between the forces of good and evil, health and sickness, growth and fragmentation. The traditional healer must simultaneously cure body and soul; otherwise, society will perceive him or her as a failure. The healer, variously called a shaman, medicine doctor, witch doctor, voodoo priest or priestess, oracle, *curandero*, or *espiritista*, enters the battle for the soul-mind-body of the patient with an armory of physical and spiritual weapons. It also helps if the healer succeeds in staging a highly dramatic performance, since traditional healing typically takes place in the presence of impressionable spectators. Healing does not merely consist of the recovery of physical strength and health but must also result in the reintegration of the patient into his or her social group. The medicine man or voodoo priestess is not only a psychotherapist but equally a transmitter of culture.

Conflicting social forces manifest themselves in the bodies of patient and healer, where they take on physical and symbolic forms. Both patient and healer experience these forces as ego-alien—that is, as forces not fully human in appearance and voice. The forces inhabit the bodies of practitioner and patient, where from the depths of the unconscious they erupt as evil spirits or "supernatural" voices of the gods.

Many of the chapters of this book describe these "supernatural" manifestations and their role in the healing process. Healing here means a process of psychic-physical-social reintegration, a process that I first observed in full detail in the shadows of the mighty Himalayas, traditionally one of the world's centers of shamanistic possession states and healing. In this book, Elan Golomb describes for us her quite similar experiences with the "oracles" of Ladakh (see Chapter 5).

During the early 1980s, I had the good fortune of finding myself among the Buddhist Ladakhis of Northwest India, a Tibetan culture in the Western Himalayas. Their culture includes a rich mixture of ancient healing practices, time-honored religious rituals, and modern allopathic medicine practiced by doctors trained in the big cities of India. In Ladakh, tradition and modernity coexist, sometimes in symbiosis and sometimes in opposition to each other.

It is not easy to convey to the modern, Western-educated reader the spiritual, social, and personal worlds that the Ladakhis have created for themselves. Always they feel themselves surrounded and at times penetrated by an array of invisible forces and beings, which may be benevolent, indifferent, or hostile to humans. It is always best to placate these beings, since otherwise they might possess a person or bring about illness and death. Persons with "small hearts" (anxious, shy, prone to neurotic problems) are especially likely to fall prey to attacks by "demons" and "angry gods"—an observation in good agreement with the findings of modern psychology.

Along the dimension of time, the Ladakhis see themselves connected to their past and future reincarnations through the relentless workings of karma. The iron law of karma states that all moral and immoral actions have inevitable aftereffects in one's present existence or in one's future lives. The theory of karma helps the Ladakhis understand their fate, their illnesses, and their long periods of happiness. According to this view, illness is not simply caused by malfunctioning or damaged organs. Instead, illness points to a lack of harmony between body, speech, and mind, and between the patient and his or her visible and invisible environments. States of health or distress in the physical organism, in the moral-spiritual realm of karma, and in the social body complement each other. Consequently, healing, medicine, and religion are closely linked, even inseparable in nature. The successful healer must be a pious person, and the theologically schooled *rinpoche* (abbot) is by virtue of his training also a healer. As such, he must know how to battle the forces of fragmentation at the physical, social, and spiritual levels and how to restore the unity of body, mind, and social organism. Traditional healing in Ladakh and elsewhere is almost always holistic in character. Traditional healers heal not merely through competent diagnosis and prescription, but also by the sheer force of their personality. Is not modern psychotherapy based upon the same principle?

The majority of Ladakh's patients are women; as in Western societies more women than men visit spiritual advisers (therapists) and doctors. The stresses and strains that Ladakhi womanhood is heir to do not differ substantially from those prevailing in most other societies, although the more extreme forms of violence are absent in peaceful Ladakh. The stresses include marital tensions, psychological abuse by spouses, death of loved ones, infertility, querulous in-laws, recalcitrant or wayward children, poverty, and the evil eyes of envious neighbors. Ladakhi women respond to these experiences with a combination of physical and psychological symptoms that include various bodily aches, problems of digestion, "weakness of the heart," sleep disturbances, states of hysteria and psychic dissociation, and tears.

As the patient enters the path of hope and despair in her search for inner peace, better health, and social integration, she can choose among many different types of healers: the village-based *lhamo* or *lhapo* (oracle or shaman), the traditional Tibetan doctor called *amchi*, the *önpo* or astrologer who casts horoscopes and thus practices primary prevention, the Western-trained paramedic and army doctor, and the high-ranking *rinpoche* who looks after the spiritual welfare of his flock. In one way or another, these healers and religious specialists help Ladakhi patients deal with the disappointments and tensions of everyday life, typically prescribing dietary changes, herbal medicines, prayer, and pilgrimages for their clients. In the main, the healers are "emotional troubleshooters."

Although traditional Ladakhis are steeped in religion, this does not mean that they attribute all or even most illnesses to the influence of supernatural beings and forces. Instead, they engage in considerable "healer shopping." Their experience proves to them that no healer is successful all the time, but all healers are successful some of the time. They ask, Are not some healers best at combatting evil spirits while others prescribe the more potent medicine? Is it not wise to go to both modern and traditional healers since the modern ones may have the more powerful drugs while the traditional ones provide better understanding and exude greater spiritual power?

Readers of this book will encounter many parallels between the conceptions of healing just described and the notions of healing that are delineated in fascinating detail by the various contributors to this book. Everywhere, successful healers must learn to speak the psychological/spiritual/cultural language of their patients; they must enter the patients' minds through a process of empathy and become sensitive to the emotional preoccupations that accompany their physical illnesses. They must evoke in the patients a sense of faith, hope, and trust in the healer's power.

Bridges are needed to cross the chasm between the mechanistic world-view governing the training of modern doctors and the holistic spiritual-psychological-social belief systems endorsed by many of their patients. This is as true in the huge, impersonal hospitals of New York City as in the small ill-equipped army hospital in the small town of Leh, Ladakh.

What better way is there to learn about the broad similarities and intricate cultural variations of healing practices than to study this volume? Above all, the chapter authors teach us to take a broad, cross-culturally and historically oriented perspective on traditional and modern healing practices. It is one of the many strengths of this volume that its contributors and editors have been diligent in their search for unity in the midst of diversity while exploring diversity within unity. In contrast, the theories of many other psychologists and social scientists mirror and reinforce the increasing fragmentation of American culture by exaggerating culture and gender-specific experiences. They claim that women and men from diverse cultural backgrounds inhabit entirely different mental and emotional worlds. For instance, cultural psychologists such as Kenneth Gergen and Girishwar Misra have postulated that the different psychocultures of the world are incommensurable and that the modern self is fragmented in a historically unprecedented way.

The contributors to this volume tend to shy away from such exaggerated claims while celebrating the diversity and richness of human experience around the globe. They do not lose sight of the fact that healers everywhere must follow the same general principles of healing if they are to be successful within their unique cultural niches.

Leonore Loeb Adler and B. Runi Mukherji are to be congratulated for compiling for this book such a fine collection of chapters describing ancient and modern ways of healing. Perhaps, one day, our modern notions will catch up with the intuitive wisdom of the past while adding scientific rigor and detail to it. The skills of the modern surgeon are indeed impressive, but surgery and antibiotics alone cannot heal many of the ailments that plague humankind. There will always be a place in healing for wisdom and compassion. Wisdom and compassion, it turns out, are precisely those two virtues that the Tibetan Buddhists of Ladakh have stressed over the centuries. For the healer these virtues will always be in season.

Introduction

Leonore Loeb Adler and B. Runi Mukherji

Spirit Versus Scalpel: Traditional Healing and Modern Psychotherapy is a unique presentation of traditional and modern healing and mental health practices. This book provides information about the concept of healing from a variety of cultural perspectives and traditions of healing in a number of different cultural contexts. *Spirit Versus Scalpel* also explores the application of these cultural perspectives in modern psychotherapeutic and health care settings.

Since the early 1980s we have seen a literal explosion of data that support the idea that states of mind have consistent and demonstrable effects on physical health. And while the effect may not be as dramatic as "thinking positive thoughts" as a cure for cancer, certainly there has accumulated significant evidence that mind/body approaches can reduce the severity and frequency of a wide variety of symptoms. Within our own culture, especially in the area of behavioral medicine, there is a growing awareness in health care settings of the need to take into account the relationship of mental states in physical illness and wellness.

This book explores the concept of illness/wellness and healing from a cross-cultural perspective. Part I: Concepts of Healing examines the broad concept of disease and treatment from historical and cultural points of view. Chapter 1 begins with the historical background. Starting with traditional societies of hunters/gatherers, then going to agricultural societies, the techniques of the healers on several continents are discussed. The thrust of Helmut E. Adler and Leonore Loeb Adler's discourse is tracing the development of medicine from the classical Greeks as the first professional

physicians to modern psychoneuroimmunology. The discussion includes
some of the latest thoughts, which suggest that stress is associated with
immunosuppression. It underscores the fact that the influence of the emotions and other mental processes on bodily functions was widely accepted
in ancient times. It has been only recently with the work of Hans Selye,
Arnold Allan Lazarus, Robert Adler, and others in the field of psychoneuroimmunology that the Western medical establishment has again begun to
acknowledge the intimate relationship of mental or cognitive factors in the
disease process.

Chapter 2 broadens the discussion from the individual to the cultural
context within which disease and intervention, the patient, and the practitioner are embedded. Author John Beatty points out that different cultures
have different cultural presuppositions, or deeply embedded values, beliefs,
and attitudes about concepts such as life and death and about the nature
of causality. These cultural presuppositions clearly influence the role and
status of the healer or medical practitioner as well as the nature of what is
deemed appropriate intervention. The close connection between life and
death in various societies is explored and related by Beatty. He admonishes
that in many multicultural communities the medical profession has to develop a sensitivity with regard to the patients' cultural background.

Chapter 3 again visits cultural presuppositions, but this time from an eth-
nosemantic approach, analyzing phrases used by Chinese patients in a clinical setting, attempting to describe their physical and psychological states.
Since successful communication depends upon a shared set of background
assumptions, Chapter 3 points to the problem inherent in the diagnosis of illness given that cultural presuppositions affect the interpretation of utter-
ances used in describing the symptoms. In this chapter several aspects of
communication are elaborated, specifically the expressions of external and
internal perspectives, as for example found in the Chinese-language data. Edward H. Bendix feels that successful communication in the medical setting
depends crucially on shared, unspoken background assumptions for interpreting what is actually uttered.

Part II: Healers and Their Methods from Around the Globe focuses on
some diverse traditional healing procedures on different continents. The
seven chapters that explore healing traditions across the world include
South Africa, Sri Lanka, India, Ladakh, Puerto Rico and the U.S. mainland,
Mexico, and Alaska. While these healing systems are distinct, and each one
evolved from a unique set of amalgamations of diverse religious and folk
traditions, there are striking similarities that emerge from them, pointing
to a commonality of human belief and experience. In all of them, the disease process is seen as an invasion of hostile forces and the healing is ef-
fected by the person who is a medium through which powerful benign
forces act. In Ladakh, this person is called an *oracle*, in South Africa it is
a *diviner*, in Sri Lanka it is a *kapurala*, and in Puerto Rico and Mexico it

is an *Espiritista*. In all of them, there is the powerful symbol of whiteness, the *Mesa blanca*, the white scarf presented to the healer before treatment, the white ash used to coat the patient's body; the use of herbs and medicinal salve or concoctions for the treatment of physical symptoms; and the "cleansing" rituals with oils, chants, and prayers. These are obvious similarities, but at the common core all systems of traditional healing see the disease process as fragmentation or dislocation of the person from their social, psychological and physical context. In Chapter 9, Spires-Robin and McGarrahan state that the disturbances have to be addressed if the patient is to be healed; Louw and Pretorius in Chapter 4 comment that satisfactory healing involves both recovery from bodily symptoms, as well as social and psychological integration of the patient into his or her community.

There is a key difference between traditional healing and modern medicine, in that all systems of traditional healing are "holistic." Indeed, the very word "healing" has its roots in Middle English *helens* and in Anglo-Saxon *haelan*, to make whole, from the root *hal*, which means whole. The focus of the modern Western medical tradition is curing, the removal of the cause of the disease or the cessation of symptoms. Traditional healing might involve curing but does not require it. This paradox is well described in Chapter 5. A woman had gone to the *rinpoche* (a Ladakhi monk) to treat her headaches. She was told that her *lhato* (small spirit altar) was not getting enough attention. When she heard this explanation, her headaches remained, but the pressure on her shoulders lessened. His analysis gave her something she could deal with.

Chapter 4 is presented by Dap A. Louw and Engela Pretorius and deals with the traditional healers of South Africa and then compares their methods with those of modern, Western psychotherapy and counseling.

A real insight is provided in Chapter 5, which describes the healing sessions with the oracles in Ladakh. Elan Golomb describes some of the oracles' procedures in a fascinating narrative, giving her personal impressions and experiences.

In a different vein, Chapter 6 by Nihar Ranjan Mrinal, Uma Singhal Mrinal, and B. Runi Mukherji introduces the traditional Indian healing practices to the reader for an interesting comparison with the other chapters. For instance, Sri Lanka has a variety of options available so that individuals can select the healer or doctor they have most confidence in to arrive at better health. In addition the choices include traditional as well as modern Western treatment.

Chapter 7 co-authors Suneetha S. de Silva and Willie J. Epps say that "Spirit faces Scalpel."

However, the discourse of Chapter 8 is mainly based on the recollections of author Angela Jorge's conversations with her grandmother, who was a practicing *Espiritista* and followed the traditional *Mesa blanca*.

Chapter 9 focuses on spiritualism as it is practiced in Mexico, as part of a religious sect. Coauthors Regina Spires-Robin and Peggy McGarrahan present and explain the worship and healing of Mexican spiritualism in an informative and scientific manner that has been thoroughly researched.

Last, but by no means least, in this section is Margaret Fischer's Chapter 10 on Alaskan shamanism. Her literary and descriptive discourse sets the mood and stage for introducing the shaman's activities and styles.

Part III: Treatment and Training is concerned with different approaches to healing in the modern community. "Restructuring" of the problem, which enables the patient to better cope, discusses the cognitive restructuring at the heart of process-oriented therapies like Cognitive Behavioral Therapy and Rational-Emotive Therapy (RET). The chapters in the third section look to the ways in which modern health care must take into account the cultural contexts of patients in assessment of illness, the types of appropriate intervention, and in the training of healthcare practitioners.

Chapter 11 by Mitchell W. Robin and Raymond DiGiuseppe is a good introduction to Rational-Emotive Therapy. While Dr. Albert Ellis developed RET some 35 years ago, the significance of this chapter is the cross-cultural and cross-ethnic endorsement of the Attitude and Belief Scale II. The authors base their conclusions on research that found "support for Ellis' hypothesis that people who endorse irrational beliefs have a greater tendency to suffer from both emotional and personal disturbance."

Quite another approach to psychotherapy is used by C. Edward Robins in Chapter 12. He presents a case study that is psychoanalytically analyzed. Robins based his theoretical reflections on the conceptions of Sigmund Freud and Jacques Lacan, and offers his conclusion of the value of psychoanalysis as a therapy.

Quite a different theme is offered by Charles V. Callahan in Chapter 13. He uses the "go-between," the referral agent, who helps the patient or client find a practitioner or therapist, skilled in the appropriate and successful treatment.

Diana Chen tackles a very important topic in Chapter 14. An outgrowth of cross-cultural research, cultural relativism is a pertinent notion with regard to mental health support systems. In current multicultural communities the concept of the "melting pot" is no longer valid; instead it was replaced by the acceptance of the "salad bowl," where each group adheres to their own traditional customs, while adjusting or accepting some of the manners of the majority population within the society. Chen describes the traditional stigma toward mental health issues. This chapter shows great insight into the problems confronting Chinese Americans, who, due to their recent immigration to the United States or other Western countries, are faced with many problems, leading eventually toward some degrees of acculturation. Her suggestion is for improved bilingual mental health and community services, in addition to "developing a new model of combining native healing methods with mainstream psychiatric practices."

In Chapter 15 Lisa Whitten broaches the topic of including the role of culture when teaching health care to future practitioners. She offers many useful suggestions to implement the important role of culture in the curriculum at various levels.

There is a growing awareness in this country for the necessity of changing the nature of health care, and while much of the national debate has focused on the need for reform in the way in which health care providers are organized and reimbursed, a rapidly growing number of laypeople, practitioners, and health care professionals have embraced methodologies and practices that come from traditional systems of healing.

In his Foreword to *The Healer Within* (Locke & Colligan, 1986) Norman Cousins wrote: "Less is known and taught about the healing system than about any of the other internal forces that govern human existence." It is hoped that this book is not only thought-provoking, but also instigates a new focus that includes traditional culture into modern health care and psychotherapy that will result in Spirit *and* Scalpel: Traditional Healing *and* Modern Psychotherapy.

REFERENCE

Cousins, Norman (1986). Foreword. In Steven Locke and Douglas Colligan, *The Healer Within*. New York: Penguin USA (Formerly E. P. Dutton).

Part I

Concepts of Healing

From Hippocrates to Psychoneuroimmunology: Medicine as Art and Science

Helmut E. Adler and Leonore Loeb Adler

Throughout human history, whenever a person fell ill it was natural to seek help from an expert to discover the cause of the disease. The healer then proceeded to treatment, based on an analysis of the case. The source of the illness might be attributed to natural or supernatural causes. Since there had to be causation, it was logical to conclude, in the absence of a natural cause, that the disease was due to sorcery or to transgression against the gods. If followed, again, that the healer, who would be best qualified, was a person who was closely in touch with supernatural forces—a priest or a magician, able to counteract the evil forces.

In very underdeveloped societies, such as hunter/gatherers, little specialization is found. Healers practice magic and provide protection based on the special supernatural powers they are able to summon. Kiev (1964) cites the Australian Murugin and the Cheyenne Indians as examples. In the next stage of development in fishing/hunting societies, where labor is more divided, preparation for healers is more elaborate and their prestige consequently is also increased. The Eskimo shaman, for example, must experience a trance, undergo physical ordeals, and observe special taboos in order to qualify (Kiev, 1964). In agricultural societies still more knowledge is required, but again, this correlates with increased prestige and remuneration. Healers must know herbs and special medicinal techniques. The Ashanti of West Africa require a three-year training period; the obeah man of the West Indies occupies an institutionalized position (Kiev, 1964).

In European history, in the absence of scientific knowledge, medicine also had to rely on suggestion, intuition, tradition, and some superstition, in the period between the breakdown of ancient civilization and the Enlightenment. With the rise of "scientific" medicine, psychiatry, and psychology, these theories and practices were discounted as merely "superstitions." But the increasing understanding of the psychological factors in disease, psychophysiology, psychoendocrinology, and psychoneuroimmunology validate some of these so-called nonscientific practices. And in some respects, this brings us back to the beginnings of professional medicine, to the classical Greece of Pericles, Anaxagoras, Thucydides, Phidias, Sophocles, Euripides, Aristophanes, and Socrates, when Hippocrates was the first professional physician.

Hippocrates, like the Greeks of his time, believed in the mutual influence of mind and body. He taught that mental illness was a consequence of brain disease. His well-known humoral theory of temperament, later extended by Galen, provided for a physiological basis of personality. He also claimed that purely emotional states may produce bodily changes. In modern terms, Hippocrates (and his followers) may be credited with a theory of neurological, endocrinological, and psychophysiological causation of normal and pathological psychological function. (Plato liked Hippocrates' view of the importance of the brain, but Aristotle and most other philosophers preferred the heart as the seat of mental and emotional processes. Therefore, paradoxically, Plato, the idealist, proposed the study of the brain, which Aristotle, the empiricist, who advocated the study of mental life not of humans only but of animals and plants as well, relegated the brain to the role of cooling the hot vapors that arose from the heart [Zilboorg & Henry, 1941].)

In the early days the first requisites of a physician were to relieve suffering and to fight against death. Physiology and anatomy came much later. In the absence of a scientific foundation, physicians created an imaginary basis, which served well as long as the world accepted their explanations. These ideas were modified according to advancing knowledge and novel, but not necessarily correct, systems of causation. Included among these were, at various times, astrological influences, spirit possession, witchcraft, and the notion that epidemics were sent by God to punish humanity.

The most important influence, after Hippocrates, was Galen (ca. 130–200 C.E.), who was born in Pergamon, in Asia Minor, studied in Alexandria, and lived and worked for most of his life in Rome. He followed Hippocrates in his teaching, but where Hippocrates would have been satisfied with observing phenomena, without explaining them, Galen theorized about the origin and course of disease. He followed Aristotle in his philosophy and thus took an empirical point of view. In his day, he was the most famous of physicians and his influence extended throughout the medieval period (Cumston, 1968).

During the Roman period, most medicine was practiced by Greeks and other foreigners. Many were slaves and freed slaves. Women were also found as physicians and pharmacists. During the decline of Western civilization, after the fall of Rome, Arab physicians kept Greek knowledge alive. They translated Greek texts into Arabic and thus saved many of them for posterity. They followed mainly Hippocrates and Galen and their students. Jewish scholars were active in the Islamic world and contributed to medical knowledge, as well as translating Greek medical literature into Hebrew or Arabic. Maimonides (1135–1204), a native of Spain, practiced in Morocco and Egypt, and was highly regarded as a physician, as well as for his scholarship. Rhazes (d. 923), another Jewish physician, recognized that fever was not a disease, but nature working to heal a disease. He was also the first to distinguish between smallpox, measles, and scarlet fever. The most famous of Arab physicians was the Persian Avicenna (latinized from Ibn Sina [980–1037]). His *Canon* became the medical bible of the Middle Ages. Other prominent Islamic physicians were Abulcasis, Avenzoar, and Geber, the latter primarily an alchemist (Cumston, 1968).

Western medicine gradually emerged from a long dark period with the founding of the first medical schools in Salerno, Italy, and Montpellier, France. Constantine, the African, was instrumental in initiating the study of medicine in Salerno. He had been born in Carthage about 1015 and after traveling in Islamic countries, settled in Salerno, where he greatly influenced the study of medicine, although he himself resided at Monte Cassino, the famous monastery not far away. Salerno had a number of female physicians, of which the most famous was Trotula. She wrote on diseases of women, labor, childbirth, and infant care, but also on other medical topics such as epilepsy, diseases of the eyes and the ears, as well as on the teeth and gums. There is, however, some controversy whether she really existed (Singer & Singer, 1968). Salerno's importance derived from its confluence of Greek, Latin, Arab, and Jewish influences, to bring together all the knowledge available at the time (Cumston, 1968; Singer & Singer, 1968).

Montpellier rivaled Salerno for students. Although it received its official statute only on August 17, 1220, its faculty of medicine had predated this event by many years. Montpellier physicians quarreled with graduates of the School of Paris in the seventeenth century. Parliament solemnly declared that one must be a doctor of the Faculty of Medicine of Paris in order to practice medicine in that city. Despite this decision, there were always some physicians of Montpellier attached to the court. King Louis XIV founded two chairs at Montpellier. François Rabelais, famous author and satirist, took his M.D. degree at Montpellier.

During the sixteenth century there was a great interest in esoteric philosophies, the kabala, alchemy, and astrology in relation to medicine. The great Michael Nostradamus was an M.D. from Montpellier. The high points of this period were the ideas of Paracelsus, actually Theophrastus Bombast von Hohenheim, born in Einsiedeln, Switzerland, in 1493. He was professor of illness (pathos) from the stress created by resisting it (ponos). It was Cannon (1929) who showed how stress of an emotional nature could cause physiological disturbances in autonomic nervous system function and thus originate a disease process. Hans Selye's (1976) well-known General Adaptation Syndrome, going through stages of alarm, resistance, and exhaustion, added the role of adrenocortical steroids in psychological and subsequent reactions. This approach is probably too general. More recent work suggests some physiological specificity to particular kinds of stressful events (Mason, 1974 cited by Taylor, 1990).

Stress is considered to play the key role in the psychological etiology of disease, and, on the other hand, the adjustment to stress, the coping behavior of the individual, is considered a major factor in recovery from illness. Evidence for the damaging role of stress comes from many quarters. Physiological causation can be traced to neurophysiological, endocrinological, and immunological sources. There have been some claims of particular personality structures as predisposing individuals to various diseases, including heart attacks, infectious mononucleosis, streptococcal infections, dental caries, and juvenile diabetes (Ader, 1981). The findings are not at all clear, however, unless we know the mechanism by which psychological causes contribute to the etiology of a given disease. With respect to cancer, B. H. Fox (1981, p. 103) puts it: "Personality factors affect the probability of a person getting cancer, but they do so both damagingly and protectively. The contribution of personality factors to cancer incidence is probably relatively small. The effect, where it exists, is specific to certain organ sites."

The relatively vulnerability of individuals to stress-induced disease is very variable. At one time a differentiation between intense, competitive type A personalities and laid-back, easy going type B individuals was thought to relate to heart-disease-prone personality type A and less-susceptible type B (Friedman & Rosenman, 1959). However, careful meta-analysis of 101 studies conducted between 1945 and 1984 did not find a definite link between specific diseases and specific personality traits, although a general negative style—marked by depression, anxiety, and hostility—may well be associated with a broad range of diseases, including coronary heart disease as well as asthma, headache, ulcers, and arthritis (Friedman & Booth-Kewley, 1987).

Stress-induced disorders have been recognized by the Diagnostic and Statistical Manual (DSM-III-R). For example, posttraumatic stress disorder, known as "shell-shock" in World War I and "battle fatigue" in World War II, was noticed as consequence of industrial accidents as early as 1882 (it was thought to be due to damage of the spinal cord), and has been widely studied. Vietnam veterans showed it, so did concentration camp survivors (Cohen, 1953). Three Mile Island disaster local residents showed raised levels of catecholamines in urine samples, a sign of long-term stress (Baum,

Gatchel & Schaeffer, 1983). Animal studies agree. Cynomolgus monkeys are subject to coronary heart disease. When stressed by keeping them in unstable social groups, they showed greater levels of atherosclerosis and susceptibility to heart disease.

A recent addition to the role of neural and endocrine factors in disease processes has been the recognition of the influence of the immune system. Robert Ader (1981) has coined the term "psychoneuroimmunology" for this factor in disease etiology. The immune system is today recognized as a complex interacting system that recognizes and deals with attacks on the body's integrity. Two major types of lymphocytes are involved. The T-cells are agents of cell-mediated immunity. They include helper, suppressor, and cytotoxic cells. B-cells are agents of humoral immunity. Their task is antibody production and destruction of viruses and cancer cells by so-called killer cells. In addition, there are monocytes, including scavenging macrophages and granulocytes.

I. P. Pavlov and his students knew about the immune system in the 1920s. Metal'nikov and Chovine in 1926 demonstrated conditioning of the immune reaction in guinea pigs. Many studies followed. Interest in the United States grew only in the work of Neal Miller (1969). J. Garcia had used taste aversion conditioning in rats as a very effective technique, pairing a sweetened drinking solution with the injection lithium chloride, a powerful noxious agent. Serendipitously, when pairing cyclophosphamide, a powerful immunosuppressant with saccharin, the rats died during extinction trials, when only saccharin was given. The immunosuppression of cyclophosphamide had become conditioned to the sweetened solution (Ader and Cohen, 1981).

Psychoneuroimmunology suggests that stress is associated with immunosuppression. It may be the corticosteroids released by stress that suppress the immune response. It has been shown that every-day stressors, such as medical school exams, sleep deprivation, loneliness, and depression affected the immune system, reduced T-cells, suppressed the production of interferon, and reduced DNA repair. Long-term stress such as care given to family members with Alzheimer's disease and residents close to Three Mile Island also demonstrated reduced immune function (Gatchel et al., 1987).

In recent years the spread of the HIV virus has taken on the proportions of an epidemic. The virus, by attacking the immune system, causes Acquired Immune Deficiency Syndrome (AIDS). The breakdown of the immune system puts the patient at risk for the invasion of opportunistic bacteria and other pathogens, causing illness that ultimately will kill the individual. Stress and depression predict the course of immune changes among HIV-infected men (Patterson et al., 1993).

Any treatment that reduces stress is linked to the lessening of the negative consequences of stress and thus to improvement of health in many cases. Cognitive factor can play a major role in this process. The perception of control over stressors, real or imagined, inoculates against stress. Learned helplessness is less damaging if the subject believes control is possible (Taylor, 1990).

In nontraditional healing techniques, the stressful interpretation of disease as uncontrolled, unpredictable, and unavoidable is replaced by procedures and interpretations that allow patients to become optimistic, helpful, and better able to cope with their symptoms. Coping with stress depends more on matching coping strategies with the beliefs of the subject than the type of coping adapted (Taylor, 1990).

Among medical practitioners, this factor is known as the placebo effect. In health psychology (Krantz et al., 1985) it is called coping. Relaxation, guided imagery, and meditation have been found to be helpful (Burish and Bradley, 1983). Perception of self-efficacy (Bandura, 1986) aids also in the relief of symptoms. In cross-cultural perspective, modern medicine has stressed germs and viruses, the Chinese have the imbalance of Yin and Yang, and the inhabitants of the Caribbean, spells and amulets. By fitting the belief system to the local culture, each of them may control or alleviate disease by activating the positive effects of cognitive factors in healing.

REFERENCES

Ader, R. (Ed.) (1981). *Psychoneuroimmunology*. New York: Academic Press.

Ader, R. & Cohen, N. (1981). Conditional immuno-pharmacologic responses. In R. Ader (Ed.), *Psychoneuroimmunology* (pp. 281–319). New York: Academic Press.

Alexander, F. (1950). *Psychosomatic Medicine*. New York: Norton.

Bandura, A. (1986). Fearful expectations and avoidant actions as coeffects of perceived self-inefficacy. *American Psychologist, 41,* 1389–1391.

Baum, A., Gatchel, R. J. & Schaeffer, M. A. (1983). Emotional, behavioral, and physiological effects of chronic stress at Three Mile Island. *Journal of Consulting and Clinical Psychology, 51,* 565–572.

Bolles, R. C. (1993). *The story of psychology*. Pacific Grove, CA: Brooks/Cole.

Burish, T. G. & Bradley, L. A. (1983). *Coping with chronic disease: Research and applications*. New York: Academic Press.

Cannon, W. B. (1929). *Bodily changes in pain, hunger, fear and rage*. Boston: Branford.

Cohen, E. A. (1953). *Human behavior in the concentration camp*. New York: Norton.

Cumston, C. G. (1968). *An introduction to the history of medicine*. London: Dawson's of Pall Mall.

Dunbar, F. (1943). *Psychosomatic diagnosis*. New York: Harper.

Fox, B. H. (1981). Psychosocial factors and the immune system in human cancer. In R. Ader (Ed.), *Psychoneuroimmunology* (pp. 103–157). New York: Academic Press.

Friedman, H. S. & Booth-Kewley, S. (1987). The "disease prone personality": A meta-analytical view of the construct. *American Psychologist, 42,* 539–555.

Friedman, M. & Rosenman, R. H. (1959). Association of specific overt behavior pattern with blood and cardiovascular findings. *Journal of the American Medical Association, 169,* 1286–1296.

Gatchel, R. J., Baum, A. & Krantz, D. S. (1987). *An introduction to health psychology* (2nd ed.). New York: Random House.

Gentry, J. H. & Matarazzo, J. D. (1981). Medical psychology: Three decades of growth and development. In L. A. Bradley and C. K. Prokop (Eds.), *Medical psychology: Contributions to behavioral medicine.* New York: Academic Press.

Kiev, A. (Ed.) (1964). *Magic, faith, and healing: Studies in primitive psychiatry today.* Glencoe, IL: Free Press.

Krantz, D. S., Grunberg, N. E. & Baum, A. (1985). Health psychology. *Annual Review of Psychology, 36,* 349–383.

Mason, J. W. (1974). Specificity in the organization of neuro-endocrine response profiles. In P. Seeman and G. M. Brown (Eds.), *Frontiers in neurology and neuroscience research: First international symposium of the Neuroscience Institute.* Toronto: University of Toronto.

Matarazzo, J. D. (1980). Behavioral health and behavioral medicine: Frontiers for a new health psychology. *American Psychologist, 35,* 807–817.

Matarazzo, J. D., Weiss, S. M., Herd, J. A., Miller, N. E. & Weiss, S. M. (Eds.) (1984). *Behavioral health: A handbook of health enhancement and disease prevention.* New York: Wiley.

Melamed, B. G. (1986). Special issue on child health psychology. *Health Psychology, 5,* 3.

Miller, N. E. (1969). Learning of visceral and glandular responses. *Science, 163,* 434–445.

———. (1983). Behavioral medicine: Symbiosis between laboratory and clinic. *Annual Review of Psychology, 34,* 1–31.

Patterson, T. L., Semple, S. J., Temoshook, L. R., McCutchan, J. A., Atkinson, J. H., Straits-Troster, K. A. & Grant, I. (1993). Stress and depression predict immune change among HIV infected men. Poster at American Psychological Convention, Toronto, August 20, 1993.

Plant, S. M. & Friedman, S. B. (1981). Psychosocial factors in infectious disease. In R. Ader (Ed.), *Psychoneuroimmunology* (pp. 3–30). New York: Academic Press.

Rodin, J. & Salovey, P. (1989). Health psychology. *Annual Review of Psychology, 40,* 533–579.

Selye, H. (1976). *The stress of life* (2nd ed.). New York: McGraw-Hill.

Singer, C. & Singer, D. (1968). The origin of the medical school of Salerno, the first university. In C. Singer and H. E. Sigerist (Eds.), *Essays on the history of medicine.* Freeport, N.Y.: Books for Library Press. (First published in 1924.)

Taylor, S. E. (1990). Health psychology: The science and the field. *American Psychologist, 45,* 40–50.

Zilboorg, G. & Henry, G. W. (1941). *A history of medical psychology.* New York: Norton.

Cultural Perceptions of Life and Death

Baron Victor von Frankenstein (a.k.a. John Beatty)

The role of culture in human society is all-pervasive. Although there are many definitions of culture, ranging from shared learned behavior to integrated symbolic systems, basically all of them include the values, attitudes, and beliefs of a people.

It has been said that humans are unique in their ability to symbolize. "All animals eat, but only humans dine" has been used to indicate the fact that no matter how basic and biological something may be, it is always caught up in that network of symbols we sometimes call culture. It doesn't matter whether it is eating or having sex—culture will modify and symbolize those events. Life and death and the nature of these two concepts appear to be of interest to all cultures. Every horror film fan will notice that the interest in the relationship between the two is well known in such films as *Frankenstein* and *Dracula*, and of course the famous "book" *Secrets of Life and Death* (which I have paraphrased in my title). Hence it should not surprise us to find that life, death, and related concepts will be found in various societies, differently integrated.

Basic belief systems are found in all human societies, although the actual beliefs vary from place to place and time to time. Whether a cultural pattern allows for a belief, for example, in many gods or in just one is a function of both time and place.

More importantly, culture is an integrated system. That is to say that the beliefs in the system are tied in to other beliefs in a system. Anthropologists have shown that there are regular correlates in the social structure with certain kinds of economic activity and so forth. As a result, it is not enough to note that different perceptions exist, but that they are integrated into the system differently. Life and death therefore may be conceived of differently in various societies and they will be integrated differently. The nature of death, the causes of death, the prevention of death will be seen differently because of the individual nature of the concepts and the various ways in which the integration of these concepts occurs in each society.

Culture has even greater problems in store for us. Far more sophisticated problems arise when dealing cross-culturally. Each society contains certain beliefs or postulates—often referred to as "cultural presuppositions"—that are deeply rooted in the culture. Cultural presuppositions are those beliefs held by people in a culture that are given little if any thought. This leads to two peculiar problems. The first deals with the nature of intercultural interaction. When people from different cultures meet, their cultural presuppositions may be quite different. As a result they may easily misunderstand one another. The second problem stems from the fact that when Westerners look at other cultures, their own cultural presuppositions interfere not only in what they see, but how they analyze what they see. Francis Hsu (1973) has discussed in some detail the nature of the problem of prejudicial judgment in science, especially anthropology.

It is really difficult to hold that the people in one culture believe that all people in the world share their cultural presuppositions, since for most people they are so deeply rooted in the belief system that they are probably, if ever, thought about overtly. For example, U.S. Americans rarely if ever consider that everyone in the world believes there are only two genders or thinks about the possibility that there might be more than just two genders—male and female. It is a general cultural presupposition in the United States that there are two and only two. Some evidence suggested by some Native American societies leads us to suspect that some cultures perceive more than two genders. Hence dealing with a person from such a society would likely lead to problems in this area, since neither would have considered the possibility that one society sees several genders while the other sees only two. The idea of cultural presuppositions is particularly important here when one understands the enormous variation possible in the perception of people (both physically and spiritually), the nature of life and death, and the nature of life after death.

These cultural presuppositions often have far-reaching consequences. This is crucial in understanding peoples' attitudes about many things. During the Vietnam War, a newsreel showing Vietnamese grieving at a funeral had a sound track in which the narrator pontificated that although many people say the Vietnamese feel differently about life, these scenes seem to argue to the contrary. The problem, of course, is that the writers simply perceived the funeral activities from the point of view of their own culture. It is rare that people are happy in general when someone dies, although cultural beliefs do have an impact on this as well. In the United States, it is not unusual for someone to say that "it is better this way" when a person dies after a long painful illness. Some Christians are willing to see death as God calling back one of his children, and hence the person who died is now "home," free from the "troubles of the world." Many cultures have dance as a part of their religion. By and large Christianity is not danced. General dancing (as opposed to theatrical dancing) is generally seen as "happy," hence funeral dances could easily be misunderstood.

Although it is clear that many peoples of the world find life an unpleasant experience and death an experience that frees the individual from worldly cares, I can find no society that openly advocates everyone dying as soon as possible. The very existence of medical practitioners in all cultures seems to argue for the idea that one ought to live and make an effort to do so.

On a very elementary and limited level, one need look only to beliefs about what is lucky and what is not to see the way some aspects of a culture that seem unconnected with life and death suddenly become quite connected. Most cultures, if not all, hold that some things are lucky or bring good fortune. Specifically what these are varies from culture to culture. United States Americans, by and large, hold that 13 is an unlucky number. The most common reason being given is that there were 13 people at the Last Supper (Christ and 12 apostles). This clearly is not universal— not everyone is Christian—and also indicates the way in which, in this case, an unlucky number is tied to a religious system.

Japan, on the other hand, regards the number 4 as being unlucky. Many buildings in Japan, including and especially hospitals, which have more than four floors, have no floor called the fourth floor.

Unlike the West where the number taboo is related to religion, the Japanese taboo is related to a verbal problem. The word *shi* in Japanese means both "four" and "death." Hence it is considered unwise to put patients in a hospital on a floor called "death." In a similar manner, the Japanese often avoid the use of the number 9 because it is homophonous with the word meaning "torment." In one town in Japan, there are eight garages, dutifully numbered 1 to 10 with the numbers 4 and 9 properly omitted.

Such linguistic problems can be seen in most, if not all, cultures. It is held that the Hospital for Incurable Diseases changed its name in order to be able to raise funds. People in the United States were apparently unable to bring themselves to give money to diseases that could not be cured.

This is, of course, one of the simpler levels at which the concepts within a culture have an effect on the rest of culture, and in this case on certain somewhat minor aspects of the health field. Things can and do get more complex. Once the holistic nature of culture has been identified, it becomes impossible to see concepts of life and death as distinct or detached from all other aspects of the culture. One need only to consider the effect it would have on the definition of something like homosexuality if a culture defined four or more "sexes." If two of the sexes were labeled "male" and two "female" in English, English speakers could clearly label as "homo-sexual" relationships that were "heterosexual" in the other culture.

One can not discuss the nature of life and death without at least a nod in the direction of such cultural variables as the cultural perceptions of the nature and cause of illness and attempts to cure it. The role of medical practitioners, for example, is seen differently in different cultures. This does not mean only whether the medical practitioner has status that is higher or lower than other people, but how the entire role is seen relative to the patient.

One Native American shaman (the technical term for a medical practi-tioner, whose ability to cure is involved with both knowledge of medicines and a strong contact with the supernatural as well), reports becoming ex-tremely upset because the patient's family had laid out the payment before the rituals involving the curing were completed. This implied to him that the act of curing was regarded as financial, rather than seeing the curing act as something that he does. Payment from the family is in the form of a gift and gifts have to be seen as symbolically different from a payment in the form of fee.

The fact that many people from other cultures have rather psychological ties to the shaman and prefer to be treated by such a person (not unlike U.S. Americans' desire to be treated by their own physicians) often com-plicates the delivery of health care in this country among Native Americans, who feel far more comfortable being treated by a practitioner of native medicine than a Western physician. In many parts of the world it has be-come apparent that having a shaman work with Western physicians as well as with the patients is a much more beneficial approach (see, for example, Lambo, 1978). The American Indian Community House in New York City attempted to develop an alcohol treatment project that would invoke tra-ditional healers and traditional values along with some Western ones. In many ways the Western physician's approach is seen as being cold, rather disinterested, and clinical compared to "traditional" ways of doctoring, which involve much communal support in terms of group rituals and the appearance not only of an "attending physician" but an "attending per-sonal support group" as well, both in terms of the spirits and the com-munity.

Lest it be thought that the Western physician is needed to supply the native one with the proper medical expertise, it should be noted immedi-ately that the West has borrowed extensively from the medical knowledge of other cultures. Each culture has its own worldview and in these cases two opinions are as valid as in the West, only in the kinds of cases discussed above, having at least one opinion from the native viewpoint is clearly a must. In many instances the actual chemicals used for cures come from other cultures, although explanations for cures do not. Several Chinese acupuncturists have asserted that Western physicians accept that acupuncture works, but that the reasons it works are unknown. The Chinese, of course, feel that the reasons are known. They have to do with too much *yin* and *yang*. This kind of explanation is unacceptable in Western medicine and hence the reason remains "unknown."

Certainly in those cases where illness results from some violation of cultural norms, it is virtually impossible for an outsider to know what things are likely to be upsetting, or how to coax such information out of the patient, or what might be needed to bring about a cure. One need only look at some of the numerous examples of "culturally specific" illnesses—such as "running *amok*" (Langness, 1965; Newman, 1964); "*windigo* psychosis" among certain sub-Arctic Indians (Bishop, 1975; Fogelson, 1965; Teicher, 1960); Arctic hysteria among the Yakut and Tungus in Siberia (Czaplicka, 1914); *pibloktog* (Foulks, 1972; Gussow, 1960; Wallace, 1972) and Kayak *angst* (Freuchen, 1935; Gussow, 1963; Honigman & Honigman, 1965) in Greenlanders; *Koro* (Hsein, 1963, 1965; Yap, 1963, 1965); *Pa Ling* (Kiev, 1972; Yap, 1951) and *Hsieh-ping* (Wittkower & Fried, 1957) both in China; *Saka* in Kenya (Harris, 1957); *Latah* in Mongolia and Southeast Asia (Aberle, 1961; Van Loon, 1926); *Imu* among the Ainu of Japan (Winiarz & Wielawski, 1936); or deaths related to Australian aboriginal bone pointing, sorcery, or the more recent work by Wade Davis (1985) on Haitian zombies—to realize that an understanding of a culture is crucial to the understanding of illness in that culture.

At this point we are examining the ethnography of doctoring. That is to say, we have been examining the role of the physician in different societies. The problems involved are far greater when we come to the situation of doctoring in an intercultural situation—that is, one in which the physician comes from one background and the patient another (as frequently happens in many of the world's cities today). It is quickly realized that examining doctoring in intercultural situations is even more complex than when both physician and patient are from the same cultural background. Not only are there likely to be different cultural presuppositions about the nature of the causes of illness and death, but also different perceptions of the medical practitioner, the methods involved in cures, and the nature of prevention. The fact that there are physicians in all societies is not to imply that no society approves of suicide or even of what we would call murder. Clearly many do and many require it under specific circumstance. The Japanese have several kinds of ritual suicides such as *seppuku* (*hara kiri*) and *shinjuu* (a complex form of either multiple suicide or suicide and murder); India has had acceptable forms of suicide; suicide among several Native American tribes has been studied as well (e.g., Fenton, 1941; Devereaux, 1961), and the famous line attributed to Crazy Horse—"Today is a good day to die" (Armstrong, 1971, p. 103)—indicates something about willingness to sacrifice one's own life. Even the West holds "greater love hath no man than to lay down his life for his friend" (John 15.13).

In addition there are the various relationships between human sacrifice and death. In many cases death is not just human but tied to larger concepts such as death and rebirth of the earth or even the entire universe. Human sacrifice as practiced by some of the Central American Indians, notably Aztec and Maya, clearly associates human death with complex theological and philosophical notions about the universe (see, for example, Spencer & Jennings, 1977 or Davies, 1981). What I am arguing here is that all societies make an attempt to avoid death as a general rule.

The conceptions of life and death and the related concepts dealing with the afterlife, souls, and the like that change and ultimately affect one's perception of the nature of life and death vary dramatically from one society to another. Dying may in some cultures be seen as an evil and the culture may struggle mightily to keep people alive—often even as vegetables—while others see life as a kind of necessary evil. This kind of heroic effort to keep people alive in Western culture has fallen under some scrutiny as limited resources become taxed. For example, with a limited supply of blood, how much should one allocate to terminally ill patients who are certain to die when others who need it might not get it? At more lofty levels are the questions about allocating financial resources to different illness.

The question raised here is not only how one perceives life and death in different cultures but how that perception affects other aspects of the culture and how one analyzes the events. Suicide, for example, is discussed by many writers (most notably Durkheim, 1963). Consider, however, the problem of simply identifying the act itself. Many Native Americans themselves have noted that a surprisingly high number of Native Americans go out drinking, get drunk, and walk home. They pass out on train tracks or a highway and are killed by passing trains or cars. This has been powerfully discussed theatrically in Hanay Geiogomah's (1980) "Body Indian." Are these simply accidents or are they suicides? Similarly a number of Mohawks have been killed in car accidents. The men, who are often involved in the highly dangerous job of constructing high-rise steel-framed buildings, manage the long drive from New York City to Caughnawaga (now Kahnawake) just outside of Montreal. After dropping off their pay with their families, they manage to get killed in a traffic accident. Some Mohawks have overtly stated that if you can't have control over your life, you can at least have it over your death.

A number of writers have examined Native American suicides (Fenton, 1941; Devereaux, 1961; and Margolin as quoted by Lorenz, 1963). The major difficulty in the latter source is the interpretation of the data. Konrad Lorenz's interpretation has been challenged (Beatty, 1969) in that Lorenz's explanation comes from a kind of presupposition rather than from the data itself. Rather than restate that argument, consider the following as a way of examining the relationships between specifics acts and the perceptions of the causes of those acts.

A cultural complex exists among Kiowa-Apaches that will indicate something of the problem. Kiowa-Apaches traditionally believe that brothers are the only people in the world you can ever really trust. In addition, there is a kind of illness among the Kiowa-Apaches known as "ghost sickness." This ailment often manifests itself as a form of paralysis, which afflicts a person who has seen a ghost. Interestingly enough, the ghost most commonly feared by the Kiowa-Apaches is one's brother's ghost. Some rather psychoanalytically oriented people have held that this is actually nothing more than a problem in sibling rivalry. Since the Kiowa-Apaches are obliged to repress any hostility toward their brothers in their lifetime, the death of a brother allows for a kind of release. The living brother who has repressed his hostility to his brother now fears his brother's hostility toward him. Hence this ghost is most likely to attack (and kill). Morris Opler and William Bittle (1961) point out that ghosts of relatives come to conduct the dying to the afterworld, and the least violent act a ghost can do is to lead a new "shade" to the afterworld. Hence there is a great deal of tension surrounding the dead, which is associated with name taboos and the showing of grief. The affiliation of the dead with the living is clear.

Of course things are never quite that simple. The Kiowa-Apaches differentiate spirits that do not take part in earthy affairs but live in a "heaven" of abundance and pleasure. Ghosts on the other hand are something different. There appear to be two kinds associated with individuals. Neither is in the newborn child and good people have little of it at death. Opler and Bittle hold that it is perhaps easiest to conceptualize it as "the evil tendencies, powers and impulses that accumulate during life." However, ethnographic reports show that brothers actually joke rather roughly with one another and roughhouse a good deal. Hence there is ample opportunity for hostility to express itself in rather ritualized ways.

If instead we analyze the situation so that the appearance of the deceased brother's ghost is likely to cause the living brother to die so they can again be together, then the danger is caused not by repressed hostility but overt closeness. The danger is not strictly in the dying, but the damage that is done to the living and the loss of a responsible member of both the family and society.

The Kiowa-Apaches are not above expressing grief over death. Ethel Tobach (1969) has wisely pointed out that grief (in general, not simply among the Kiowa-Apaches) is the recognition that a social bond is permanently broken (a situation she maintains is possible only among humans). Nonetheless, death itself is seen as a necessity by many of the Apache.

It is the relationships between the concepts of life, death, afterlife, and the supernatural that are most likely to have an effect on the way the health care is seen and delivered. The perception and integration of concepts concerning the very nature of causality, or the flow of life into death is likely to have enormous ramifications in this area. Keith Basso (1970) reports that Apaches, for example, regard death as a normal part of life, but, additionally, they feel that if no one died, no one could be born. That is, in a highly stressed ecological system the number of people, animals, and such is quite limited, hence there is a limited number of people who could possibly exist at any time. If people didn't die, there wouldn't be space for others being born. The result is that there isn't a particular interest in "keeping people alive."

Not long ago the Puppet Center at Brooklyn College in New York was preparing a set of puppet shows based on stories from other cultures. Among them was a story called "Perez and Martina" from Puerto Rico. In this story a cockroach finds some money which she decides to use for makeup to make herself attractive to possible suitors. Many different animals come and are attracted to her, and she finally decides to marry Perez— a rodent. After the marriage she prepares a large kettle of food, which Perez falls into and dies. The story ends with her bemoaning his death.

The story puzzled many of the people working in the Puppet Center and an attempt was made to find out what the story might mean. Although scholarly works mentioned its distribution as odd (India and Puerto Rico), and some mentioned the fact that the various animals have rather different voices, which allow the narrator to demonstrate great verbal skills, none of the works seemed interested in what the story meant.

Interviews with a number of Puerto Ricans (including academicians) frequently held that the story meant nothing. It was occasionally likened to "Rockabye baby on the tree top" in the sense that it was felt that that had no meaning either. While there is no doubt that analyses can be made from many theoretical viewpoints, starting with the fact that both protagonists are "pests" that compete for food with humans, the most common analytic statements made by those interviewed dealt with the nature of death as seen by Puerto Ricans. They claimed that the story, if anything, indicated that death is very much a part of the life cycle, and that people accept it as such. It was felt that this was a major difference between Puerto Rican culture and the surrounding "Anglo" culture. Although it is hard to pin down exactly what the difference between the two cultures' perception of life and death are, it is clear that many of the people interviewed felt that there was in fact a difference in the perception of life and death.

Japanese conceptions of life and death are tied not only to a Buddhist interpretation of the world, complete with reincarnation, but also with a complex question of the nature of causality. The idea of a kind of random element is common in Japanese interpretation of events. Two examples will give some idea of how this appears in the culture.

It is reported that a Japanese soldier threw a hand grenade into a building where there were a number of people, killing several and wounding others. When he was asked why he killed the people, he replied he hadn't, the hand grenade had.

A second example deals with the Japanese unhappiness with domestication of animals and their preference in hunting rather than domestication. (Native Americans from the Plains share this attitude with the Japanese, although it is not clear that it is from the same cause.) In Japan, at least a part of the argument is based on concepts of life and death—or perhaps more specifically about ways of dying.

Japanese belief does not like to deal in certain ways with predestination. Americans tend to contrast predestination with free will and the concepts involved tend to apply only to humans. Free will is of less interest than a kind of chance occurrence. In the hand grenade episode, there is a serious problem concerning the cause of the killing. For the Japanese who threw the grenade, he did not do the killing. Even U.S. Americans would probably agree that at the most elementary surface level this is true. The actual deaths were caused by shrapnel entering the bodies of the individuals. U.S. Americans, of course, do not stop there. It is, to a degree, like arguing that the man who shoots the gun does not actually do the killing, the bullet does. The Japanese, of course, would recognize the same next step—that is, the man who throws the grenade has some responsibility. However, at a higher level, the Japanese continue to ask what brought that person, in that mental state, to that place at that time, as well as what brought the victims there as well. This kind of questioning is occasionally seen in the United States and is left as an imponderable. When an "innocent" victim is shot in a shoot-out between two drug dealers, we may ask ourselves "why that person?" but the questioning rarely goes further and there seems to be no general philosophical answer pursued. The Japanese, on the other hand, are far more accepting of this kind of event and use these random events in a general philosophy. This is made clearer in the hunting example.

The Japanese feel that in hunting, the factors that bring the hunter to the animal are partially the skill of the hunter, but partially the randomness of the universe. Why that animal was in that spot when the hunter arrived, and why that hunter was able (or unable) to take the animal at that time are all clearly part of a randomness in the universe (rather than God's unknowable reasons—that is, it is all part of some vast unknowable scheme). The animal from birth has a chance to escape and live and die without ever being taken by a hunter.

To some degree in Japan this allows for acts of self-sacrifice. Buddha in a previous existence is said to have once met a lioness and a cub who were starving. Rather than let the animals kill him for food, Buddha threw himself from a cliff and thereby allowed the animals to have their food without taking his life. This self-sacrificial act has relevance to Buddha's later reincarnation at a still higher level.

Similarly, animals, which are believed to have souls, are seen as being able to "evolve" up the Buddhist "evolutionary hierarchy" through such self-sacrificial acts as well. All around Japan, for example, there are plaques devoted to whales that have beached themselves, thereby supplying food to a local village that was in difficulty.

In one sense this is particularly significant because whale meat in Japan is seen as "fish"—that is, the cultural classification of the animals is not in line with the Western evolutionary one. (Nor, it should be added at once, is the popular version of the concept of animals vis-a-vis the scientific one. "Insects" are often not held to be "animals" by many U.S. Americans. "Animal" in common English tends to refer to "mammals.") The ground rules for the classification of animals is rather different in various societies as well. In a sense, a whale's self-sacrifice is dramatic since it is a "lower" form of life, being a "fish." To argue that the Western classification system is correct and the Japanese are wrong or naive is to miss the point that the grounds for classifying are cultural, in both Japan and the West.

It is also interesting to note that Takahashi (1988) has pointed out that Japanese dieticians consider the foods for school lunches rather differently than Western dieticians. Japanese dieticians hold that the meals should not only be nutritious, but should be used to make points about the nature of Japanese food both nationally and regionally. Hence the lunchroom experience is also partly classroom, in which dietary principles are tied to local and national customs. The dietary aspect here is especially relevant because of the importance of nutrition in health. What cultures regard as food or what they will or will not eat is also important to our understanding of the kinds of health care delivered to the population.

Ed Karanja (1990) has pointed out that among Kikuyu in Kenya the change from life to death is simply another developmental step, not unlike going from adolescence to adult status. Interactions between the living and the dead continue, but the sharply defined line between life and death that is found in Western culture is not there in Kikuyu.

Similarly Victor Turner (1967) has argued that among the Ndembu, masks often are half male and half female or half human and half animal or half living and half inanimate. This fusion of what appear to be opposites in the West is regarded quite differently among the Ndembu, in that the principles that distinguish one from the other are not so sharp. The world appears to be more of a continuum than a set of compartmentalized boxes.

Thus the opinions and beliefs about all aspects of the nature of life and death can have far-reaching consequences for any culture. These ultimately can be shown to affect the way a given population feels about the function of medicine, the delivery of health care, the ways in which treatments are administered and so on.

In today's shrinking world with people of many cultures living together in single nations, the members of the medical profession clearly need to develop a sensitivity about the ways in which they deal with people in treating their illnesses as well as the overall concern about the nature of health care in the society. There is a need to understand that other cultures see the world differently than do Westerners and that the differences are not so much right and wrong ways of seeing the world, but simply different perspectives on the world.

REFERENCES

Aberle, D. F. (1961). "Arctic hysteria" and Latah in Mongolia. In Y. A. Cohen (Ed.), *Social structure and personality: A case book* (pp. 471–475). New York: Holt, Rinehart and Winston.

Armstrong, Virginia Irving (Compiler) (1971). *I have spoken American history through the voices of the indians.* Athens, OH: Swallow Press.

Basso, Keith H. (1970). *The Cibecue Apache.* New York: Holt, Rinehart and Winston.

Beatty, John (1969). Taking issue with Lorenz on the Ute. In M. F. Ashley Montagu (Ed.), *Man and aggression.* New York: Oxford University Press.

Bishop, Charles A. (1975). Northern Algonkin cannibalism and Windigo psychosis. In Thomas R. Williams (Ed.), *Psychological anthropology.* The Hague: Mouton.

Czaplicka, M. A. (1914). *Aboriginal Siberia: A study in social anthropology.* Oxford: Clarendon.

Davies, Nigel (1981). *Human sacrifice.* New York: Dorsett Press.

Davis, Wade (1985). *Serpent and the rainbow.* New York: Simon and Schuster.

Devereaux, George (1961). Mohave ethnopsychiatry and suicide: The psychiatric knowledge and the psychic disturbances of an indian tribe. Bureau of American Ethnology, no. 175. Washington, DC: U.S. Government Printing Office.

Durkheim, Emile (1963). *Suicide.* Glencoe, IL: The Free Press.

Fenton, William N. (1941). Iroquois suicide: A study in the stability of a culture pattern. Anthropological paper no. 14, *Bureau of American Ethnology Bulletin,* 128. Washington, DC: U.S. Government Printing Office.

Fogelson, Raymond D. (1965). Psychological theories of Windigo "psychosis" and a preliminary application of a models approach. In Melford E. Spiro (Ed.), *Context and meaning in cultural anthropology.* New York: Free Press.

Foulks, E. F. (1972). The Arctic hysterias of the north Eskimo." In Maybury-Lewis (Ed.), *Anthropological Studies.* Washington, DC: American Anthropological Association.

Freuchen, Peter (1935). *Arctic adventure.* New York: Farrar and Rinehart.

Geiogamah, Hanay (1980). Body indian. In *New Native American drama: Three plays by Geiogamah.* Norman: University of Oklahoma Press.

Gussow, Z. (1960). Pibloktoq (hysteria) among the Polar Eskimo: An ethnopsychiatric study. In W. Muensterberger and S. Alexrad (Eds.), *The Psychoanalytic Studies of Society.* New York: International University.

——— (1963). A preliminary report of Kayak-Angst among the Eskimo of West Greenland: A study in sensory deprivation. *International Journal of Social Psychiatry,* 9, 18–26.

Harris, G. (1957). Possession "Hysteria" in a Kenya tribe. *American Anthropologist,* (1), 117–135.

Honigman, J. J. & Honigman, I. (1965). *Eskimo Townsmen*. Ottawa: University of Ottawa.

Hsein, R. (1963). A consideration on Chinese concepts of illness and case illustrations. *Transcultural Psychiatry Research*, 15, 23–30.

——— (1965). A study of the aetiology of Koro in respect to the Chinese concepts of illness. *International Journal of Social Psychiatry*, 11, 7–13.

Hsu, Francis H. K. (1973). Prejudice and its intellectual effect in American anthropology: An ethnographic report. *American Anthropologist*, 75 (1).

Karanja, Ed (1990). Personal communication.

Kiev, A. (1972). *Transcultural psychiatry*. New York: Macmillan.

Lambo, Thomas Adeoye (1978). Psychotherapy in Africa. *Human Nature Magazine* (March).

Langness, L. L. (1965). Hysterical psychosis in the New Guinea highlands: A Bena Bena example. *Psychiatry*, 28, 258–277.

Lorenz, Konrad (1963). *On aggression*. New York: Harcourt, Brace and World.

Newman, P. L. (1964). Wild man behavior in a New Guinea highlands community. *American Anthropologist*, 66, 1–19.

Opler, Morris & Bittle, William E. (1961). The death practices and eschatology of the Kiowa Apache. *Southwestern Journal of Anthropology*, 17, 383–394.

Spencer, Robert F. & Jennings, Jesse D. et al. (1977). *The Native Americans*. New York: Harper and Row.

Takahashi, Junichi (1988). *Women's tales of whaling*. Tokyo: JWA.

Teicher, Morton I. (1960). *Windigo psychosis. A study of the relationships between belief and behavior among the indians of northeastern Canada*. Proceedings of the American Ethnological Society, Seattle.

Tobach, Ethel (1969). The comparative psychology of grief. In Bernard B. Schoenberg, Arthur Carr, David Peretz and Austin H. Kutscher (Eds.), *Loss and grief: Psychological management in medical practice*. New York: Columbia University Press.

Turner, Victor (1967). *The forest of symbols*. Ithaca, NY: Cornell University Press.

Van Loon, F.H.G. (1926). "Amok and Latah." *Journal of Abnormal and Social Psychology*, 21, 434–444.

Wallace, A.F.C. (1972). Mental illness, biology and culture. In F.H.K. Hsu (Ed.), *Psychological anthropology* (pp. 363–402). Cambridge, MA: Shenkman.

Winiarz, W. & Wielawski, J. (1936). Imu—a psychoneurosis occurring among the Ainus. *Psychoanalytical Review*.

Wittkower, E. & Fried, J. (1957). "A cross-cultural approach to mental health problems." *American Journal of Psychiatry*, 116, 423–428.

Yap, P. M. (1951). Mental illness peculiar to certain cultures: A survey of comparative psychiatry. *Journal of Mental Science*.

——— (1963). "Koro or Suk-Yeong—an atypical culture-bound psychogenic disorder found in southern Chinese." *Transcultural Psychiatric Research*.

——— (1965). "Koro: A culture-bound depersonalization syndrome." *British Journal of Psychiatry*, 111, 43–50.

Unspoken Assumptions in Communicating about Inner States: Chinese External Versus Internal

Edward H. Bendix

This chapter is concerned with a pervasive distinction between external and internal perspectives on states of the person found in Chinese speakers' comments regarding expressions referring to such states.[1] A further concern is with inter- and intracultural variation (Garro, 1986; Weller, 1984; Pelto and Pelto, 1975) in conceptions of the inner person, how such differences in background knowledge may affect communication, and, in particular, what the implications are for cross-cultural communication in mental health settings.

Quite frequently Chinese speakers consulted in connection with a research project on illness concepts spontaneously distinguish expressions of the kind we will look at in terms of external descriptions of someone else versus internal descriptions of oneself. There are no explicit linguistic elements, such as special morphemes, in these expressions to mark them as external or internal, and Americans looking at translation equivalents of these expressions do not exhibit this theme of classifying them for such a distinction. In addition to providing such translation equivalents, bilingual Chinese will often offer somewhat looser translations in which they add one of the English verbs "looks" or "feels" (i.e., external or internal), although the original Chinese expressions do not contain the equivalents of these English verbs.

The theme is encapsulated in the Chinese compound noun expression "outside-inside," which one bilingual dictionary translates as "(i) the outside and the inside; one's outward show and inner thoughts [what we might call in other terms 'public and private']; (ii) (Chin. med.) exterior and interior." This is item (1) in Figure 3.1.

Figure 3.1
List of Expressions in English and Chinese

(1) outside-inside: "(i) the outside and the inside; one's outward show and inner thoughts; (ii) (Chin. med.) exterior and interior"; biao3 li3 / biu2 leui5

(2) not comfortable: "not comfortable; unwell"; bu4 shu1 fu2 / m4 xu1 fug6

(3) essence-spirit wrong/poor: "looks lousy, no vitality; low spirit"; jing1 shen2 cha1 / jing1 san4 caa1

(4) essence-spirit not good: "looks lousy, no vitality; feel (one's) spirits low, in low spirits"; jing1 shen2 bu4 hao3 / jing1 san4 m4 hou2

(5) (I) feel; (wo3) jue2 de . . . / (ngo5) gog3 dag1 . . .

(6) essence-spirit problem: "mental problem, psychological problem"; jing1 shen2 wen4 ti2 / jing1 san4 man6 tai4

(7) essence-spirit illness: "mental illness"; jing1 shen2 bing4 / jing1 san4 beng6

(8) essence-spirit-on get-not-arrive full-enough: "spiritually (be) not satisfied"; jing1 shen2 shang4 de0 bu4 dao4 man3 zu2 / jing1 san4 seung6 dag1 m4 dou2 mun5 zug1

(9) not enough essence-spirit: "in weak spirits, not energetic enough"; bu4 gou4 jing1 shen2 / m4 gao3 jing1 san4

(10) essence-spirit not enough: "not enough vitality"; jing1 shen2 bu4 gou4 / jing1 san4 m4 gao3

(11) collapse-lose: "depressed, dejected, dispirited"; tui2 sang4 / teui4 song3

(12) no essence strikes color: "listless, no desire to do anything"; mei2 (wu2) jing1 da3 cai3 / mou4 jing1 daa2 coi2

(13) no spirit no energy: "one looks tired and listless"; * / mou5 san4 mou5 hei3

(14) pickup-not-raise power: "can't raise (one's) power; don't feel like doing anything"; ti2 bu4 qi3 jing4 / tai4 m4 hei2 ging6

(15) pickup-not-raise essence-spirit: "can't raise (one's) spirit; don't feel like doing anything"; ti2 bu4 qi3 jing1 shen2 / tai4 m4 hei2 jing1 san4

(16) bowed-head lose-energy: "(looks) miserable, disappointed"; chui2 tou2 sang4 qi4 / seui4 tao4 song3 hei3

(17) no heart-think (heart-motor): "lack of motivation; no desire to do anything"; mei2 xin1 si1 / mou5 sam1 gei1

(18) feeling-state low-drop: "in low spirits; mood very low"; qing2 xu4 di1 luo4 / qing4 seui5 dai1 log6

(19) heart-feeling not good: "bad mood, moody, not happy"; xin1 qing2 bu4 jia1 / sam1 qing4 bad1 gaai1

(20) heart-feeling not open-clear: "bad mood"; xin1 qing2 bu4 kai1 lang3 / sam1 qing4 m4 hoi1 long5

(21) essence-spirit not quick: "depression, moody"; jing1 shen2 bu4 kuai4 / jing1 san4 bad1 faai3

(22) chest closed; xiong1 men4 / hung1 mun6

Figure 3.1 (continued)

(23) closed-closed not happy: "depressed, in low spirits"; men4 men4 bu4 le4 / mun6 mun6 bad1 log6

(24) develop closed-energy: "be sulky"; sheng1 men4 qi4 / *

(25) gloomy-gloomy not happy: "depressed, melancholy, joyless"; yu4 yu4 bu4 le4 / wad1 wad1 bad1 log6

(1)　　表里

(2)　不（唔）舒服

(3)　精神差

(4)　精神不（唔）好

(5)　（我）觉得…

(6)　精神問題

(7)　精神病

(8)　精神上得不（唔）到满足

(9)　不（唔）夠精神

(10)　精神不（唔）夠

(11)　頹喪

(12)　沒（無）精打彩

(13)　有神有氣

(14)　提不（唔）起劲

(15)　提不（唔）起精神

(16)　垂頭喪氣

(17)　沒心思，（有心机）

(18)　情绪低落

(19)　心情不佳

(20)　心情不（唔）开朗

(21)　精神不快

(22)　胸悶

(23)　悶悶不樂

(24)　生悶氣

(25)　鬱鬱不樂

Each item in Figure 3.1 starts off with a rough morpheme-by-morpheme gloss of the expression that, in this discussion, will be used as a mnemonic identifier for English-speaking readers, for which purpose the transliteration of the Chinese expression would not serve so well. Although suggestive, the roughness of the gloss should remind the reader that it is not a translation and that our focus on variation in people's understanding of an expression is incompatible with offering an authoritative translation. Following this identifier are one or more translations that have been offered by bilinguals. After the translations comes the Pinyin Romanization of the Mandarin form of the expression followed by a slash and one style of Romanization of the Cantonese form. The Cantonese forms are given since most of the expressions were originally collected in Cantonese. An asterisk marks absence of an equivalent expression in Mandarin or Cantonese. For those who read Chinese, the items are also given in characters. Where a Cantonese word (or whole expression) is not a cognate of the Mandarin equivalent, the Cantonese character is given in parentheses after the Mandarin.

I will use the word "meaning" in the general sense to avoid the technical semantic and pragmatic discussion, which really is necessary but goes beyond the scope of this chapter.

We must first consider the issue of reference. For the domain of expressions we are discussing, there is the general problem for the hearer of interpreting what the speaker is referring to when talking about an internally experienced state. Here there are no concrete, physical objects that both speaker and hearer can see and of which they can thus have a more clearly shared perception. For example, if you say item (2) in Figure 3.1, that you (or some part of you) are "not comfortable," I have to take your word for it that you are indeed referring to some inner constituent variable of a person, of which we may share a common conception, such that one of its values can be the state "not comfortable." My acceptance of this presupposition is logically prior to my acceptance of the truth of your assertion that the present value of this constituent variable in you is indeed the state "not comfortable."

For item (2), "not comfortable" is the usual translation, but this is somewhat misleading since the understanding is stronger than that of the English translation. Better would be "discomfort" or "unwell" with some degree of understatement. "Not comfortable" is acceptable as a valid excuse for absence from work or in a parent's note to the teacher to excuse the child's absence. This is one social use of the term. It can be a complaint about any part of the body and can be used to refer to psychological experience as well. However, the usual interpretation is physical. I am here reporting bilinguals' use of English terms "psychological" and "physical" in explanations, not using the terms myself. Thus, the use of the terms by Chinese may or may not reflect acceptance of a Western dualism, which also need not be there for other users of the expression "not comfortable" (compare, e.g., Zheng et al. 1986).

We can look at one more example of this problem of invisible referents, something that can be roughly glossed as "essence-spirit" and found in several of our expressions. What does the apparent component of a person called "essence-spirit" refer to? Does it refer to anything? Do the different English translations we will see indicate that there are different classes of entities that one could make reference to with this one term or just different properties of a single entity? There is, then, a set of questions that has to be kept in mind. Do people differ in the nature and specificity of the conceptions that this term expresses for them? Or further, what is the variability among speakers as to whether this is a straight referring term or a metaphor embedded in different fixed expressions (Keesing, 1985)? When would such variation in their underlying understandings get in the way of their ability to communicate? Some of these expressions must indeed be taken as metaphors, at least in their original coinage some time in the past, for which there are no literal equivalents, a type known technically as catachresis (see, e.g., Sapir, 1977). Some present-day speakers may of course take the metaphors literally (Sandor, 1986).

In what follows, when I seem to be giving translations of expressions or describing the interpreted referents, I will only be reporting what I have been told in English—the data of bilinguals explaining and translating into English. Although phrased as generalizations, they are unquantified reports, with no claim that the variation presented is a representative sample of intracultural variation.

As for "essence-spirit," then, items (3) "essence-spirit wrong/poor" and (4) "essence-spirit not good" in Figure 3.1 can be translated "looks lousy," that is, you can see it in another person. It can be something physiologically wrong or due to sadness; here "essence-spirit" refers more to the person's "looks" or, better, "vitality." The difference between "not good" and "wrong/poor" is minimal here. For "essence-spirit" the meaning "mental" in some broad sense emerges with item 6 "essence-spirit problem"—that is, "mental problem," or with (7) "essence-spirit illness," "mental illness," or with (8) "spiritually not satisfied." If (3) "essence-spirit wrong/poor" or (4) "essence-spirit not good" are used about oneself, then they mean not one's "looks" but "spiritually, mentally." (Remember I am reporting; personally I would not use the English words "spiritually" and "mentally" as though they were synonymous.) So, when using (3) or (4) about myself, I am referring to my feelings, "I feel lousy," and one tends to use (5) "(I) feel" with the expression—thus, (5) plus (3), "I feel essence-spirit wrong," or (5) plus (4), "I feel essence-spirit not good." Items (3) or (4) are not necessarily psychological problems but can be the physical manifestations of what may have a physical cause, the person "doesn't look good."

If these expressions are translated as "(be in) low spirits," as they can be, it is really Chinese, not English, "spirit," although the bilingual is using the English word "spirit." They are understood as being a more physical-mental problem (as opposed to an emotional one)—namely an "essence-spirit" problem, which can be perceived internally as well. When they are said about oneself, the internal perception is implied as evidence for making the assertion about one's condition. That is, when said about oneself, the meaning "feeling" may be only implied, not a necessary meaning, and the tendency is to make it explicit by using (5) "(I) feel" with (3) and (4). The physical weakness or problem is, for example, the person "didn't sleep well last night (also not eating well, working too hard)." There may be other reasons for the insomnia, but the result is that now the person does not look good. If used about oneself, one is not feeling enough energy, cannot concentrate, does not feel like doing anything, is tired, wants to sleep.

Items (9) "not enough essence-spirit" or (10) "essence-spirit not enough" also contain the word "essence-spirit," like (3) "essence-spirit wrong/poor" and (4) "essence-spirit not good." Items (3), (4), (9), and (10) are semantically different strictly speaking, yet in the right context they can be interpreted as referentially synonymous in the sense that they can be used to refer to the same state in an underlying conceptual system involving the "vitality" sense of "essence-spirit." Item (11) "collapse-lose" is like inner defeat, loss of self-esteem—one is demoralized, destroyed. Although not containing the word "essence-spirit," (11) refers more to one's "essence-spirit," but in the "spirit," not "vitality," sense of "essence-spirit," thus not in the physiological sense.

So what do we make of there being these two senses of "essence-spirit" if we assume there is an intended reference? Might one speaker see them as only two different aspects of one and the same inner constituent category, and another, more acculturated speaker, as two different constituents of the person labeled by the same word in different contexts? That is, these different uses of the word "essence-spirit" need to reveal nothing about a holistic or dualistic view of the person. How would these two speakers fare when talking to each other, given that they do not share the same background beliefs of how the inner person is constituted?

In the class of expressions being described here, the external-internal distinction is covert in the sense that there are no obvious linguistic morphological features of the expressions to flag them for this distinction.[2] In some instances two expressions may be paired as both being capable of referring to the same condition or state, one for the condition or state as externally observable and the other as internally experienced. Of course, one can talk about oneself from an outside perspective, using certain of the external expressions, or guess at another person's internal state, if not told about it directly by the person. In some, but not all, instances, such as items (3), (4), (9), and (10), expressions interpreted as external without further context can be used internally with the explicit addition of (5) "(I) feel."[3]

It is not the case that every expression must be either clearly external or clearly internal. Some expressions can be more or less easily used both for talking about how someone looks or about how one feels oneself. Such use varies in part with the degree to which a given category of internal feeling or emotion has observable correlates, but it is still two different uses of the same expression and thus maintains the general external-internal distinction. As we shall see increasingly as we explore our theme, observability is a major consideration.

In this sense, then, we can look at some more examples. Items (12), (13), (14), and (15) can be grouped together:

(12) no essence strikes color: "listless, no desire to do anything";

(13) no spirit no energy: "one looks tired and listless";

(14) pickup-not-raise power: "can't raise (one's) power; don't feel like doing anything";

(15) pickup-not-raise essence-spirit: "can't raise (one's) spirit; don't feel like doing anything."

The difference is that (12) and (13) are from the outside perspective, observable; (14) and (15) are from the inside, more complaints about oneself, although they might additionally have some external manifestation; (12) and (13) mean " 'blah' (washed-out)" and are said about others since I cannot see myself; they mean "looks 'blah.' " (The metaphor in (12) is explained later.)

(16) bowed-head lose-energy: "(looks) miserable, disappointed."

In context, (16) is quite close to (12) and (15), but again, (15) is about inner feeling, from the inside, whereas (16) and (12) are from the outside. Thus you do not use (16) and (12) that easily about yourself without creating a special effect. Instead, for yourself you can complain of (15) "can't raise my spirit." For example, to some people it would sound amusing if you asked (12) or (16) about yourself: "Do I look 'no essence strikes color'?" or "Do I look 'bowed-head lose-energy'?"

As said, whether items are external, internal, or both, they can also differ in the degree to which they are reported as observable and what it is that the observables are evidence of. Item (12), "no essence strikes color" shows more on the outside, thus external; you can guess the internal condition associated with (12) about a third person with greater certainty although not necessarily how the person is experiencing it. Items (17), "no motivation" and (15) "can't raise one's spirit" may additionally have some external manifestations, but these are not as clearly observable from the outside as (12) is. Item (17), like (15), then, is not suitable for external reference.

(18) feeling-state low-drop: "in low spirits; mood very low";

(19) heart-feeling not good: "bad mood, moody, not happy";

(20) heart-feeling not open-clear: "bad mood";

(21) essence-spirit not quick: "depression, moody."

Among expressions for internal experiences, (18), (19), (20), and (21) are still less observable externally than (17), thus are harder to infer from external evidence than (17); (18) is more observable than (19), (20), and (21).

Observableness refers to physical manifestations and leads to another question: How does one familiar Western distinction, that between physical, psychological, and emotional, undergo syncretization when introduced into Chinese conceptual systems? If these English terms, or their technical translation equivalents into Chinese, are used by a Chinese, how is their underlying mind-body dichotomy affected when meeting a conceptual system that is said not to have this dualism so fundamentally? Item (12) "no essence strikes color" is reported as more "psychological" than "emotional" since it has a more observable, "physical" manifestation: the person is listless. That is, "psychological" is closer to "physical" than "emotional" is. Emotions are more subjective. Given this last characterization of psychological, physical, and emotional by a bilingual, one may wonder whether it would affect, for example, a mental health professional's communication in a cross-cultural medical setting with a patient who has these conceptions but who seems to the professional to be expressing something closer to the professional's conceptions when the patient uses such English terms as "psychological," "physical," or "emotional." (On the blur between psychological and physical symptoms more generally, compare Mechanic, 1980.)

We continue with distinctions made along the external-internal dimension.

(22) chest closed;

(23) closed-closed not happy: "depressed, in low spirits";

(24) develop closed-energy: "be sulky";

(25) gloomy-gloomy not happy: "depressed, melancholy, joyless."

Item (22) is said about oneself. To use it about someone else, the person first has to tell you; otherwise you can see the person is uncomfortable but you do not know what is wrong. Items (23) and (24) are used more about someone else than to describe oneself; the person is sullen in appearance but not in an offending way. For (23) the individual who made these evaluations also said that it is almost never used about oneself; to do so sounds funny, like putting on a big act. We could account for this reaction by saying that using this external expression for one's inner state of the moment can be interpreted as an insincere exaggeration, since one could have used an equivalent internal term, which would be interpreted as a more sincere mode of self-expression for such a disturbed inner state.

Item (24) is more "objective," it is used more as a comment on someone else than as a personal complaint. But (24) can be used to describe oneself on a past occasion, which is more like describing someone else, an outside perspective. Or (24) can even be used to describe oneself in the present (that is, we might wish to add, if a culturally or at least personally recognizable context can be evoked in which objective self-description can be seen as a fitting mode of expression). Thus (24) lies between (22) and (23) in appropriateness for use about oneself.

Although individual expressions are presented here as varying in their appropriateness for use about others or about oneself, note that the criterion of external versus internal reference itself, however, remains consistently relevant as a question to ask about different expressions.

For (23) another person's evaluation, in contrast to that of the individual above, was that you can use it to describe yourself. However, since it sounds vague as a way of describing yourself when you know enough about yourself to be more specific, it is more appropriate for an external description of someone else. That is, you know your internal experience and could use a more direct and specific expression than (23); so why use it about yourself? (This last comment would seem to be invoking the maxim of quantity of Grice [1975].) Thus, this evaluator and the previous one ultimately agree on the awkwardness of using (23) for oneself. The same evaluations just given for (23) also go for (25).

For (22) "chest closed" I had difficulty in getting a more elucidating English translation. It seemed to be an unclear concept in English terms and was better evaluated with such characteristics as the following offered by one bilingual. Item (22) is probably physiological, probably one of those concepts that are in between psychological and physiological. The air cannot get out of your chest easily. But who knows what the air contained in your lungs is? Is the air exterior? Or is it interior—that is, part of your body? By itself the form "closed" in (22) (men4/mun6) otherwise is an emotional psychological feeling but the whole expression (22) is more clinical. (It is not clear whether this person is contrasting "emotional psychological" with "physical psychological.") Item (22), she continues, seems to be one of those expressions that are meant more metaphorically or more concretely—such as by a patient, depending on the speaker's psychiatric status (compare Kleinman, 1982; Mechanic, 1980).

With regard to the English word "air" used by this bilingual, the word translating English "air" (qi4/hei3) can also translate English "energy" and

"anger." She assented to "a force" as a good characterization out of several
others offered and rejected (including "energy") for the air in the chest.

Most of the items in Figure 3.1 should probably be taken as fixed unit
expressions. Some characteristics of the concepts they are used to refer to
can be evoked by testing whether such intensifiers as translated "very" or
"too much" used with a given expression are meaningful for a speaker.
For example, "very" (hen3/hou2) with (22) "chest closed" would come out
as "chest very closed." The following are some sample reactions rejecting
intensifiers, using items (22), (23), and (24):

(22) no intensifier, not even "very"; (22) is a disease term.

(23) no intensifier, not even "very"; (23) is a description by itself, not gradable, a
     category, an end point.

(24) no intensifier; (24) is a unit term.

You can just say (24) with an adverbial like "often" (chang2 chang2). To
indicate an ongoing action, people would say "she or he is at (24)" (ta1
zai4 + (24), "she or he is being sulky"), which is the usual form in which
one hears (24).

A useful diagnostic for the external-internal distinction is (5) "(I) feel"
used with an expression. Not all expressions that have external reference
work equally well used with "feel" to indicate internal reference. (The word
"I" can be omitted with "feel" and is inferable from context.) We can
illustrate this use with item (12). In (12), "no essence strikes color," translating as "listless, no desire to do anything," "strikes" is used metaphorically in the sense of striking or giving off sparks, and "color" can stand
for vitality. In other words, "no inner essence is manifesting vitality." For
some people (12) is more exclusively a report of an external manifestation,
the potential underlying causes being more varied or indeterminate and not
clearly part of the reference of the expression, at least not in the more
recontextualized situation of being questioned about it. Thus using "feel"
with (12) to say something about oneself can present difficulties of interpretation for such people on such an occasion since it is harder to identify
what a speaker's intended internal referent might be. The more likely interpretation would be an "essence-spirit" problem, "lack of vitality," in
which case a better way of saying it about oneself is "no essence-spirit,
not-have essence-spirit" (mou5 jing1 san4), used with or without "feel."

For others questioned, this interpretation comes more easily for (12) used
about oneself: "having no motivation to do anything, feeling low, not energetic, lazy," and the cause could be emotional or psychological and not
necessarily physical. Still, an adverbial or other addition is needed in such
usage of (12) for oneself. Most commonly "feel" must precede (12), or
"feel" plus an adverbial "always/often/etc." plus (12) (zung2 hai6 "al-

ways"; zao1 xi4 "often.") Without specifying "feel," you can still say "always" plus (12) about yourself, but then you are not so much talking about your internal experience of the moment as describing yourself more generally—that is, less expressively and more descriptively or externally.

Some expressions are ordinarily said without "feel" when describing oneself. The reason given is that the meaning "feeling" is already "in" them. Thus people's reactions to using "feel" with such expressions allow us to use "feel" as a diagnostic for the meaning "feeling" already being there. Such would be, for example:

(18) feeling-state low-drop: "in low spirits; mood very low";

(19) heart-feeling not good: "bad mood, moody, not happy";

(20) heart-feeling not open-clear: "bad mood";

(21) essence-spirit not quick: "depression, moody";

(25) gloomy-gloomy not happy: "depressed, melancholy, joyless."

Using "feel" with such expressions as these five evokes the reaction that "feel" adds an implication of uncertainty, the combination coming out something like "I feel (as if) I feel. . . . " You do not have to guess what you are feeling and so do not need to say "feel."

Regarding (15) "can't raise (one's) spirit, don't feel like doing anything" and (17) "lack of motivation, no desire to do anything," these two items, although designating states that have some external manifestations, are more about oneself, internal. But, in contrast to the five items just discussed, (15) and (17) are more easily usable with "feel." They do not directly have the meaning "feeling," and thus using "feel" with them does not create the clashing redundancy "I feel (that) I feel . . . " found with the above five items. Items (15) and (17) express the absence of something rather than the presence of a feeling. Without "feel," they can still frequently be translated "feel low, sad," but this is a common, contextually inferred reference to the cause behind the "lack of motivation or vitality" of (15) and (17).

It would be interesting to investigate the difference between Chinese and American reactions to using "I feel" with expressions that already contain the element of meaning "feeling." For example, saying (5) plus (21), "I feel unhappy, I feel depressed" is judged to be awkward said in Chinese; (21) alone, "I'm unhappy, depressed," is the direct self-expression. Americans asked consider "I feel unhappy" a fully acceptable utterance and are puzzled that it should be awkward for Chinese.

In summary, it appears that the expressions or terms are not semantically encoded or marked for the distinction external versus internal. Rather this distinction is imposed and inferred from properties that the speaker or hearer attributes in his or her conceptions of the inner states that the expressions are used to refer to. For example, the properties are those of being more observable or less observable from the outside. The less observable the state is, the more likely the term is to be evaluated as internal. Thus, to the extent that there is an emphasis on making the distinction external versus internal, it appears to be the pragmatic result of a cultural theme and not part of the definitions of these expressions. Not having this cultural theme, Americans do not automatically classify inner states for the distinction.

Given not only the inter- but also the intracultural differences in conceptions of the inner person, the mental health professional is on guard against unquestioning assumptions about sharing underlying conceptual systems when communicating with clients or patients about unobservable inner states, especially in the cross-cultural medical setting. Interviewers must include conscious awareness not only of their own conceptions, but of the various ways in which the clients or patients may differ from theirs and among one another in their conceptual systems, including differences in degree of acculturation to Western models.

Although professionals are already aware of this need, it is especially easy to lose sight of when interacting with bilinguals who seem superficially to be using English expressions with the same understanding that the mental health professional gives them. That is, interviewers must include attempts to find out and clarify underlying differences in conceptualizations beyond those expected between an interviewer and an interviewee who share a common cultural background. As we have seen in the Chinese examples discussed here, the reluctance to use "I feel" with an expression referring to inner feeling should not be interpreted unquestioningly as an attempt to avoid expressing one's feelings since, on the contrary, it may be an attempt to avoid objectifying them.[4]

NOTES

1. The materials in this chapter are drawn from a research project funded by the National Institutes of Mental Health under grant No. MH40495.

2. In some languages further south in Asia, by contrast, external-internal have been grammaticized as evidential categories of the verb (e.g., Bendix, 1993).

3. In Japanese the construction *gatte iru*, "looks," is added to expressions of an internally perceived experience when such expressions are used about others. For example, the adjectival verb *atui*, usually translated as "be hot" but better glossed as "feel hot," is an expression one can use naturally about oneself. Using it in this simple form about someone else is rejected by speakers on the grounds that one cannot know what that other person feels. To say "(she or he) is hot," the most usual way to say it is *atui gatte iru* "(she or he) looks hot" (Aoki, 1986).

4. Matters are compounded when an interpreter is needed in the interview, since words then flow through three underlying conceptual filters, and the professional may not know how much of what the interpreter translates is the patient's conceptualization (Cicourel, 1981).

REFERENCES

Aoki, H. (1986). Evidentials in Japanese. In W. Chafe and J. Nichols (Eds.), *Evidentiality: The linguistic coding of epistemology*. Norwood, NJ: Ablex.

Bendix, E. H. (1993). The grammaticalization of responsibility and evidence: interactional potential of evidential categories in Newari. In J. Hill & J. Irvine (Eds.), *Responsibility and evidence in oral discourse*. Cambridge: Cambridge University Press.

Cicourel, A. V. (1981). Language and medicine. In C. A. Ferguson and S. B. Heath (Eds.), *Language in the USA*. Cambridge: Cambridge University Press.

Garro, L. C. (1986). Intracultural variations in folk medical knowledge: A comparison between curers and noncurers. *American Anthropologist, 88*, 351–370.

Grice, H. P. (1975). Logic and conversation. In P. Cole and J. L. Morgan (Eds.), *Syntax and semantics 3: Speech acts*. New York: Academic Press.

Keesing, R. M. (1985). Conventional metaphors and anthropological metaphysics: The problematics of cultural translation. *Journal of Anthropological Research, 41*, 201–217.

Kleinman, A. (1982). Neurasthenia and depression: A study of somatization and culture in China. *Culture, Medicine, and Psychiatry, 6*, 117–190.

Mechanic, D. (1980). The experience and reporting of common complaints. *Journal of Health and Social Behavior, 21*, 146–155.

Pelto, P. J. & Pelto, G. H. (1975). Intra-cultural diversity: Some theoretical issues. *American Ethnologist, 2*, 1–18.

Sandor, A. (1986). Metaphor and belief. *Journal of Anthropological Research, 42*, 101–122.

Sapir, J. D. (1977). The anatomy of metaphor. In J. D. Sapir and J. C. Crocker (Eds.), *The social use of metaphor*. Philadelphia: University of Pennsylvania Press.

Weller, S. C. (1984). Cross-cultural concepts of illness: Variation and validation. *American Anthropologist, 86*, 341–350.

Zheng, Y. P., Xu, L. Y. & Shen, Q. J. (1986). Styles of verbal expression of emotional and physical experiences: A study of depressed patients and normal controls in China. *Culture, Medicine and Psychiatry, 10*, 231–243.

Part II

Healers and Their Methods from Around the Globe

The Traditional Healer in a Multicultural Society: The South African Experience

Dap A. Louw and Engela Pretorius

One of the many challenges that come with the dismantling of apartheid in South Africa is the creation of a health system that will be applicable to the needs of all the people of the country. Up to now this unfortunately has not been the case. With a white minority government in control, the health system has also been "white"—that is, based on the Western approach to medicine. This automatically meant that the traditional African approach to healing—favored by many of the 85 percent black population—has been left out in the cold. Not only was this approach not officially and legally recognized, but it was also disparaged by the white establishment.

With a new political dispensation being envisaged in South Africa, this state of affairs will and must change. As in many other African countries, traditional healers next to the medical doctor, the psychologist, and other (mental) health professionals deserve a place in the health team. This of course will be difficult and even unacceptable to professionals trained in Western medicine. Opponents of this concept should, however, realize that Africans are not Americans nor Europeans—and will never be. They are from Africa, where unique cultures rule and where needs differ. When it comes to healing people there is no place for cultural arrogance, no time for lengthy discussions on whether a certain method has a placebo or "scientific" basis. People have the right to be healed according to their culture and their belief system. Of course, this will not always have to be the case, but often it is the only effective way.

WHAT PRECISELY IS A TRADITIONAL HEALER?

What is today commonly known as the traditional healer was until relatively recently known as a witch doctor. This term is growing obsolete as
a result of the negative connotations—by virtue of a semantic shift—that
are ascribed to it. "Witch doctor" should, in fact, denote a doctor who
must "heal" witchcraft, as an eye doctor treats eyes. Eventually the term
took on the meaning of a doctor who is a witch (Last, 1986).

Most scientists agree with the World Health Organization's definition of a traditional healer: Someone who is recognised by the community in which he lives as
competent to provide health care by using vegetable, animal and mineral substances
and certain other methods based on the social, cultural and religious background
as well as the prevailing knowledge, attitudes and beliefs regarding physical, mental
and social well-being and the causation of disease and disability in the community
(Oyebola, 1986, p. 224).

This definition corresponds with Tessema's (1980, p. 48) description of
traditional healing as the "solid amalgamation of dynamic medical know-
how and ancestral experience."

Traditional healers, just like the practitioners of Western medicine, can
be divided into various fields of specialization. In South Africa there are
two broad groups of traditional healers: herbalists and diviners (PASA,
1989). As there is an overlap in their roles, the distinction is not always
clear-cut and obvious. As a matter of fact, the same person can function
as a diviner as well as a herbalist at different times. It also seems that some
cultural groups draw a relatively clear distinction between the diviners and
herbalists, while the differentiation is less clear-cut among others.

Herbalists

In contrast to diviners, herbalists are not mystically called by their ancestors (Schoeman, 1989). They decide out of their own free will to undergo training with an established herbalist and subsequently practice on
their own. The period of training is usually not less than a year, after which
the trainee pays the trainer a cow or its equivalent in money (Blackett-
Sliep, 1989).

According to Pretorius (1990) the job description of herbalists is very
wide. They are expected to help in virtually all situations over which a
person has no control or in which he or she feels uncertain. Although the
focus of healing falls primarily on the use of herbs, magical techniques also
play a decisive role as the belief is that all herbs contain ingredients with
magical power. Van Rensburg, Fourie, and Pretorius (1992) point out that
the medicine of the herbalist often carries a strong symbolic meaning. For

example, the Tswana herbalist often uses the skin of a water iguana (large lizard) or crocodile, which symbolizes coolness, to "cool off" a patient. Or the Zulu herbalist may use the heart, eyes, fat, or meat of the lion, elephant, and other powerful animals to cure fear or anxiety. Most of the traditional herbs are of vegetative origin (herbs, bark of trees), although a small number may be of animal origin.

Diviners

Whereas herbalists decide out of their own free will to undergo training, diviners are called by their ancestors to become healers. Although diviners are known by different names in the different South African cultures (e.g., *amagqira* in Xhosa, *ngaka* in Northern Sotho, *selaoli* in Southern Sotho, and *mungome* in Venda and Tsongo) they are referred to as *sangomas* (from the Zulu word) by most South Africans.

According to Schoeman (1989) the calling by the ancestors occurs through an experience known as *thwasa*, which in Western terms would be regarded as an episode of (physical and especially mental) illness. The term *thwasa* is derived from a Xhosa verb meaning to be reborn. Symptoms of *thwasa* include anxiety, various physical aches and pains, palpitations, sleeplessness, and conversion disorders. Vivid and extensive dreaming are common, and the dreams are usually disturbing in nature. According to Bührmann (1984) the person usually also becomes withdrawn and irritable when spoken to, and restlessness, violence, and aggression are not uncommon. Psychotic symptoms (in Western terms) like auditory hallucinations—usually the voices of the ancestors—and negligence of personal appearance and hygiene complete the picture.

Usually another diviner is consulted to determine whether it is a real illness or a calling by the person's ancestors (Van Rensburg, Fourie & Pretorius, 1992). If the latter is the case, the person is immediately placed in the custody of a diviner. This marks the beginning of the training for which the trainer, as in the case of the herbalist, is also financially compensated. The duration of training is five to six years. Ngubane (1977) points out that the training period also has some unpleasant characteristics. The trainee must, for example, abstain from several enjoyments like sexual intercourse and certain foods, while withdrawal from society and loss of contact with friends and family form an integral part of the training.

As the person was in actual fact "appointed" by his ancestors, they are consulted regularly. The diagnosis of an illness is often made by means of divination (e.g., the throw of divining "bones" and other special objects in order to interpret the message of the ancestors). It is of the utmost importance to keep the ancestors satisfied. More specifically the ancestors should be able to "sleep" in order to create a world in which humans can live in prosperity and good health. To this end it is sometimes necessary to sacrifice an animal, an event described by Berglund (1976, p. 198) as "a sharing of the slaughtered beast and a renewal of kinship bonds with each other which implies mutual concern for each other." In cases where sorcery seems to be at the root of the patient's problems, he or she is also given a lucky charm to thwart the sorcery.

The treatment used by traditional healers in general, and diviners specifically, varies greatly and depends on the healers' own knowledge and skills as well as the nature of their patients' illness (PASA, 1989). It especially includes ritual sacrifice to appease the ancestors (as described), ritual and magical strengthening of people and possessions, steaming, purification (e.g., ritual washing, or the use of emetics and purgatives), sniffing of substances, and blood letting. Hammond-Tooke (1989, p. 123), South African anthropologist and foremost authority in this field, summarizes the essence of traditional healing as follows:

Ultimately the treatment consists of coming to grips with fractured relationships—either between agnates (and therefore with ancestors) or between close kin and neighbours (witchcraft). Disease is thus conceived in terms of a breakdown of human relationships, and the healing rituals and witch executions, both in their different ways restore or attempt to restore, harmonious social life. In this sense, then, traditional healing is "holistic." It treats disease, not only by powerful medicines, but also with rituals that place the patient in the centre of a social drama in which emotions are not only highly charged but symbolically expressed. The afflicted person is not only made to feel important and the object of social concern, but the ritual also relates what is happening to her wider cosmological and social concerns. . . . Thus satisfactory healing involves, not merely the recovery from bodily symptoms, but the social and psychological reintegration of the patient into his community, whether it be the lineage, neighbourhood, possession cult.

Faith Healers

The faith healer or prophet is a relatively newly added category to the traditional healing profession. This category actually indicates a syncretism, a reinterpretation of orthodox Christianity in such a way as to be reconcilable with traditional culture. In this regard faith healers often declare that they receive their power and abilities from both God and their ancestors. As faith healers are part of both the traditional and modern Western belief systems, they are in a unique position to therapeutically help people in a country like South Africa where both belief systems prevail.

Faith healers deliver their services within the framework of the Independent Churches of Africa (ICA). The number of ICA denominations in South Africa has grown from about 30 in 1913 to more than 3,000 in 1990 (Pretorius, 1990). More specifically, 6 million followers—that is, 30 percent of the total black population in South Africa and 39 percent of the total Christian population of the country—are involved. According to Oosthuizen (1985) there are approximately 12,000 of these churches in Africa, with an estimated membership of 30 million.

Pretorius (1990), using the work of Sundkler (1961) as basis, points out several parallels between faith healers and diviners:

- Both the diviner and faith healer are called to their vocations by means of a special type of illness. In the case of the diviner the illness is attributed to the spirits of the ancestors, while in the case of the faith healer the illness is attributed to the action of the Holy Spirit.
- Certain taboos (e.g., specific foods) apply in both cases.
- Both the diviner and faith healer are responsible for health and vitality.
- Both regard witchcraft and sorcery as important causes of illness.
- Both acknowledge that the spirits of the ancestors can cause illness and infertility, and that it is necessary to placate them with sacrifices.

As far as the specific treatment methods are concerns, West (1975) lists the following as typical of the faith healer:

Prayer	in 100 percent of cases
Holy Water	in 79 percent of cases
Baths	in 52 percent of cases
Enemas	in 45 percent of cases
Steaming	in 42 percent of cases

THE POSITION OF TRADITIONAL HEALTH CARE IN SOUTH AFRICA

Historical Overview

Traditional healing is neither antiestablishment nor antiwhite and therefore was not established as an antipode for the "white man's medicine." Quite the contrary. According to Halse (1992) traditional healers were already practicing in Africa about 4,500 years ago, before there had been any knowledge of the Western medical system. It is also generally accepted that before the European colonization of Southern Africa, traditional medicine—intertwined with magic and religion—exerted great political influence in public and private affairs. This, however, changed with the arrival of the first colonists in South Africa: the Calvinistic-oriented whites regarded the black as "heathens" and "primitive" and it was almost blasphemy to accept or even acknowledge the existence of such "barbaric" methods like traditional healing. Under missionary influence and also as a result of repressive and imperialistic political policy trends, the colonial administrators prohibited traditional medical practices (Ulin, 1980). Other factors that strengthened the fight against traditional medicine were, inter alia, Western upbringing, the integration of African subsistence economies into the world capitalist system, while increasing racial tension and racism also played an important part. This brought about new values, preferences, and behavioral patterns, and eventually contributed to the dismantling of African traditional cosmology and culture.

These factors, however, could not prevent traditional healing from remaining the choice healing method among a large proportion of South African blacks. In 1947 the Dingakas Association of traditional healers petitioned the South African Medical and Dental Council (SAMDC) for registration as health practitioners alongside doctors, dentists and nurses (Halse, 1992). The SAMDC (with which South African psychologists also at present register) requested the traditional healers for further details regarding their examination of patients, diagnosis, and treatment. Most probably as a result of the "secret code" of traditional healing (which the healers did not want to break), they refused. A golden opportunity was therefore missed for better understanding and maybe even collaboration between the two groups. A year later, in 1948, apartheid was legalized and better understanding and collaboration became almost impossible—and in the hearts of most white South Africans also undesirable.

With the political changes taking place in the 1990s, the rift between Western and African thinking is fortunately beginning to narrow. Most, if not all, South African psychologists and other mental health professionals have now come to realize that collaboration with traditional healers is not only desirable in the new South Africa, but will become a necessity. This will ensure a holistic approach to healing, where individuals will benefit by receiving treatment tailored to their unique needs within the framework of their cultures and belief systems.

In this regard it should be mentioned that a country like Zimbabwe (South Africa's northern neighbor) formally recognized traditional healers in 1981 with the enactment of the Traditional Medical Practitioners Act (No. 38 of 1981) (Dauskardt, 1990). Under this act, the establishment of a national association for traditional healers was encouraged. The association that was founded, the Zimbabwe National Traditional Healers' Association (Zinatha), today maintains practicing standards, controls research and training and incompetent and abusive practices, and rationalizes healing procedures, in essence creating and maintaining an ethical environment for the traditional systems (Cavender, 1988).

Availability and Accessibility of Traditional Healers

Owing to lack of official statistics, the national healer:population ratio in South Africa is estimated at 1:200 (Pretorius, 1990). This is much more favorable than the physician:population ratio in the modern sector, which is approximately 7.4:10,000 (Van Rensburg, Fourie & Pretorius, 1992). This apparently favorable ratio could, however, be deceptive, if the type and quality of care in this (traditional) sector were not taken into account. In the current economic climate in South Africa and amid concomitant unemployment, there is a marked increase in the ranks of traditional healers, among whom are quite a number of charlatans. It is calculated that of the 80,000 persons practicing traditional healing in the Vaal Triangle (an area south of Johannesburg), only about 10 percent are bona fide healers— that is, healers who abide by the strict ethical code of this vocation. The effect of these charlatans is illustrated by the finding that 15 percent of patients with poisonous intoxication admitted to a hospital near Pretoria were due to traditional "medicines" (PASA, 1989).

It has often been stated that traditional healers are accessible because, compared with modern medical practitioners, they have the advantage of cultural, social, psychological, and geographical proximity. As Blackett-Sliep (1989, p. 43) states, "they live where the people live." Considering the healer:population ratio, geographical proximity is indeed a reality, although distance does not seem to act as a deterrent when seeking the services of a traditional healer. As a matter of fact, a person often prefers to consult a healer in another area, on the one hand because the client expects the traditional healer to identify the problem without prior information, and on the other hand because the person (e.g., a neighbor) who has harmed the client, may also consult the same local healer.

The tendency to describe traditional medicine as readily accessible often obscures the relative inaccessibility brought about by the high costs often associated with this kind of care. A survey of Mangaung (a so-called black township near Bloemfontein) indicated that the consultation fee of diviners is twice as high as that of Western medical practitioners, white and black (Pretorius, 1990; Pretorius, De Klerk & Van Rensburg, 1991) (see Figure 4.1). The fact that the average black who visits a traditional healer earns much less than the average white who visits a Western medical practitioner puts this finding in perspective. Blackett-Sliep (1989), on the other hand, points out that traditional healers are often more accessible than medical doctors and therefore more affordable. This is due to reductions in transport costs. The traditional healer also usually starts with an initial minimal fee. The balance is then paid only after the patient has been cured, a system of "you pay for what you get," which is more acceptable to many.

The Acceptability of Traditional Healers

In any discussion about the services of traditional healers it is not only its acceptability to the local population that needs to be illuminated, but also its acceptability to the policymakers and the ranks of the practitioners of modern medicine. There can be no doubt about acceptance and utili-

Figure 4.1
Comparative Consultation Fees of Western and Traditional Medical Practitioners

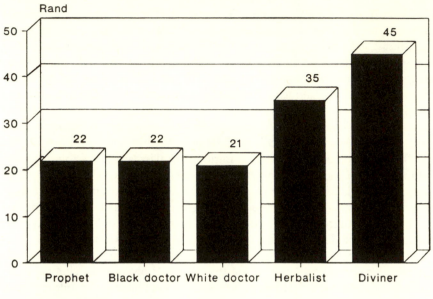

(Pretorius, 1990)

zation by a specific clientele in South Africa. Although some researchers in the recent past have made mention of a decrease in the clientele of traditional healers, many others are of the opinion that traditional healers are attracting a larger clientele, especially from the higher social strata (Anyinam, 1987; Cavender, 1988; Mkwanazi, 1987). Although it would seem that most Western medical practitioners are indifferent to traditional healers, some do advocate their use enthusiastically. The persons who object to traditional medicine tend to be those who encounter the failures of traditional healers and have to rectify these. As a result of the naturalistic orientation of most herbalists, these traditional healers enjoy greater acceptance than diviners and faith healers.

The numerous legal approaches in respect to the acceptance in societies of traditional healing by the authorities concerned can be divided into four broad categories: exclusive, tolerant, inclusive, and integrated systems (Stepan, 1983). In South Africa a tolerant system characterized by a laissez-faire policy exists at present. Only systems based on modern medicine are recognized, while the existence and significance of the traditional sector are virtually ignored, although the Council for the Associated Health Service Professions—a statutory body not affiliated with the Medical and Dental Council—makes provision for the control of traditional healers.

THE ROLE AND UTILIZATION OF TRADITIONAL HEALERS IN SOUTH AFRICA: EMPIRICAL FINDINGS

It is understandable that traditional healing in South Africa has largely been shrouded in mysticism, misconceptions, and ignorance. The apartheid system that kept races apart, vast cultural and language barriers, the dominance of biomedicine, as well as an unwillingness to allow outsiders on this holy ground were at the root of this. However, with the political changes in South Africa also came an eagerness among the different cultural groups to become better acquainted. This fortunately also applies to the scientific world, where researchers have during the last few years uncovered new data on various previously unknown and even hidden information on many cross-cultural aspects, including traditional healing.

One of the most recent surveys on the utilization of traditional healing is that by Pretorius (1990; also see Pretorius, De Klerk & Van Rensburg, 1991). The research was carried out in Mangaung, as previously mentioned, a so-called black township near Bloemfontein in the Orange Free State. Some of the most important findings are discussed below:

1. *Percentage of respondents consulting traditional healer.* Of the total number of respondents (207) 35.6 percent indicated that they consult with traditional healers. It should be pointed out, however, that this finding may not reflect the true state of affairs. Because consultation of traditional healers is not accepted by a large (and especially the Christian) part of the black community, many respondents might have been unwilling to admit to it.

2. *Frequency of consultations with traditional healers during preceding 12 months.* About 32 percent of the respondents visited a traditional healer during the preceding 12 months. The details are given in Table 4.1. It should be taken into account, however, that due to overlapping, individuals consulted more than one kind of healer.

3. *Reasons for consulting traditional healers.* The reasons the respondents gave for visiting traditional healers are given in Table 4.2.

4. *Responses to certain statements.* In order to see how important the respondents regard the role of the traditional healer in the health system, they were given the following statements: "Traditional healers should be banned" and "Medical doctors should know more about traditional healers." The responses are given in Table 4.3. It is interesting to note that only 9 percent agreed with the statement that traditional healers should be banned, and that 76.6 percent were of the opinion that medical doctors should know more about traditional healers.

Table 4.1
Frequency of Consultations with Traditional Healers during
Preceding 12 Months

Number of Consultations	Traditional Healers		
	Diviner	Herbalist	Faith Healer
	%	%	%
1 - 2 times	50.0	50,0	52,3
3 - 4 times	29.2	15,0	15,9
5 - 10 times	8.3	5,0	9,1
More than 10 times	12.5	10,0	15,9
None	-	20,0	6,8
TOTAL	100.00	100.00	100.00

(Pretorius, 1990)

TRADITIONAL HEALING VERSUS WESTERN PSYCHOTHERAPY AND COUNSELING

All systems of healing have certain similarities and differences. This is also the case with traditional healing and the Western approach in the form of psychotherapy and counseling. Concerning similarities, Bodibe (1992) states that both approaches emphasize the importance of building a relationship based on trust; both aim at personality integration and positive growth; both emphasize the expression of feelings. Bodibe, however, rightly points out that there are also vast differences between the approaches (see Table 4.4).

- The African approach is symbolic, intuitive, and integrally part of the traditional African belief system, while the Western approach is based largely on scientific and logical principles that have no direct link with any unscientific beliefs.
- Traditional healers are directive in their approach. They give advice to their clients by functioning as the mouthpiece of the ancestors who possess superior wisdom. Guidance is therefore from the unconscious and not from the ego of the healer. Western counseling is based on the principle that clients have to take responsibility for their own actions and decisions, and are therefore nondirective.
- The African tradition emphasizes the unity of body and mind, and tends to be

Table 4.2
Reasons for Consulting Traditional Healers

Reasons for consultations	Traditional Healers		
	Diviner	Herbalist	Faith Healer
	%	%	%
They are trusted	91,3	95,0	86,4
They live nearby	4,2	5,0	11,4
Illness	87,5	100,0	86,4
They are effective	66,7	55,0	74,4

(Pretorius, 1990)

more holistic in its approach to diagnosis and treatment. In Western healing the psychological sphere is given preference (i.e., the person's feelings, thoughts, and behavior).

• Western healing usually places more emphasis on the individual, while traditional healing emphasizes the unity of a person with a community.

• Traditional African healing, with its vibrant dance and the accompanying songs, involves an emotive and active experience of participation as opposed to the more cerebral, abstract, sedentary activity within Western healing.

LINKING TRADITIONAL HEALING AND BIOMEDICINE

While anthropologists and professional health practitioners for many years were of the opinion that traditional and modern medical systems were rivals, there was, for the majority of patients, no inconsistency in the dual utilization of the systems (Jansen, 1983; Mankazana, 1979; Spring, 1980; Yoder, 1982). This was possible because Africans have a dualistic outlook on life that accommodates both the conspiracy theory of "witchcraft" and the "scientific" theory of modern medicine. This phenomenon of dual utilization is significant because it provides a basis for linking traditional and modern medicine. In order to create a new syncretic type of national health care system, traditional healing can be made relevant and its efficacy increased by means of either complementarity or integration.

Table 4.3
Responses to Statements

	Response Categories					
Statement	Definitely agree	Agree	Uncertain	Does not agree	Definitely does not agree	Total
	%	%	%	%	%	%
Traditional healers should be banned	5,0	4,0	27,4	40,8	22,9	100,0
Medical doctors should know more about traditional healers	29,3	47,3	17,6	4,4	1,5	100,0

(Pretorius, 1990)

Complementarity

Complementarity ensures a safe position between the difficulties of pro-
hibition on the one hand, and, on the other, the problems associated with
official recognition of traditional medicine in the case of legislation, especially the possible scorn of the Western medical sector (Dauskardt, 1990).
This is no "cowards way out" but according to this chapter's authors the
only practical workable way to avoid a conflict between the Western and
traditional systems. After all, after having seen and experienced the negative
effect of legislation that tried to interfere with cultural customs and values
for too long, most South Africans at this stage are wary to fall into the
same trap again.

Complementarity thus signifies that traditional and modern medicine coexist, independent of each other, each respecting the unique character of
the other. There is cooperation between the two systems, creating a better
working relationship between them: appropriate referrals occur regularly,
certain skills of the traditional healer are upgraded, while the cultural sensitivity of modern health care practitioners is enhanced (Green & Makhubu, 1984).

Integration

Integration generally denotes the application of traditional healers in the
official medical sector as an inexpensive way of increasing the availability

Table 4.4

Differences between Traditional Healing and Western Psychotherapy/Counseling

Traditional healing	Western psychotherapy
Focus is on the individual client and his whole family.	Focus is usually on the individual client (although family therapy is often used).
Main tool is divining bones. Also makes use of rituals like music and dance.	Main tools are the psychotherapeutic interview, assessment and specific therapeutic counseling strategies.
Exploration of the client's standing with his ancestors and neighbours, as it is believed human machinations of witches and sorcerers can cause problems.	Promotion of insight, exploration feelings and the use of specific intervention and techniques.
Usually treats patient in in community where he/she lives.	Usually treats patient in consulting rooms outside community.
Makes use of systemic thinking.	Utilises the eclectic approach.
Unlicensed but governed by high moral code. Many charlatans exist.	Licensed and bound by ethical code. Very few charlatans are found.
Main inclinations: sort things out between patient and ancestors.	Main message: develop inner resources and strategies to deal effectively with external factors and intrapsychic conflict.

(Adapted from Bodibe, 1992.)

of efficacious medical services. The underlying idea is that the characteristics and skills of certain traditional practitioners receive appropriate training with a view to managing certain modern practices and advocating certain medical views. The best example in this regard is the successful integration that has been accomplished with traditional midwives in various countries.

Given the possible options for linking traditional healing to modern medicine, the present authors are of the opinion that integration of the two systems would be potentially detrimental to both. Such a syncretism is also not likely to develop because of the fundamental irreconcilability of the cosmological views of the two systems. Conversely, complementarity could facilitate the transfer of important values to both systems and eventually the universal goal of "health for all" could be realized.

THE FUTURE ROLE OF THE TRADITIONAL HEALER

Despite the fact that traditional health care—in terms of, inter alia, a legal and a Christian point of view—has no "right of existence," it has nevertheless continued to exist up to the eve of the twenty-first century. There are also signs that this kind of care is gaining prominence in South Africa, and not only among the clientele. Numerous academics (notably psychologists) have for some time now been advocating cooperation between the modern and the traditional medical sectors, and have even involved traditional healers in actions connected with holistic medicine. Initiatives regarding cooperation with traditional healers have actually come from, inter alia, the South African National Tuberculosis Association, the National Cancer Association of South Africa, and the Department of National Health and Population Development (regarding AIDS). The organizations do not only employ traditional healers in the therapeutic roles in some of their clinics but realize that they can play a most important role in changing their communities' attitudes concerning vital problems like AIDS and population growth. In addition, traditional healers, through their various organizations, strive after legitimation by the South African government and recognition from the South Africa Medical and Dental Council. What will most probably give a strong impetus to traditional healers' attempts to gain recognition are the demands of workers via labor unions for such recognition. According to the organizers of labor unions, the demand is not only for the recognition of an already acceptable method of healing, but it also has a political dimension: the demand reflects the right of people to the medical care of their choice. The nonrecognition of traditional medicine is viewed as forcing one specific medical system on the people, which constitutes part of the system of oppression in South Africa.

If the principle is accepted that the therapy patients receive should be in accordance with their cultural and worldview, traditional medicine cannot be phased out in the near future. As a matter of fact, should this occur, an essentially psychological vacuum could be created for those who believe in and benefit from it (Glasser, 1988). Of course there are the difficult questions that will have to be answered (e.g., Is it fair, taking the training of the medical doctor into account, that the consultation fees of the traditional healer be similar? Should traditional healers become beneficiaries of medical aid systems?) More difficult questions, however, have been solved all over the world when people were willing to work together—respecting the seemingly incomprehensible practices and customs of the other. There is no reason why South Africans cannot do the same. As Engel (1977, p. 135) rightly states:

But nothing will change unless those who control resources have the wisdom to venture off the beaten path of exclusive reliance on biomedicine as the only approach to health care. . . . In a free society, outcome will depend upon those who have the courage to try new paths and the wisdom to provide the necessary support.

REFERENCES

Anyinam, C. (1987). Availability, accessibility, acceptability, and adaptability: Four attributes of African ethno-medicine. *Social Science and Medicine, 25,* 803–811.

Berglund, A. I. (1976). *Zulu thought-patterns and symbolism.* Cape Town: Philip.

Blackett-Sliep, Y. (1989). Traditional healers and the primary health care nurse. *Nursing,* RSA, 4, 42–44.

Bodibe, R. C. (1992). Traditional healing: An indigenous approach to mental health problems. In J. Uys (Ed.), *Psychological counseling in South African context.* Johannesburg: Maskew Miller Longman.

Bührmann, V. (1984). *Living in two worlds. Communications between a white therapist and a black counterpart.* Cape Town: Human & Rousseau.

Cavender, T. (1988). The professionalization of traditional medicine in Zimbabwe. *Human Organization, 47,* 251–254.

Dauskardt, R.P.A. (1990). Traditional medicine: Perspectives and policies in health care development. *Development South Africa, 7,* 351–358.

Engel, G. L. (1977). The need for a new medical model: A challenge for biomedicine. *Science, 196,* 129–135.

Glasser, M. (1988). Accountability of anthropologists, indigenous healers and their governments: A plea for reasonable medicine. *Social Science and Medicine, 27,* 1461–1464.

Green, E. C. & Makhubu, L. (1984). Traditional healers in Swaziland: Toward improved co-operation between traditional and modern health sectors. *Social Science and Medicine, 18,* 1071–1079.

Halse, D. (1992). The role of traditional healing in the future South Africa. *Natal Psyche*, Winter 1992, 3–4.

Hammond-Tooke, D. (1989). *Rituals and medicines. Indigenous healing in South Africa*. Johannesburg: Donker.

Jansen, G. (1983). *The doctor-patient relationship in an African tribal society*. Assen: Van Gorcum.

Last, M. (1986). Introduction: The professionalization of African medicine: Ambiguities and definitions. In M. Last & G. L. Chavunduka (Eds.), *The professionalization of African Medicine*. Manchester: Manchester University Press.

Mankazana, E. M. (1979). The case for the traditional healer in South Africa. *South African Medical Journal*, 56, 1003–1007.

Mkwanazi, I. (1987). Witchcraft and modern surgery. Presentation at Congress of Theatric Study Group. Bloemfontein: July 24–25, 1987.

Ngubane, H. (1977). *Body and mind in Zulu medicine*. London: Academic Press.

Oosthuizen, G. C. (1985). The African Independent Churches' centenary. *African Insight*, 15, 70–80.

Oyebola, D.D.O. (1986). National medical policies in Nigena. In M. Last & G. L. Chavunduka (Eds.), *The professionalization of African medicine*. Manchester: Manchester University Press.

Pretorius, E. (1990). *Die rol en benutting van tradisionele helers in 'n swart woongebied by Bloemfontein* (The role and utilization of traditional healers in a township near Bloemfontein). Unpublished D.Phil. dissertation. Bloemfontein: UOFS.

Pretorius, E., De Klerk, G. W. & Van Rensburg, H.C.J. (1991). *Die tradisionele heler in Suid-Afrikaanse gesondheidsorg* (The traditional healer in South African health care). Pretoria: HSRC.

Psychological Association of South Africa (PASA) (1989). *Mental health in South Africa*. Pretoria: PASA.

Schoeman, J. B. (1989). Psigopatologie by tradisionele swart Suid-Afrikaners. (Psychopathology among traditional black South Africans). In D. A. Louw (Ed.), *Suid-Afrikaanse handboek van abnormale gedrag*. (South African handbook of abnormal behavior). Johannesburg: Southern.

Spring, A. (1980). Traditional and biomedical health care systems in Northwest Zambia: A case study of the Luvale. In P. R. Ulin & M. H. Segal (Eds.), *Traditional health care delivery in contemporary Africa*. New York: Maxwell School of Citizenship and Public Affairs.

Stepan, J. (1983). Legal aspects. In R. H. Bannerman, J. Burton, & C. Wen-Chieh (Eds.), *Traditional medicine and health care coverage: A reader for health administrators and practitioners*. Geneva: World Health Organization.

Sundkler, B.G.M. (1961). The concept of Christianity in the African Independent Churches. *African Studies*, 20, 203–213.

Tessema, S. S. (1980). Traditional African medicine: Past growth and future development in East Africa. *The East African Medical Journal*, 57, 48–54.

Ulin, P. R. (1980). Introduction—Traditional healers and primary health care in Africa. In P. R. Ulin & M. H. Segal (Eds.), *Traditional health care delivery in contemporary Africa*. New York: Maxwell School of Citizenship and Public Affairs.

Van Rensburg, H.C.J., Fourie, A. & Pretorius, E. (1992). *Health care in South Africa: Structure and dynamics*. Pretoria: Academica.

West, M. (1975). *Bishops and prophets in a black city. African Independent Churches in Soweto*. Johannesburg: Philip.

Yoder, P. S. (1982). *African health and healing systems: Proceedings of a symposium*. Los Angeles: Cross Roads.

5

Oracles in Ladakh: A Personal Experience

Elan Golomb

While the performance of the two oracles working side by side in Chog-lamsar, Ladakh, was riveting, it is the knowledge of oracles, their ability to predict and heal, that is sought by people everywhere. In the West, the apocalyptic visions of Christ, who could be considered a kind of oracle, shaped many lives. A recent slew of New Age mediums offered themselves to people who sought an all-knowing, out-of-world perspective.

Mediums are human beings who act as conduits for the communication of nonhuman spirits. For the sake of intellectual abbreviation, I call the mediums *oracles*. Not all Western oracles are religious. I know of a stock exchange mogul who charges $10,000 for five minutes of his time and gets it. He does not have enough time to meet all applicants.

For intellectuals who scoff at spiritual seekers and disdain money seekers, there are the oracles of science. Albert Einstein, who looked into the work-ings of the physical world, was one. Instead of seeing people as amorphous recipients and the product of innumerable, indecipherable forces, he said the world has reason. Humankind needs to think that the world has reason, teleological direction, and a predictable shape. Looking for purpose and design in nature, people want to believe that they and the world are evolv-ing into a predictable position.

It is too great a blow to their egos for people to see themselves as nothing but a chance concatenation of cells. They can not allow that although they can impinge on the environment, they lack higher meaning and will even-tually disappear. In Pali, the language of the earliest North Indian Buddhist texts, *anicca* is the word for change. Westerners have resisted the basic Buddhist concept that the only thing we can count on is change.

Where do Ladakhi oracles fit into this? Oracles speaking through earth representatives are important to many Ladakhis. The forms taken by Ladakhi spirits have been shaped by three traditions. The first comes from the plains of India, the second from China through Tibet, the third is from a pre-Buddhist religion known as Bon, which propounded the concept of cosmic cohabitation. Bon practitioners dwelt in a sacred habitat for all things and worshipped aspects of their environment as the abode of cosmic deities.

The Ladakhi tradition that grew out of this is tantric and animistic. It created shamanic rituals, meditations, and magic to gain access to the spiritual forces, whose actions are seen in the ever-changing visible world. It evolved sacred sites and propitiated the gods of this tree, that field, and that stream. The animistic relationship to the specific, local environment evolved into a religion known as Bon.

Bon has influenced the schools of Mahayana Buddhism as practiced in Tibet and Ladakh; Bon was influenced by Buddhism in turn. One way for antagonistic and competing forces to survive is to mutually absorb one another. Of course, Bon is not entirely local, since even the Bon viewpoint did have outside influences such as the Iranian way of handling the dead. Where, originally, Ladakhis burned their corpses, this was replaced by the Zarathustrian practice of leaving the dead out for vultures to eat.

Ladakh, which is often known as Little Tibet, is in Kashmir, India, on the border of southwest Tibet, with shared geology, altitude, and religion. Ladakh, like Tibet, has high, dry, windswept plains surrounded by enormous mountains. Some Ladakhi valleys are fed by the waters of glacial runoff that are captured and directed by irrigation canals. Such valleys are planted. At 13,000 feet, the land may be seeded with high-altitude barley and, above this, grazed in summer by yak and sheep.

Ladakh is a land of mystery. The setting for its *Gompas* (solitary temples) sometimes looks like the surface of the moon. Everywhere there are *chortens* (receptacles for offerings) erected more than 300 years ago, mounds of stone or clay topped by a series of plates, a crescent moon, a global sun, and a tongue-shaped spike that represents the *nadhi* (sacred flame of Buddha). The *chorten* in symbolic form gives the Buddhist view of life: earth, fire, air, and water. By reminding us of the basic substance from which we come it urges our minds to go to the formlessness behind it.

Ladakh is a land divided by *mani* walls, rectangular structures of gathered stones. The *mani* wall ends in a *chorten*. It is about five or six feet high with a sloping roof covered with rocks that have *Om! Mani padme hum* carved on them. There are small *mani* walls and large ones. Outside Leh, a huge *mani* wall runs along the road but you cannot walk along its right side, the "proper" approach, because the *mani* wall leads you into the Indian army camp, which is off limits.

Some *mani* walls were erected by prisoners serving their terms when Ladakh was ruled by kings. All the *mani* walls, until recently, were added to each year by local people. Like spinning a prayer wheel, adding to a *mani* wall is thought to help *self* and the world as well.

Along roads in Ladakh, are *thoyor*, stone monuments erected by individuals, stone piled on stone to create small pyramids. These stand alone in the dry, desert soil that is occasionally swathed by yellow and purple flowers. *Thoyor* are an original human statement. Some were erected to convince the spirits to keep floods from the crops. Others were built as resting places for the spirits of the newly dead before they move on to be reborn.

In the mountains are *tsa-tsa*, molded clay figures into which are put the ashes of the dead. Honorary *tsa-tsa* sit on stone monuments topped by rag flags, juniper twigs, arrows, and banners. *Tsa-tsa* platforms are erected to help a person achieve higher rebirth.

At one time Ladakh and Tibet were undivided. Tibet was invaded and influenced by China, whose imagery trickled into Ladakh. A stronger religious magnet to the resident Ladakhis was the Buddhism that came to Tibet-Ladakh from India. Initially, Indian Buddhism was godless, which is why we have the Zen adage, "Slay Buddha if you meet him on the road." This saying means find your own view of reality; accept no other, not even that of Buddha.

The demonic and tantric actions associated with Padma-Sambhava, who is said to have brought his version of Buddhism to Tibet from India, put the native spirits under vows. Padma-Sambhava is considered to be the founder of Tibetan Buddhism, which currently is divided over the deification of reality. Some religious groups accept more Bon and Hindu images. However, within a single religious group there are conflicts and divisions. Today, it is considered a sign of higher education to reject the spirits, but not many monks do so.

Starting in the eighth century A.D., many monks took on Bon-shamanic practices that generated services for lamas to sell to citizens to help them advance their *self* into a higher rebirth. They paid the monks for personal readings, fortune telling, and propitiation. It is in such an atmosphere that the use of oracles developed. Today, some monks reject god imagery and the vision of oracles. Others are guided by what they think of as genuine, unseen spirits.

The Bon religion performed animal sacrifice. When Buddhism arrived, it steadily cut down the frequency of sacrifice until it has almost disappeared. Animistic Bon gods now are honored in mostly verbal rituals. Lozang Jamspal, a Ladakhi Tibetan scholar (personal communication, September 12, 1993), remembers in his childhood that a charismatic monk who was an oracle came to the four families (including his own) that shared religious practices and said "don't kill animals." Impressed by him, they stopped killing goats to please the spirits.

According to Buddhism, all life is sacred. I asked Dr. Jamspal, what about eating meat? He smiled and said that "the idea of killing animals and eating them have separated. Now it is considered wrong to kill animals but OK to eat them."

Accepting aspects of Bon into the Buddhist religion was one way to assimilate new practitioners. Frightening and colorful Bon imagery is painted on Tibetan *Gompa* walls. These represent the forces that support or tear at humanity from within and without: health or disease, greed or compassion, the fertility of people, beast and crop, water or desert, death.

Along the *Gompa* entry are depicted ferocious forces that religion can help people to defeat. Death as shown in the paintings of dancing skeletons is an ever-present stimulus toward action. Blue monster deities with an aura of fire wear necklaces of human heads. Partly swallowed human bodies hang out of their mouths and they stand on struggling bodies. By such imagery, people are reminded of their spiritual enemies.

After passing these frightening depictions, you see paintings of high *Lamas* ("superior ones") and Buddhas whose hands are held in *mudra* (mystic finger attitudes) positions that signify inner peace, physical healing, and spiritual evolution. You see the depiction of the *Yab-yum* (father-mother, conjugal deities), a standing Buddha in sexual union with his female consort, one of whose legs is folded around his waist, her arm around his neck. The *Yab-yum* signifies the bliss of enlightenment as beyond the ecstacy of sexuality in terms that people can understand. The united male and female figures imply that enlightenment means unity of self with all things.

In Ladakh, illness is often thought to be brought about by the invasion of hostile outside forces. Once sickened, you need to get rid of the invading spirits. Even madness is thought to be the result of spirit possession. You regain your sanity by casting out the demons. You turn to lay oracles and oracle-monks to help you do it.

People feel compelled by more than current discomfort to deal with their interpersonal problems, because Buddhism states that unsettled issues create *karma* (ethical retribution), which consigns them to an endless string of lives troubled by the same or connected issues. If there is a connection between this life and the one that went before, the one who now steps on your foot was mistreated by you in a previous life. Oracles and monks offer explanation of how things came to be. Some work on your physical condition, others on your mental. Through such treatment, people try to gain control.

The importance of the *Gompas*, monks, and nuns continues but since tourism has brought money to Ladakh, a country that previously did not much rely on it, a new form of evaluation, monetary worth, threatens to undermine the culture. Without money, people were shaped by the Buddhist principle of friendship. Extended families cohabited, shared work, and all of life's events. They helped one another, helped people from their villages and even strangers. Although accounting was done, it was not merely a matter of numbers. It was more like the following: I give you what you need and you do the same for me. When you work for me, I supply the food and *chang* (barley beer). We work, party, and mourn together, accompanied by ritual song. We sing the traditional songs that are associated with each event and feel close.

As mentioned earlier, Ladakh is a land of stones; structures are made of them; grassy fields are bounded by stone walls. When the grass is high, the people sing as they cut the grass, which helps them to set a steady pace. The words of the song are: "it is good to work hard." Men and women sing alternating verses with considerable volume and excellent pitch. They interrupt work for lunch, which is shared by a large group, all part of the family. While the women sit in a group at one end of the circle, and the men are at the other end, the women and the men converse together.

I was invited with my companions Peter, a photographer, and Wahab, my Ladakhi Muslim driver, to have lunch with our hosts. Part of the meal consisted of buttered and salted tea, yoghurt with spiced greens, and *chang* (a drink). *Chang* is made in large pots and uses up about three-fourth of Ladakh's barley. When I told my hosts that my stomach was upset, they advised me to drink some *chang*—which, to my surprise, settled my stomach quite a bit. I learned that when the people get sick they often consult their local *amchis* (herbal healers), diviners *Bonpo* (secular and monks), as well as oracles. *Amchis* are trained herbal practitioners, who dispense ancient herbal and physical remedies.

Then we met a neighbor of my friend Sonam, called Norzin. She lived in a farmhouse and raised barley, wheat, vegetables, and sheep for meat and wool. This woman asked us into her house and all of us sat in the kitchen, where there was a large standard metal stove with engraved sides. In Ladakh such a stove serves for both cooking and heating. A warmed kitchen around mealtime is the household center. Norzin served her visitors salted *solja* (tea) with milk, homemade yoghurt, and unleavened wheat bread. While Sonam translated our conversation, Norzin talked about her family and herself, saying that she had one difficulty, namely that she could not see well at a far distance. Although there were treatment centers in Leh, she was too busy to take the bus ride to the city. However, our photographer Peter asked Norzin to try on his drugstore reading glasses; and they greatly helped her. Before we left, Peter gave Norzin the glasses as a gift.

Next, Norzin talked about what seemed to be severe arthritis. Her legs couldn't easily support her weight. With the coming of tourism, sugar has entered the local diet and sugar is often associated with arthritis. The other most frequent health problem of Ladakhis is high blood pressure, brought on by their continuous consumption of *solja* (salted tea)—30 cups a day is considered not a lot.

She said that her painful back had been treated by a local *amchi*, who burned the ailing part as well as a portion of her scalp. She showed me a small area in the middle of her head that had no hair. When asked about the consequences of burning, she said it took away the problem. I later heard that my hostess, Sonam's mother, had her knee burned by an *amchi*, which also cured the disorder. Perhaps burning is like the Chinese *moxa* (herb) burning that brings blood to site of the malfunction.

Norzin's husband returned from working in the fields. He sat silently on the bench beside her and listened to her talk while he drank a cup of *chang*. He showed us similar burn scars on his back and also said that burning caused his problem to depart.

However, his wife's poor eyesight and arthritic hip could not be burnt away. Given insufficient time or money to go for *amchi* herbs or a Western doctor's medicine, she suffered. To go to a Western doctor did not occur to her. Neither did she think of getting glasses for presbyopia. Like most local people, she regarded her troubles as imposed from without and not something she could solve. She accepted her pain as part of life and worried about the other family members.

Diviners, oracles, and *amchi* are a big part of the Ladakhi villagers' approach to medicine. The three oracles I saw in Choglamsar all come from Stok. There is no saying to whom an oracle will present itself. Many villages have oracles and *amchis*. Western medicine is harder to find. After seeing the oracles work on patients, I asked oracle Lobsang Dolma for an interview.

When first we entered her room, she brought us tea. Most Ladakhi meetings start with salted tea. When I asked her how she became an oracle, she said that it was not her choice. The oracle came to her unbidden. The husband who sat beside her had once been the channel for an oracle that no longer came to him. She also said that one of her children had been chosen by another oracle.

When an oracle occupies a medium, the medium becomes an oracle, in effect. It seems that being the voice of an oracle is an accepted Ladakhi profession. However, before you are seen as a valid vehicle, it must be proved by what you say and do and the help you bring to others that your actions are not the work of madness, which is the result of a possession.

Now that Lobsang has accepted her role, the oracle takes away her consciousness. After spirit possession has ended, she has no memory of what she has done and said. In her adjacent working room, she showed us a small cup set on the altar in which her *self* resides during the time that the oracle uses her. She said that the hardest thing to do after possession is to reenter her body.

Now in her early sixties, Lobsang was first visited by a spirit some 40 years before. At that time, she did not want to grant entry. She remained set against oracle possession, although fighting it took energy. Two years prior to our visit she felt ready to allow the oracles to use her. Once this started she felt relieved and even happy.

I asked her what kind of training she got in curing people. She said that the oracles educated her. I asked if real people also were involved in this teaching. No, all her teachers were oracles. Oracles other than those spirits that possessed her came to test her powers. They hid things, cloths of a certain color, ritual objects that she had to find. She said that it was easy to find these things. She also had to remove pins from the body of a sufferer. Swallowed pins and other ingested objects are a common Ladakhi complaint. Body pain is often seen as the consequence of something that must be removed. The oracles gave her many such tests, all of which she passed.

Although there are six oracles that use her as a medium, the one who is strongest and most often present is the resident oracle-deity of Hemis, a famous Ladakhi *Gompa*. The Hemis oracle came to her without her previously knowing of it. She said that her ability to be a vehicle for spirits has been tested by some *Rinpoches* (advanced monks). She said that when she first started working with the oracles, good and bad spirits came. Then her Hemis oracle performed a ritual that made her only available to the good.

She was passed by the local Choglamsar *Lama* (guru, teacher) Togdan *Rinpoche*, a learned *Tulku* (reincarnated *Lama*) who was born in upper Ladakh and educated in Tibet. A child who is believed to be a *Tulku* is tested by the *Rinpoches* who are searching for the "right" successor. They ask the candidate to choose the objects that once belonged to him from many others. A reborn *Rinpoche* will choose his own and reject the rest. After priestly divination and testing has declared a child to be a *Tulku*, the reincarnation of an important, deceased religious figure, he is taken into the Tibetan church for retraining.

While waiting in his living room, Togdan *Rinpoche*'s wife, Gangchen Dolma, told us that her own son was a *Tulku*. Before his birth, she had been told by a *Lama* to keep sacred objects about the room and meditate upon them, to treat her child's birth as special. She did this and had dreams that told her of the birth of an important person.

All this became a distant memory after her infant arrived and soon began to show special signs. When he was aged two and was asked to choose between sacred objects that were of the Gelugpa or Kargyupa sect, he would choose only from the Kargyu. At about three, he spoke of the place in which he would one day live and clearly described the building. He said that people from that building would come to get him.

Unable to ignore this, she took the child to a *Lama* for evaluation. He said that her child was a *Tulku* and to expect the people to come for him.

When it happened, her son was happy to go and live in the building he had described. He liked to visit his family but was overjoyed to return to school. He acted like a child for a while but then returned to his adult demeanor.

His mother told me of this in a way that was devoid of pride. She had devoted herself to the healing work of Togdan *Rinpoche*, her husband, translating for his many foreign patients. Before this she had been a nurse for 20 years, working with Tibetan refugees who had gotten quite sick after leaving Tibet. Some came up from southern India where they suffered from the change in climate and the introduction to many new germs.

She said that her husband was a great healer and showed me a document signed by the Dalai Lama that declared it. She told us that he had taken away her migraine headaches after several months of his medicine. Hearing this, Peter, my photographer friend, who has periodic migraines, perked up. The next time we came with our friend Tashi to have the *Rinpoche* treat her headaches, Peter also saw him.

Togdan *Rinpoche* prescribed physically and spiritually healing amulets for Peter. He was told to take them on a bimonthly basis for two months, then once a month for four months. *Rinpoche*'s wife said that she'd get them for Peter while we visited the oracle. We later learned that she had to send an emissary to several local Tibetan pharmacies since such tablets were popular and hard to get.

I saw large pills that were wrapped in colorful red ribbons. I wondered how they were to be swallowed but refrained from questioning. I did not want my questions to interfere with whatever help they offered.

After she told Peter how to take them and he asked her the cost, she said there was none. She only asked us to deliver a package from the *Rinpoche* to one of his patients, an *Ani*, a Mongolian Kalmuk of the Tibetan tradition, living as a nun in a New Jersey town. We said we would and thanked her.

I was interested in how the *Rinpoche* functioned, how and what he knew, and so we came back to see him with Tashi and her brother. Tashi's repeated headaches have usurped her attention, made her disconsolate and disinterested. It does not help that she has had a law degree for one year and cannot find a legal job that makes use of her training in New Delhi. I told her, "Your headaches will go away once you find a job in law."

We went into the *Rinpoche*'s study. I saw an altar on which there were bowls filled with oil, butter lamps, and sacred objects like a conch shell, *dorje* (thunderbolt scepter) and bell. On the wall was a photograph of the Dalai Lama. Togdan *Rinpoche* sat at his desk. Between us was a table covered with honorific white scarves that each patient ritually puts there before being treated. Next to the scarves was the money the patients leave in an amount of their own choosing for his service.

Although surrounded by religious objects, Togdan *Rinpoche* seemed to be sensible and thoughtful. He wore glasses and had short hair. His wife also looked quite modern in a long Tibetan dress, blouse and apron, lipstick and earrings. Her hair also was short and pinned back.

The *Rinpoche* explained that Tashi's headaches came from the approach that her older brother took to the household *lhato* (small spirit altar) on his roof. Her brother lived in the "large family house," which had a name. In Ladakh, people lack a last name but are known by the name of the house in which they live.

Every house flies spirit flags and often has rooftop altars. Religion is everywhere. People spin hand-held spirit wheels while sitting and relaxing. They silently or quietly chant *Om! Mani padme hum* (Om! The Jewel is in the Lotus! Hum), a *mantra* (short prayer) that is thought to help all creatures move toward enlightenment.

The goal of Mahayana Buddhism is to help all living things move toward higher rebirth until they permanently become one with their essence. *Om! Mani padme hum* is printed on the large prayer wheels that are set on the right wall of the *Gompas*. You spin them when walking past to send this *mantra* into the ears of deities, particularly that of Avalokiteshwara, the most powerful Tibetan deity that is associated with compassion and mercy.

Tashi was told by the *Rinpoche* that her *Lhato* was growing ever smaller and was not getting enough attention. This untended family shrine angered the spirits that guard the house, anger that they directed at her, which gave her headaches.

According to a more educated *Lama*, superstition rules many Ladakhis, including its priests. He added that any explanation can have a positive effect whether or not it is realistic. When Tashi heard the *Rinpoche*'s explanation, her headache remained but pressure on her shoulders lessened. His analysis gave her something she could deal with.

The *Rinpoche* then spoke to Tashi's younger brother Norbu, who was very depressed without having analyzed the source of his difficulty. Perhaps he didn't want to face it. Another sister had previously told me that Norbu was in an arranged marriage, as are about 95 percent of the Ladakhi population in his thirties age range. He has been married for three years to a childish woman who does little for him and will not discuss matters. She has borne two children and would happily leave him and take the children with her. This he doesn't want.

In the *Rinpoche*'s living room where Norbu and I waited, I asked if his wife was concerned with his depression. He said she never brought it up. It must be hard to be with a person who is so cut off. His "chosen" wife is not much better than the husband who was "chosen" for his other sister at age 18. This man was an in-law of her sister's husband. She did her sister a favor by marrying him. They were married three months when he spoke of leaving her to live in a monastery one day soon. The date for his

departure was unclear. Married life was a disaster, which she had the courage to quickly end.

Despite her considerable beauty and intelligence, Tashi is now in her
thirties and has not remarried. She claims to be too old to get a man, and
says that none are left. To the Muslims who have proposed, she says she
must marry a Buddhist. Burned by her first marriage, she seems determined
to enjoy a life filled with friends and family without the hindrance of a
mate. Her mother weeps over her unmarried state and she herself sometimes worries about her approaching older years, but that is the only impact
at present.

To Norbu, *Rinpoche* said that he must try to speak to his wife since the
children will suffer in such a marriage. He gave her brother a flag to hang
in his home on which were painted Sanskrit phrases. For Togdan *Rinpoche*,
spiritual needs are part of the cure.

The *Rinpoche* spoke to a Western woman in our party, who told about
her boyfriend back at home, with whom she was always fighting. What
did the future hold for them? *Rinpoche* tossed three dice in a cup and then
asked if she liked direct talk, to which she answered yes. He said that she
should not marry this man since it would not work out. On what did he
base his comment? Could he feel the pain in her heart?

Rinpoche is a spiritual man with many levels of skill. Perhaps while using
the dice in a superstitious way, he also got a message from his well-
developed intuition. Mediators learn to ignore personal needs so that they
can more accurately read another's mind and feelings. His wife said that
he has helped people with severe physical and emotional problems, has
brought people out of their psychotic states. Still, it was strange to hear
him make such a definitive statement about her relationship. I did not think
he spoke like that to scare her into seeing him more often, for which she'd
have to pay him. He charged a nominal fee for entry, a small sum for the
honorific white scarf to be left on his table, next to which you left whatever
money you wanted to give. If anything, his wife said that he was eager to
return to his meditation.

I felt close to him and to his wife. Perhaps it is the psychological development of these people that makes you feel that no difference comes between you. It is the vanity of false ego that keeps people apart. Yet she and
I were utterly different when it came to the depths of our faith. It was
about this that I later questioned the *Rinpoche*. Raised by militantly athe-
istic people, I respected my scientific attitude. I only ask of myself to be
open and to look at everything so that I can later decide for myself.

I spoke to him about my lack of faith in what I cannot test. He sat there
tossing his dice for a while. I do not think he understood my question but
his wife who was quite articulate said that no one can give you faith and
no one should. You have only to keep observing and eventually decide
what to believe.

I later learned from Dr. Jamspal that the *Rinpoche* based his comments on the throw of three dice while communicating in his mind with the Tibetan protector deity, Palden Lhamo. I saw a rather monstrous painting of this spirit on a *thanka* (spiritual scroll painting). Among other horrific things, Palden Lhamo sits on her dead son's skin. He was murdered by her to punish her husband for continuing to kill animals. The *thanka* shows Palden Lhamo and her *mo sho*, her dice. According to Dr. Jamspal, there are 15 chapters written on the predictions of Palden Lhamo, all of which are memorized. Odd dice are considered good and even dice are bad. What seemed to have been an analysis that came out of the *Rinpoche*'s intuition actually came from a book.

The Gelugpa sect of Tibetan Buddhists in general and the Dalai Lama himself often turn to Palden Lhamo for instruction. The Dalai Lama went to his own high oracle when the Chinese started marching into Tibet. The oracle told him to flee Tibet, which he did. It was a wise move.

According to Dr. Jamspal, there are many levels of oracles. Some are on a low level and can only effect physical cures. Others will not do this. Higher oracles will describe the future. They earn their reputation through the accuracy of their predictions. Dr. Jamspal said that sometimes the oracles have a healing effect that you cannot understand. He called this the law of "dependent arising," a relationship that lacks evident explanation in the present moment but has real cause and effect.

He gave several examples of "dependent arising." One came to him from a skeptical friend, a scientist who was Ladakhi born but did not believe in local superstition. Talking to Dr. Jamspal on a visit to Princeton University, he said that his one-year-old daughter had developed abscesses on her chin that medicine could not cure.

Encouraged to do this by his wife, he took her to the caretaker of a *Gompa* who uttered mantras when he saw her abscessed face and blew into the air with some spit in it, onto her face. Blowing is often a part of sacred healing. The abscesses disappeared over the next two days. Her father, who had tried all kinds of Western medicine to cure his child, had no answer. She was too young to think and to be affected by another's verbal explanations or expectations. The only thing he knew was what he saw, that her abscessed faced was cured.

Dr. Jamspal told me another story of the "dependent arising" of healing. He knew a man who had a tattoo on the back of his hand that he wanted removed but did not know how to do it. This man visited a monk in a Ladakhi monastery who grabbed his hand in greeting and when he released his grip, the tattoo was gone. The monk had not heard of the man's desire to get rid of it and did not state his intention to remove it. Somehow it happened. After this, the man became quite religious.

A third example came from a woman who suffered from severe headaches. She desperately asked Dr. Jamspal, who was visiting her city on a lecture tour, to give her a healing mantra. He recited the Medicine Buddha Mantra, which asks that sickness be removed from all sentient beings. Several months later he returned to the city to be met by an overjoyed woman who thanked him for his healing. He responded, "I get no credit for this. It all has to do with your faith."

After seeing Togdan *Rinpoche*, Peter, Tashi, our friend from the United States, and I walked across the road and through some interconnecting yards to the oracle's home. We went into a small, rectangular room painted robin's egg blue. There was an altar at the far end on which sat tiny bowls of oil. Hanging over the altar on the wall was the drawing of a threatening, nonhuman face. I later learned that this was a portrait of her main oracle, the one that came from the Hemis *Gompa*.

Peter and I seated ourselves behind the altar on a bench. A Western woman with short hair, a floppy cap, and a sweatshirt that said, "I love Kathmandu," asked several individuals in the growing crowd whether Peter's videotaping would ruin the oracle's treatment, but no one else seemed concerned.

Two oracles appeared one at a time with water running off their faces. I assumed that letting in the spirit involved throwing water in their faces in the other room. First to come was Lobsang Dolma. She threw seeds and rice into corners of the room as if to ready it. Throwing seeds and rice is a ritual that was later repeated many times by both oracles, especially while they sang and played on a triangle and *damaru* (small drum).

Lobsang started chanting while beating on her *damaru*. In came a second oracle with water streaming off her face to join in the chanting while striking a triangle. They set up a strong rhythm, sometimes only singing, drumming, or ringing while they lighted candles, took butter, and put it on the edge of one oil-filled cup. They removed the cup with a buttered edge from one table to the next. The butter is thought to bring luck.

While singing in a rhythmic, steady way, they were joined by a third woman whose behavior was more dramatic. Her eyes rolled back in her head to show only the whites. Sometimes she stared out of the corners of her eyes while shaking her hands and fingers. She let out little repetitive, high-pitched cries that sounded like a rooster about to be slaughtered. Her behavior was so extreme that Tashi got up from her seat near the woman and came to sit next to me.

She sang in harmony with the singing oracles, but with her own periodicity. Then Lobsang put a white shawl around this oracle's shoulders as if to treat her. She was not acting as were the other two, who put on halters and aprons as they sang, tied paper crowns on their heads in the shape of three ovals on which were painted Buddha figures, who put on handkerchiefs as masks that covered their foreheads and came down close to the eyes. One tied a handkerchief across her mouth.

This dressing went on as they played and chanted, a way to assume a role that did not represent their *self*. When later questioned about it, Lobsang said that her *self* leaves her body when the oracle comes, and goes to the small altar cup. She said that her *self*'s departure from her body was easy, pushed out as it was by the oracles. It was the reentry that was difficult. It took real effort and left her tired.

She told me that she was relieved when our interview was over because the oracles were pushing on her to enter. When I later discussed the distinction between good and bad oracles with Dr. Jamspal, he said that a relative of his, a niece who is a medium, when first visited by oracles in her early twenties, was thought to be going mad. The usefulness of spirit possession proved her sane. Repeated practice turned her "madness" into oracle empowerment. Now she was able to help people with it.

After the women had sung and played for over half an hour, they began to treat patients who came forward and sat near them. They sucked through iron straws, or directly on their patient's flesh, or blew on or pressed it with objects. They simultaneously treated different people, sometimes stopping to chant or beat a drum. People waiting for treatment were seated around the edge of the room, on the floor, or stood at the door.

The entranced woman who behaved most wildly and put on no special garb treated no one. She continued to chant, roll her eyes, shake her hands, and emit the sound of roosters. After one oracle had treated several people, she turned to this woman, bent down the woman's head, and poured drops of oil that were taken from a cup on the altar. She slowly brought the woman out of the trance. I later heard from Tashi that this entranced woman had refused to treat anyone and so was asked to leave. This woman, herself sometimes an oracle, was one of the oracle's patients and possibly a mental one. She exemplified the fact that acting as a conduit for spirits creates a thin line between doctoring and madness. Possibly, while doing this, one can be mad for a while and then become sane again.

I had a firsthand experience of their treatment since I had injured my left knee by falling on a stone while trekking in the mountains of Kashmir. I now know that I had displaced my tibia, which made it impossible to bend my knee or lean on it as I thoughtlessly did when trying to pull down a window. Agony immediately followed. The injured knee had me walking up and down stairs like a baby, one foot lowered onto the next level and the other brought beside it. I was unwilling to rest my foot as advised while on vacation and hoped that the oracle would find some cure.

After I rolled up my pant leg, the younger oracle sucked on parts of my knee and ankle through a metal straw. Without my telling her what part hurt me, she worked on what hurt me most. The pressure she put on my knee was considerable; each time the oracle sucked out some kind of invisible substance, she spat clear liquid into a pot.

Tashi's older brother sat by me to give me courage. He also held my leg, but I breathed deeply enough to distract myself from the pain. After the treatment was over, I was able to walk down stairs one step after the other in a normal fashion.

Perhaps this was only the result of the power of suggestion or of cognitive dissonance that asked, how could so painful a treatment have no effect? Perhaps, after being helped by the oracle, I used the knee too much, which injured it again. Did the oracle's treatment actually help me? I do not know.

It was interesting when the Western woman using Tashi as her translator asked the oracle the same question she had asked the *Rinpoche* about her troubled relationship. I was curious to hear how oracles answered such questions. Unlike the *Rinpoche*, the oracle said that it would slowly work out. Was she more accurate than he, more accurate than a Chinese fortune cookie? Was she telling her clients what they liked to hear? Most people like to hear good news and what she said was soothing.

The oracles went from client to client. One person said she had kidney stones. The oracle directly sucked on the patient's back starting below the waist and working up, also above her breasts and down her arm, and to the end of each finger. Sucking left many hickeys. The patient sat naked to the waist in the crowd, holding her sweater to cover her breasts. She seemed relatively unselfconscious despite a room filled with strangers. She was there for healing as were they. Her baby was held by a man who sat on a nearby bench. Perhaps he was a relative, friend, or stranger. He played with the baby and when the baby got upset, took him out for a little walk. Like most Ladakhis, he loved children. She seemed quite unconcerned about the child. Good care was expected.

At a certain point, the oracle sucked and then spat, into her own hand, a black clot with about a half-inch diameter. This she pressed open with a knife. It was of a dirty, soft substance, presumably a kidney stone. Later, she took a stone out of a man who suffered from pain in the stomach from drinking. Removing substances was not a regular feature of the treatment but one that occasionally happened, that and sucking and then spitting filthy water.

She worked on the abdomen of the woman who wore the "I Love Kathmandu" shirt as she leaned against the knees of the oracle's husband with her shirt rolled up and stomach distended. After sucking on her abdomen through a straw, the oracle repeatedly spat out blackened water. Where did that black color come from? I had seen the oracle pour water through the straw to clean it between patients. Was it a matter of concealment?

The string of people waiting to be worked on by the oracle stretched out the door. I wanted to wait until all were done, especially to see if there was a finishing ceremony, but I did not know when it would be. I asked Tashi if there was a formal completion and she said no. Treatment went on this way until the end. The closest thing I saw to a completion was bringing the nonfunctioning oracle out of her trance. The treating oracle had been very direct in reaching the woman, whose hands stopped shaking, eyes dropped into a normal position, and who uttered no more rooster cries. After standing for a few minutes doing nothing, she left the room.

An oracle sees many patients. Do oracles believe in what they are doing or is it all a hoax? If you read L. Austine Waddell (1972), on oracles, particularly among the *Lamas*, he thinks it to be a form of usury based on fear generated by those who want to sell their services.

I did hear (via translation), an oracle scold the man with stomach pain for waiting so long before coming for treatment. Was she ensuring further trade? In my interview with Lobsang Dolma, I asked if she had seen any real cures as a result of her practice. She said that while she was not directly aware of her "practice" since she was only a vehicle for the oracle, she has heard that paralyzed people were helped to walk again.

There are many oracles in Ladakh. People come from far away to see them. In the treatment that I attended, there was a couple from Jammu, a distance of some 400 miles from Choglamsar.

There is a vast but shrinking population of monks and nuns. The priests do not have as much leadership as they had ten years ago so their income is not as well assured. Still, the Tibetan faith is everywhere in the countryside and even in much of the city of Leh. Do Ladakhis believe what they practice? I think so. Do oracles make use of remarkable showmanship? Yes.

Are the oracles only putting on a show? Dr. Jamspal thinks that they have some power but sometimes fake the results. He told me of a man who had a chicken bone stuck in his throat that his medical doctor was unable to remove. The man was so desperate that he went to an oracle who easily got the bone to jump out of his throat and into his fingers. The man did not think of showing the doctor his retrieved bone. The doctor said that action by the oracle was unrelated to the dislodging of the bone. Thus do we all cling to our self-supporting beliefs.

Dr. Jamspal told me a contrary story of an oracle who claimed to remove a nail from the heart of a man who had tried to kill himself by stabbing. The man felt better for a year and then deteriorated. When an X ray was taken, the nail was found to be still in his heart.

How did the oracles I witnessed in a fully lighted room with everybody sitting close and watching get dirty water into their implements to spit out after sucking on the patient's sickness? Where did the soft object come from that appeared at the end of their metal straw after sucking on the patient's body? Not all oracles suck on their clients. Some dance their way to knowledge like the oracle who dances for hours at the roof edge in the Hemis *Gompa*. What in this gives them balance?

Dr. Jamspal and his friends—a psychiatrist, Dr. H. and his scholar wife, N.—saw a Ladakhi oracle easily bend a *phurba* (heavy sword) between two fingers to show how the spirit that entered him made him strong. Mediums bring a lot of energy to their touching. The intensity of their focus and the faith that people bring to it can cause healing. Even in the

West, meditation has entered medicine. The mind affects the body. So does touching.

My knee was not healed by the oracle's treatment in a lasting way. Peter has not had a headache since then but still has five months of treatment and it is too soon to know if the headache pills will work. How much of the oracle's healing depends on faith? How much depends on a placebo effect? That some are healed or changed by their treatment is indisputable.

ACKNOWLEDGMENTS

Many thanks go to Dr. Lozang Jamspal for the very helpful information he gave about the attitudes Ladakhi monks take toward spirits and oracles and the effectiveness of the oracle's treatment. Most important, the author extends her appreciation to Dr. Jamspal for introducing her to his family, including Tsering, Phuntsok, and Rinchen, who drew her into Ladakhi life.

REFERENCES

Jamspal, Lozang. "The Five Royal Patrons and the Three Maitreya Images in Basgo, the Ancient Capital of Ladakh." In the *Proceedings of the International Association for Ladakh Studies* (to be published).

Waddell, L. Austine (1972). *Tibetan Buddhism with its mystic cults, symbolism and mythology.* New York: Dover.

6

Traditional Healing in India

*Nihar Ranjan Mrinal, Uma Singhal Mrinal,
and B. Runi Mukherji*

This chapter explores traditional methods of healing in India, where there is a wide array of medical and healing traditions. In the words of Vakil (1966), India is

a large and marvelous museum in medicine as well as other fields, the magic practices of primitive peoples, the cults of stones and trees, the beliefs in amulets and charms, traveling physicians and ambulant doctors, the scholastic, pedantic, dogmatic, and the most modern type of specialists—in actual practice, shoulder to shoulder.

In modern-day India, where there is a large and well-developed system of Western medicine, doctors and physicians congenially coexist with traditional healers such as the *vaids* of the Ayurvedic and Siddha systems, *hakims* of the Unani Islamic tradition, and herbalists. In addition there are the faith healers, the *swamis, sannyasi, maharaj babas, matas, fakirs, siddhas* (diviners), sorcerers, shamans, palmists, horoscope experts who practice unique blends of religion, magic, alchemy, astrology, medicine, and faith. The following sections of this chapter present a summary of the historical development, underlying philosophical principles, and methods of disease identification and intervention of the major healing traditions that are still widely practiced in India today.

VEDIC SYSTEMS

Between 3,000 and 1,500 B.C. an extraordinarily sophisticated civilization developed in the valley of the Indus River in northern India. Great, intricately laid-out city-states encompassing over 500,000 square miles flourished, sharing an elegant system of pictorial writing, a remarkably accurate system of weights and measures, organized sanitation, transportation, and agricultural support networks. While the script on the seals from the Indus Valley civilization has yet to be deciphered, the oldest extant body of sacred literature arose from this stable and prosperous culture. These are the *Vedas*, the four sacred books of Hinduism. The *Vedas* were transmitted orally from generation to generation for many centuries, and only more recently have been committed to writing. Thus, the actual dates of origin of the *Vedas* can only be estimated. It is believed that the *Rig Veda* is the oldest, and may be about 4,000 years old. It is a collection of hymns and constitutes our earliest knowledge of the religious system that is the foundation of Hinduism. It also contains the names and description of over 70 herbs used in healing and describes many of the practices of medicine and healing in ancient India. The *Atharva Veda* is the most recent, dating back about 3,200 years, providing further information about healing and medicine. The *Ayurveda*, which is the text on which current Ayurvedic medicine is based, is considered to be an *Upaveda*, or supplement to the *Atharva Veda*.

Ayurveda

The term *Ayurveda* comes from two Sanskrit words *ayur*, meaning life, and *veda*, meaning knowledge. Ayurvedic medicine is thus described as a "knowledge of how to live," emphasizing that good health is the responsibility of the individual. In Ayurvedic medicine, illness is seen in terms of imbalance, with herbs and dietary controls used to restore equilibrium.

The *Ayurveda* was believed to have consisted of 1,000 chapters and about 10,000 verses. Only some eight of those chapters remain. Legend has it that the *Ayurveda* was taught to the great sage Rishi Bharadwaj, and this knowledge was transmitted to his disciples, and later passed on to Atreya, who is known as the father of Indian medicine. He established a school of medicine near Taxila, around 600 B.C. The earliest written medical text that is still available to us is the *Charaka Samhita*, written by the Ayurvedic teacher Charaka about 700 B.C. The *Charaka Samhita* contains extensive information about the practice of medicine and the use of herbs in healing. About a century later, Dhanavantri established an Institute of Surgery at Varanasi (modern day Benaras). His pupil Susruta wrote the *Susruta Samhita*, which focuses on the practice of surgery in Ayurvedic medicine. Surgery was taught with the help of the dissection of fruits, plants, animals, and with dead and artificial bodies.

The practice of medicine in those early days was limited to the higher priestly classes, who were typically extensively educated in related subjects such as astronomy, mathematics, philosophy, and music. It is believed that these experts traveled to many far-flung parts of the world such as Scandinavia, Egypt, Greece, Babylonia, and Persia. It is well-documented that Hippocrates (468–377 B.C.), who is considered the father of Western medicine, had absorbed many of the ideas from the Indian medical tradition.

The Ayurvedic System and the Identification of Disease

In the Vedic tradition, as with ancient Greek and traditional Chinese medicine, the microcosm of the individual is linked with the cosmos. The Ayurvedic system considers three primal forces: *prana*, the breath of life; *agni*, the spirit of life and fire; and *soma*, the manifestation of harmony. All matter is considered to consist of the five elements: earth, water, fire, air, and ether. Ether, this nothingness that fills all the spaces of the Universe, was also recognized by the ancient Greeks. According to the Vedic view, *agni*, the digestive force, converts all the elements into three humors, which influence individual health and temperaments. In the Vedic view, if digestion were perfect, there would be no imbalance of the humors. When there is an imbalance of the humors, ill health and disease follow. The elements air and ether produce the humor of *vata* (wind); the element fire produces the humor *pitta* (fire or bile); and the elements of air and water produce the humor *kapha* (phlegm). The dominant humor is considered to control the character or temperament of the individual, producing the *vata*, *pitta*, or *kapha* type of constitution in the individual.

Though Hippocrates is considered to be the father of modern Western medicine, for many centuries Medieval Europe followed the teachings of Galen (A.D. 131–199), who wrote extensively about the four humors of the body and was influenced heavily by these concepts from India. His melancholic personality resembles the *vata*-type temperament, *pitta* matches the choleric type, and *kapha* the phlegmatic.

Further, in the Ayurvedic classification, the body is considered to be made up of seven types of vital tissues or *dhatus*, which work together to ensure the smooth functioning of the body. They include *rasa* (plasma), *raktta* (blood), *meda* (fat), *mamsa* (muscle), *asti* (bone), and *majja* (marrow). Two other concepts are also important in Ayurvedic medicine: *srotas* and *ama*. The *strotas* are the vital body channels through which energy moves. While the *srotas* are like blood vessels and nerves in their transference of energy, they are not the physical forms of these bodily passages, rather they are the energetic equivalents of them. The concept of *srota* is an integral part of most Far Eastern medicine: Tibetan medicine speaks of the energy body or the energy field of the body, and energy flow is the basis of the concept of *chi* or *qi* in Chinese medicine, and in medical practices such as *qi'gong* and acupuncture. *Ama* is the waste that accumulates in the body. In the *Ayurveda*, foods *are* medicine, and all foods are characterized in terms of their ability to aid digestion, balance the humors, sustain and replenish the vital tissues of the body, and cleanse vital channels and remove accumulated waste.

The Ayurvedic physician or *vaidya*, depends upon his or her senses as key diagnostic tools. Pulse rate, body temperature and feel of the body, the tonal quality of the voice, and overall appearance are very important in the Ayurvedic system. Some 600 types of pulse rates are described in the Sanskrit literature. Bhattacharya (1949) has described various types of pulse rates and their significance. In addition, the *vaidya* will inquire into the heredity, life condition, and dietary habits of the patient.

Therapy

> From food are born all creatures, which live upon food and after death return to food. Food is the chief of all things. It is therefore said to be the medicine of all diseases of the body.
>
> > *The Upanishads*, c. 500 B.C.

Imbalance of the humors *vata*, *pitta*, and *kapha* are seen as the root causes of disease. All foods and herbs are described in terms of the effects they have on digestion, and the diet is strictly controlled to restore the balance of the humors. Many of the interventions also are classified by the resemblance of the herb in shape, color, or structure to the disease it might be used to treat. For example, lungwort, whose leaves resemble diseased lungs, is used to treat bronchitis and tuberculosis, and yellow-colored herbs or flowers such as celandine are used to treat liver disorders. This ancient Vedic doctrine of "like affecting like" found echoes in the work of Paracelsus (1493–1541), who began revolutionizing health care in the 1530s in Europe. He treated illness based on the *Doctrine of Signatures*, which maintained that the outward appearance of a plant gave an indication of the ailment that it would cure.

The Ayurvedic approach also adds another important ingredient to the process of healing: the thoughts of the person seeking the healing. Both the *Susruta Samhita* and the *Charaka Samhita* refer repeatedly to the feelings and will of the individual, noting that the maintenance and efficacy of a therapy is directly related to the belief of the person seeking the healing (Bhishagratna, 1981).

Ayurvedic Practice Past and Present

Ayurvedic medicine flourished in India for many centuries and saw its greatest expansion under the rule of the Ashoka (ca. 269–232 B.C.), who established a huge, stable, and prosperous empire in India. Ashoka was a Hindu warrior-king who, disgusted by the violence of war, became a devout Buddhist. With the spread of Buddhism throughout Asia, Ayurvedic medicine also flourished. Ashoka sent his ambassador-emissaries to Tibet, Ceylon, Syria, Egypt, and other Hellenic kingdoms, and with them the concepts of Ayurvedic medicine spread to become the foundation of many systems of medicine and healing, both Eastern and Western. The practice of Ayurveda was severely curtailed for several centuries with the advent of Muslim invaders, the Turco-Afghans and Moghuls, during the eleventh and twelfth centuries, and the practice of Ayurvedic medicine was forcibly replaced by the Unani system of medicine (which will be described later). With the desecration and destruction of the Buddhist shrines and monasteries, many of the texts were also lost. Ayurvedic medicine was dealt a particularly lethal blow under British rule. In 1833 the British closed all schools of Ayurvedic medicine that were still functioning in India.

The government of India today is making a tremendous push to rejuvenate the practice of Ayurvedic medicine. Many new schools and colleges of Ayurvedic medicine have been started, and in a January 1994 speech, Prime Minister Narasimha Rao of India stated that he intended to start a separate ministry in the government to popularize Ayurvedic medicine (*Hitavada English Daily*, January 7, 1997, p. 3). Today it is fairly common in India to have a doctor who practices Western or allopathic medicine also prescribe Ayurvedic herbal remedies along with modern drugs. Also the Ayurvedic concepts of maintaining the equilibrium of the body by regulating the diet, and the characterization of everyday foods in terms of their effects on the body, have passed into the social and cultural ethos and are part of everyday practice among most Indians.

Yoga

Etymologically, the word *yoga* derives from the root *yuj*, to bind together, hold fast, or yoke, which also governs the Latin *jungere*, or *jugum*, and the French *joug*. The word *yoga*, in general, is used to designate any ascetic technique and any method of meditation. There is a form of "classic" yoga, which was propounded by Patanjali, in the second century B.C., in his celebrated book, *Yoga-sutras* (Shivananda, 1950). There are also countless forms of popular yogas, Buddhist yogas, Jainist yogas, and many yogas that are considered magical or mystical. The ones described here are the classic forms. Tantric Yoga will also be described, as will mantras, yantras, and mandalas, which are important related concepts.

Over and over again, Indian texts repeat the thesis that existence is suffering. Almost all of the Indian religious texts can be characterized as soteriological—that is, having as their ultimate objective salvation or deliverance from suffering: suffering from celestial misery provoked by the gods, terrestrial misery caused by nature, and from inner or organic misery.

According to the sacred texts, this deliverance or salvation (*moksha* or *mukti*) can come through knowledge (*vidya, jnana*) or by means of techniques, such as yoga. The practice of yoga gives the *yogin* (the practicer of yoga) various psychic powers, which are collectively known as *siddhi*.

There are several forms of yoga, among which the best known in the West are Hatha Yoga and Rajya Yoga. Hatha Yoga is concerned exclusively with the physiology—that is, performing and perfecting a series of physical postures that concentrates body and mind toward a single point (*ekagrata*). This concentration of the body on the various postures along with the correct breathing (*pranayana*) enable the purification of the internal organs and the elimination of alimentary residues and toxins. Rajya Yoga, often confused with simpler forms of meditation, is the series of practices for the control of mind and thought. The practice of any yoga should be done under the supervision of a teacher or *guru*, and typically involves a series of related practices or disciplines such as taking a vow of silence (*mown*), and the practice of steady gazing (*tratak*).

According to Patanjali, yogic techniques imply several categories of physiological and spiritual practices, which are the ways to control or set up a "mental dam" against the whirlwinds (*chittavritti*) of mental activity. These categories of activity are known as the limbs or members (*angas*) of yoga and each class of disciplines has a definite purpose. The eight members or *ashtangas* are:

1. Restraints (*yama*): The first step toward asceticism is self-restraint. The five important forms of restraint are not to kill (*ahimsa*), not to lie (*satya*), not to steal (*asteya*), sexual abstinence (*brhahmacharya*), and not to be avaricious (*aparigriha*).

2. Disciplines (*niyama*): The *yogin* must practice a series of bodily and mental disciplines, of which the most important are cleanliness (*saucha*), serenity (*santosha*), and asceticism (*tapas*).

3. Bodily attitudes and postures (*asanas*): These are stable body postures that must be practiced in a fixed sequence on a daily basis on an empty stomach, in an open space where fresh air is available. There are several hundreds of *asanas* that have been described, but there are 32 *asanas* that are of particular therapeutic importance: *tadasana*, which is used for relief of sciatic pain, gastric troubles, numbness in the shoulder or waist, and promoting blood circulation through the torso; *garunasana* for hernia and hydrocele; *vakrasana* for indigestion, obesity, and diabetes; *padmasana* for indigestion, control of respiration, and tremor; *shavasana* for controlling blood pressure, relaxation, lowering autonomic arousal, and so on.

4. Respiration (*pranayama*): These are exercises for control of breathing and respiration, and alter the metabolic rate of the body. It was recognized long ago that all functions of bodily organs are preceded by respiration, and that all emotional responses involve a change in respiration, therefore the path to control over the body and mind must include the control of res-

piration. Yogic treatises recognize four distinct states of consciousness, all associated with a particular respiratory rhythm. *Pranayama* begins with slowing of the respiration, which sets the stage for the passage from normal states of consciousness to other modalities of consciousness.

5. Emancipation of sensory activity from the domination of external objects (*pratyahara*): In this stage, the *yogin* is able to free himself or herself from external distractions, and therefore frees the intellect to contemplate existence in a more truthful way, to unite with the Universal Consciousness. This is the last stage of psychophysiological self-discipline, and it sets the stage for the concentration that is necessary for the latter three stages of yogic meditation.

6. Concentration (*dharana*): The word (*dharana*) comes from the root (*dhr*), which means to hold fast. Here the intellect (*chitta*) is focused on a single point, idea, symbol, or object in order to understand or comprehend, to penetrate the veil of darkness and arrive at the purest state of knowledge through the power of the intellect. This concentration of attention on a single point beyond the disturbance of the senses generates enormous psychic "will" or power.

7. Yogic meditation (*dhyana*): The completion of *dharana* is *dhyana*. Meditation follows concentration, and keeps the flow of one idea continuously. In concrete meditation, the object of meditation is concrete, while in abstract meditation, the object of concentration is abstract, such as a quality like mercy or tolerance. We will return to these objects of meditation, which are mantras, mandalas, and yantras, later in this chapter.

8. The final stage of yoga, the state of highest consciousness that is complete liberation from suffering, is *samadhi*. This is a state where the practitioner is completely submerged in the object of the *dhyana*—for example, God, symbol, or mantra. The ego (I, me, mine) completely disappears. There are two types of *samadhi*: sa-*vikalpa* and *nir-vikalpa*. In sa-*vikalpa samadhi* the triad of knower, knowledge, and knowable still exists, and serves as a support for the mind in its search; while in *nir-vikalpa samadhi* reality is dominated by knowledge and there is the final fusion of all the modes of being. It is believed that this final stage breaks through the cycle of birth and death.

These eight stages of yoga should be practiced in order. If one is able to perform *yama*, *niyama*, *asanas*, and *pranayama*, one gains control over all bodily functions, and may exert control to maintain a state of physical health. *Pratyahara*, *dharana*, *dhyana*, and *samadhi* are spiritual practices for control over one's mental and psychological states, and the totality of these practices balances the control of one's physical and mental well-being (Shivananda, 1950; Sushil, 1993; see also Eliade, 1990, for a more complete discussion of yoga practices). The use of systematic meditational practices, biofeedback techniques, controlled breathing, and postural exercises in the control of diabetes, blood pressure, migraines, sleeping disorders, and pain control is well-documented and has now entered mainstream Western medicine and need not be further elaborated here.

Tantras, Mantras, Yantras, and Mandalas

Tantric yoga or Tantrism is difficult to define. The root word *tan* means to extend, continue, or multiply, and a commonly accepted meaning of *tantra* is "what extends knowledge." Many scholars believe that the roots of Tantrism can be found in the *Vedas*; however, Tantrism came into its ascendancy in the fourth century of our era, and by the sixth century had become extremely popular in India, Tibet, Burma, and had reached into China and Southeast Asia. Tantrism has been assimilated into all the major religions of India. There are extant traditions of Buddhist Tantrism, known as the "Diamond Vehicle," Jainist Tantrism, and Islamic Tantrism. Tantric concepts have strongly influenced literature, philosophy, ritual practice, ethics, and iconography. It is believed that Tantrism influenced and was itself influenced by such Christian philosophies as Gnosticism and Hermetism, and Persian Sufism (see Woodroffe, 1929).

Central to Tantrism, is the concept of *Sakti*, the Divine Woman and Mother, the genesis of the "cosmic force." Here, the feminine principle comes to symbolize the essence of creation and the mystery of Being. It is believed that the roots of the Tantric concept of *Sakti* is rooted in the ancient religion of the Mother, which reigned over a huge territory, spanning the eastern Mediterranean regions, Africa, and most of Asia, and entered the Aryan Hindu religion through the influence of the Dravidian religious rituals and beliefs. Tantrism recognizes that the act of sexual conjugation is a metaphor for the awesome power of creation, and that one may harness the generative power of the universe through control and domination over one's bodily organs and functions. The path to the realization of this power is through *sadhana*, or the perfection of mental and bodily control through incessant practice. Mantras, yantras, and mandalas are the sustaining vehicles through which this power is attained. While the power of the mantra, the "mystical sound," was recognized by the *Vedas*, Tantrism raised the mantra into a special place, as being a direct vehicle of power. It is believed that mantras are literally *dharanis* or breast plates that protect the practitioner, or *sadhak*, from demons, diseases, spells, and spirits. Each word or sound of the mantra has a specific meaning, which is revealed only during meditation, the power of which is manifested when pronounced. Mantras are secret, often unintelligible to the uninitiated, and can only be learned from the mouth of the guru. Once the mantra has been "received" from the guru's mouth, it has unlimited powers or *siddhi*. There are many millions of mantras—for example, the *loknatha* mantra can absolve all sins, the *ekajata* mantra preserves the person from all dangers; there are mantras to guard against certain diseases, to obtain power over people, protection from evil spirits, to gain money, even salvation. All mantras must be chanted having observed purification rituals of body and of mind. The unlimited efficacy of the mantras arises from the fact that during correct recitation the mantra can *become* the "object" that the mantra represents.

Many mantras have as their source the *Vedas*; there are many to be found in the *Upanishads*, and the *Puranas*. It is interesting to note that Tantrism developed in the two border regions of India, known in those early times as the Greater Aryavat: in the Northwest, along the Afghan border extending onto Iraq and Iran; and in the Northeast in Assam, Bengal, and up into Tibet, Nepal, and Bhutan. Tantrism remains a strong force to this day in these regions, particularly in the Northeast. The Islamic practice of *dhikr*, which is the incessant chanting of the name of God along with the regulation of body postures and breathing, is believed to have arisen from the influence of Tantrism.

Over the centuries, mantras have arisen in local languages and dialects. These translated mantras, called *Shabar mantras*, have been found to be as effective as the original Sanskrit mantras, and are used by local shamans and practitioners. One particular set of *shabar mantras*, which are considered particularly potent in healing and are still used to this day, was said to have originated with Guru Gorakhnath, founder of the Nath cult, in the twelfth century.

Mandalas and yantras have a unique place in the Tantric liturgy, and it is believed that the widespread use of these elaborate patterns and designs arose from the spread of the Tantric philosophy, even though the concept of the power of "magic designs" is far more ancient. The word *mandala* literally means "circle." In many Buddhist texts, the concept is translated as "center." It is a complex design, usually with a circular border, having concentric circles enclosing a square divided up into triangles. A *yantra* (literally, "engine") is the simplest, linear form of mandala, and is usually composed of a series of triangles. Just as the mantra is the auditory vehicle of power, the mandala is the iconographic vehicle. The mandala is believed to be the image of the universe, and the area defined within its borders, a sacred space. The power of the mandala is twofold: when the design is drawn, with appropriate ritual and purification ceremonies, on the ground or on a wall, the mandala consecrates the space and protects against demons or evil spirits entering the space; when the design is drawn on a cloth, and used as the vehicle for meditation, it concentrates the energy of the *sadhak*, or practitioner, serves as a defense against the onslaught of distracting thoughts, and allows him to reach his spiritual center.

Ritual drawings as a protection against evil spirits and for healing are found in many cultures. There is a well-developed system of healing iconography in many North and South American tribes, and there is an extensive literature of the complex and elaborate mandalas that are used for meditation and healing in Buddhist and other religious practices in Tibet, China, Japan, and Southeast Asia, especially in Java. In India, the unique power and quality of each god in the Hindu pantheon is represented by a specific yantra, and the invocation of gods such as Vishnu (the Protector), Ganesh (the Elephant-headed God) Surya (the Sun God), and others must always be preceded by the ritual of drawing the yantra, and inviting the god to descend into the sacred space in the center of the pattern.

The *Shri Yantra* is believed to be one of the most potent yantras. It consists of nine triangles, four pointing upward and five downward, surrounded by concentric circles and lotus leaves. It represents the innate cosmic power of *Sakti*, the cosmic force, and it is believed that the house where the *Shri Yantra* exists is a place of power and prosperity where no distress may enter. There are many specific other yantras that represent and invoke the power of other powerful female deities such as Kali (the female form of Shiva, the Destroyer), Tara, Bhuvaneshwari, and so on. There are many yantras that are commonly used to this day to protect the person from specific afflictions or symptoms: the *Jwar-nashak Yantra*, to relieve fever; *Stambham Yantras* to protect against enemies; yantras to remove sterility, to prevent migraines and headaches, for painless labor, and so forth.

One of the simplest yantras and yet one of the most powerful and revered symbols, is the *swastik* (卍). It is a very ancient symbol, and has been found on seals from the Indus Valley civilization in Mohenjo-daro and Harappa. It is believed that in pre-Aryan times the *swastik* was the yantra of the ancient goddess of knowledge, with the four arms of the *swastik* representing the four *Vedas*. Later it became the symbol of Saraswati, the goddess of knowledge and learning. The *Swastik Yantra*, which symbolizes knowledge, enlightenment, progress, and life, is given deep respect by all Hindus, and is a common sign found on homes, temples, and other places of worship. The *Swastik Yantra* is also abundant in Buddhist and Jain literature. It is unfortunate that in the West, the swastika (卐), the mirror image of the Hindu *swastik*, has become a contemptible symbol of the Nazis. It was adopted by them as an Aryan symbol to denote racial purity or Aryan descent.

Gemstone Therapy

Interest in the curative properties of gemstones and crystals has seen a resurgence in recent years and is a well-known part of the New Age movement in healing. The use of metals and minerals as dietary supplements is a well-established practice in Western medicine. The roots of the use of gemstones and their curative properties are described in detail in the ancient *Vishnu Puranas* and also in the *Varamihir Samhita*, which is an ancient text on astronomy. Gem therapy is used by astropalmists, solar therapists, and by many Ayurvedic physicians.

Since changes of temperature and pressure on minerals present in the earth are responsible for the formation of gems, gem therapy principles are akin to solar therapy. The seven colors present in sunlight have differential effects on health and physiological functioning. The reduction of any "color" has adverse effects on health. The gem therapist first ascertains what "colors" may be imbalanced in the patient and then prescribes the wearing of a gem, mineral, or metal next to the skin or the ingestion of preparations containing the specific metal or mineral. For example, the reduction of "red" may be implicated in diseases of the blood, fever, edema, and anemia. For these types of symptoms, gems controlled by the sun and Mars such as ruby and coral may be prescribed. The pearl, which is believed to be affected by the moon and influenced by diurnal rhythms is often prescribed for stabilizing mood and emotional disturbances.

The ashes of gems and metals are sometimes prescribed in Ayurvedic treatment. For example, the ash of emeralds is used for elimination of toxins, flatulence, and for gouts and migraine; topaz ash is used in the treatment of jaundice, kidney disorders, pneumonia, and cough; ruby ash is used to heal wounds, dysentery, and for treatment of impotency; diamond ash is used in treatment of venereal disease and weakness.

Architecture

The *Vastu Shastra* is a set of writings that is attributed to various ancient *rishis* and *munis* (sages and scholars), including Jamadagni and Brahaspati. It is a collection of writings about the effects of architectural design and configuration and is believed to have been compiled about the time of *The Upanishads*, which date back about 2,000 years.

According to the *Vastu Shastra*, direction should be determined by a compass, and not by the sun or stars, attesting to the use of magnets in ancient times. There are various proscriptions that must be followed when buying property and constructing a house, in order to maintain the health and well-being of the occupants: big trees and higher land should be to the west or south; wide open spaces with a river nearby, and small trees to the east or north are considered excellent areas to build. In construction, living space should not be made less than 12 × 12 feet, while the kitchen and bathroom should be more than 9 × 9 feet. A house should not have an equal number of doors and windows, and the main entrance to a house should face east. When setting up the furniture in a room, the arrangement should allow the windows facing east and north to be kept open, and the head of the bed should point to the south. It is believed that orientational "faults" can be the source of illness and distress. Faulty orientation to the south is believed to bring on various disorders in females; children's diseases arise from faults in eastern orientation; and faulty east-south corners invite litigation and enemities.

UNANI MEDICINE

Unani medicine came into existence after 700 B.C., a relative newcomer compared to Ayurvedic medicine, but it soon became the major system of medicine and healing in Asia Minor and parts of Africa and Europe. There is record of a major school of Unani medicine at Judhi Shahpur in the seventh century A.D., and this continued to flourish even after the spread of Islam in Persia. There were many schools and universities of Unani medicine in Egypt, and many of the Unani texts were translated into Persian, Arabic, and Egyptian. One of the earliest known books is the *Al-Hawi*, written by the great scholar Al-Rizvi. The second book, *Kitab al-Qanum* (Canon of Medicine), was written by the gifted physician Ibn-Sina, or Avicenna (980–1037). This book was translated into many languages and exerted a powerful influence over the development of modern Western medicine.

Unani medicine came to India with the successive Muslim invasions, which began with the ferocious assaults of the Turkish-speaking Afghani ruler, Muhammad of Ghazni, in A.D. 1023. There were several waves of invasion by Muslim invaders during the following centuries. By the early thirteenth century a Muslim Empire was firmly established in India, and the practice of the Unani system of medicine was widespread. Muhammad bin Tughlaq (1325–51), the first king of the Tughlaq dynasty, opened at least 70 hospitals in various places around his capital, Delhi, and employed some 1,200 *Hakims* or Unani physicians. Firozshah Tughlaq (1351–88), his successor, was a great builder and scholar. It is said that he had a passion for building, and in fact was responsible for the construction of many dams, hospitals, schools, and reservoirs. He is also reputed to have authored a book on medicine called the *Tibbi-e-Firozshahi*, and distributed 1,000 handwritten copies.

The Tughlaq dynasty was replaced by the Lodi kings, who ruled India from 1451 to 1526. During the period of the Lodi kings there was considerable cross-fertilization between the Islamic and Hindu cultures. In fact, the stage for this tolerance had been set during the benign rule of Firozshah. During the reign of Sikander Lodi (1489–1505), a book was written by Miyan Bhava, *Mad-al-un-shifa Sikandashahi*, which for the first time studied both the Ayurvedic and Unani forms of medicine and indicated the similarities of their theoretical systems. Many medical centers were also started in Kashmir, Gujarat, and Avadh.

The Lodi dynasty was succeeded by the Moghul emperors. It was during this period that Unani medicine claimed its ascendancy. Babur (1526–56), the first Moghul king, was one of the most brilliant Asiatic princes of his age, and he invited many Unani physicians to visit India during his reign. It is believed that he paid the salaries of some 29 different Unani specialists. Successive Moghul emperors continue this tradition and worked vigorously for the spread and development of the system. Under most of the Moghul rule, medical facilities and medical care were provided free of charge to the general public. After the fall of the Moghul empire, in about 1740, *Hakim* Azmal Khan established the Unani school of medicine, Tibbiya College in Delhi. Unani medicine was actively supported by the British, and it continues to be a popular alternative to Western medicine in India today.

Identification of Disease

Unani and Ayurvedic medicine have many similarities: In both philosophies the elements of matter are earth, water, fire, air, and sky. Both systems believe that phlegm, bile, and air are produced in the body and that an imbalance between these products is responsible for various disorders. The Unani system adds some new features to the Ayurvedic system: temperature, respiration, and activity are also seen as key aspects of health. It is believed that elements of matter are used to synthesize specific parts of the body at different temperatures. Blood is also given importance in the Unani system, since all the elements of food and air (oxygen) are distributed by the blood. Further, a key belief in the Unani system is that the body intrinsically has the power to renew, rejuvenate, and restore itself. The *hakim* tries to utilize this power inherent in the body to restore health. Key features used in diagnosis in the Unani system are the condition of the skin, eyes, tongue, and hair, as are sleep and food habits.

Therapy

In this system, an effort is made to cure the disease by removing the external symptoms and causes. Like the Ayurvedic *vaidya*, the Unani *hakim* gives importance to food habits and an adherence to a strict diet. As in the Ayurvedic system, foods and medicines are characterized by their effects on the body in terms of cold, hot, dry, or moist. Diseases caused by cold are challenged by "hot" medicines, diseases due to heat are treated by "cold" medicines, and excess water in the body by "dry" types of medicines. Cures are often lengthy, but effective.

TRIBAL AND FOLK MEDICINE

A significant proportion of India's population consists of tribal peoples, who are collectively called *Adibashis* or Ancient Peoples. There are many hundreds of diverse tribes that flourish all over India, each having distinctive modes of dress, food, language, religious beliefs and practices, tribal organization, and customs. One important common thread that links the diversity of the tribal peoples is their beliefs about, and reliance on, plants and herbs. The many tribes that have been systematically studied show

similarities in their reverence for certain trees and herbs that are held sacred, and that hold importance in ritual functions. While different tribes
have distinctly different religious systems and rituals, there are important
commonalities, distinct from the Vedic and later Hindu traditions, which
are believed to point to a common pre-Aryan religious origin. Many of the
tribal practices in the use of plants and herbs have filtered into mainstream
Hindu and Muslim practices over the centuries, and in fact, for many tribes,
the gathering and sale of plants and herbs to Ayurvedic, Unani, and other
herbalists is an important form of sustenance and livelihood.

In an ethnobiological study among the tribal peoples of Uttar Pradesh,
a state in Northern India, Maheshwari and Singh (1985) found widespread
use of *renja* root (*Mimosaceae, Acacia leucophloea*) in the successful treatment of jaundice and dysentery. *Chirchira* (*Amaranthacea*) root is used for
treatment of snakebite. This root also has ritual significance and is used in
Tantric and Mantra *sadhana* practices. To keep evil spirits away, the wood
of *bel* (*Rutacea*) is kept burning during childbirth and the ash is sprinkled
over the child. The newly born child is given a smoke bath by burning
ajawain (*Umbelliferae*) seeds. Griffiths (1946) found that the Kol and
Tharu tribes also sprinkle *ajawain* seeds in the delivery room. It is interesting to note that the use of *ajawain* for bathing newborns and decoctions
of *ajawain* in treating childhood stomach disorders and colic is widespread
in Hindu families. *Ajawain* is also used in folk medicine for the treatment
of asthma. *Ajawain* seeds are burned on a fire, and the asthma sufferer is
made to inhale the fumes. Similarly, *tulsi* (*Lameaceae*) which is considered
a sacred herb in the Hindu tradition and is used in many Hindu rituals
(particularly for the dying), is used by many tribal peoples to ward off evil
spirits. Many tribals keep *tulsi* leaves on the mother's stomach to prevent
miscarriage and to protect the child from evil spirits.

The Bhil tribes, who live in the northwestern Indian states of Rajasthan,
Madhya Pradesh, Gujarat, and Maharashtra, have an interesting method
to keep away disease and evil spirits from their villages. Some flowers and
thorns of the *himal* tree (*Bombax ceiba*) are collected in a pot (*diwani*)
with oil and the blood of a sacrificed fowl. After performing some magical
rites, the sorcerer or shaman takes the *diwani* out of the village and puts
it on the road. It is believed that the disease goes away with someone that
passes that way. It is forbidden to look back after putting the *diwani* down
on the road (Sebastian & Bhandari, 1987).

During the festival of Holi, which is a spring and harvest celebration, a
himal tree is decorated with dried cow dung (a common form of fuel and
kindling in much of India) and red and white streamers. Some wood and
hay are also placed around the tree, and on the day of Holi, the tree is
burned. It is assumed that the evil is burned away with the tree. The direction that the burned tree falls is considered an omen. If the tree falls to
the east or to the north, it portends a good harvest, if not, it is a sign of

impending damage to crops or to disease among the Bhils (Koppers & Jungblur, 1976). The Bhils also treat ailing persons or diseased animals by a method called *jhadapad*, which consists of waving twigs of the *aakdo* (*calotropis procera*) over the patient or animal. It is believed that the shrub has the power to draw away the disease from the patient.

The *peepal* (*ficus religiosa*) and the *baad* (*ficus bangalensis*) trees are held as sacred by both Hindus and the tribal peoples. It is believed that many kinds of spirits, both evil and demonic, and other powerful spirits live in these trees. Many Hindu women put offerings of water and flowers under the trees to placate the spirits, and to seek help from the spirits in warding off evil. Bhils do not construct houses under the shade of this tree, and newly married girls are not allowed to take shelter under these trees. The tribals believe that the aerial roots of the *baad* tree will sink their roots into the breasts of the bride and cause infertility (Koppers & Jungblur, 1976).

Similarly, the *neem* (*azadirichta indica*) tree is considered sacred by Hindus, Muslims, and tribal peoples. The Bhils use the twigs of this tree for many religious and magical rituals. Muslim sorcerers use the branches of *neem* to cure jaundice in a practice similar to the *jhadapad* described earlier: twigs of *neem* are passed over and around the patient, who sits in front of a basin of water. It is believed that with each passing, the jaundice is drawn out of the patient and into the water. The water becomes yellow after the ritual is over. This practice is quite widely used with surprising efficacy. The twigs and leaves of *neem* have long been used for medicinal purposes. The twigs of *neem* are used as a dentifrice all over India, and in fact one of the most popular brands of toothpaste marketed in India is made with *neem* extract. *Neem* leaves and extracts are widely used in Ayurvedic medicine as a potent way to rid the body of accumulated wastes and toxins, and as a dietary supplement.

The Tharu tribe, which lives on both sides of the Indo-Nepal border, places immense faith in plants and sorcery. For rickets, the branch of a local tree called *gheelond* is tied around the neck of the child. For rapid healing of bone fractures, a paste made out of the leaves of the *hadjudee* tree is applied. The stones taken from the stomach of river crocodiles that have been killed are preserved and used in the treatment of patients suffering from gallbladder or kidney stones. The leaves of the *dauna* tree are used for curing headaches, and the roots of the *gaddi* tree for toothache. For muscle pains around the torso, the hard scale found on the back of a local snake is tied around the waist. Ear pains are treated with cow urine, and burns by applying burnt tortoise shell paste to the affected body parts.

Ghoshal (1981) has discussed various common treatments used with surprising efficacy in folk medicine across the country. In the western state of Gujarat, garlic curry is used in the treatment of cholera to lessen the frequency of bowel movements, and a boiled mixture of lime and molasses gives immediate relief in vomiting.

Stomachaches in the navel region and frequent loose bowels are believed to be caused by the displacement of the chord in the belly. Massage with warm oil is used to provide relief. Alternatively, the patient lies on his or her back, and a lighted earthen lamp is placed on the stomach and covered with a glass. When the available oxygen is used up, the flame dies, and the resulting vacuum makes the glass adhere to the stomach. It is believed that the glass remains fixed to the stomach until the chord moves to the right place. Other remedies include stretching exercises of the fingers and toes, and the application of gentle pressure to the area.

Treatment of migraine is often done with the practice of *adha-shish*, or half breath, which is a common practice in yogic *pranayana*, or controlled breathing. The migraine sufferer lies down and closes one nostril with his or her hand, and the physician or medicine man puts in a few drops of garlic extract in a salt solution in the other nostril, which is then inhaled by the patient. This is done with alternating nostrils.

For treatment of headache and cough, leaves of the *ankra* tree are fried and tied around the head before going to sleep, to bring relief by morning. For toothache, a paste is made with the carbon deposited under cooking utensils, and salt, which is then applied to the gums. Exzema is treated with *neem* extract, and it has been found that regular application of *neem* paste to the affected area produces a complete cure. *Neem* paste is also widely used in India as an antiseptic wash, as is the spice turmeric. Turmeric has been known since Vedic times as an antiseptic; it is also believed to have antiinflammatory properties and is commonly used in poultices for sprains and fractures. Skin diseases such as ringworm are often treated with a paste made from garlic and saliva. Inflammation of the eye is commonly treated by placing hot tea leaves in a cotton pad and binding it over the eyes. Fried onion scales are often used to hasten healing of abscessed wounds. In many parts of India, asses' milk is used as a preventative for tuberculosis.

The chanting of mantras or spells to remedy ailments is a common practice in folk medicine. Acute birth delivery pain is eased by chanting spells in a glass of water. This water is then given to the patient to ease the delivery. Rheumatic pains are eased by the medicine man by chanting spells and then blowing the wind from his mouth on the affected part. It is believed that young children who cry for no apparent reason, or who start losing weight, are suffering from the evil eye cast upon them by some jealous person. To determine the person who cast the evil eye, the diviner or medicine man will put some alum on the fire. The smoke from the alum is believed to rise in the shape of the person or spirit causing the problem. The family can then protect the child from the person or spirit. One way to cast out the evil eye, which is used in many parts of India, both north and south, is to pass a handful of salt and red chilies over the child an odd number of times, such as seven or eleven, and then cast the handful into a fire, to burn away the evil. In some places a wick dipped in oil is used in place of the red chilies and salt. The wick is then hung on a wall and lit at the bottom. If part of the wick falls to the ground while still burning, it is believed that the evil eye was very powerful.

This is a very brief discussion of the wide variety of plants, roots, and herbs that are commonly used in India among the tribal people and in common folk remedies. As has been pointed out, many of these practices have endured for centuries, and are effective in curing or ameliorating common ailments. It is sad that India, like many other Third World countries, is rapidly losing the marketing rights to many of the traditional medicinal plants that are indigenous to it. For example, a *neem*-based insecticide has been patented by a firm in the United States; *adrak* (ginger) extract, has been patented by a drug company in the United Kingdom, where it is now used to counter nausea after chemotherapy in cancer and surgical operations; *haldi* (turmeric) extract has been patented by a German company for use as an antiinflammatory agent and is currently being used to replace the use of steroids, which have harmful side effects. Indian laboratories are increasingly collaborating with research institutes and agencies of more developed countries, which provide support for research and development; but in return for funding, India is signing away the rights of exploitation of indigenous plants to these international agencies for only marginal recognition of their work (*Hitavada*, 1994).

FAITH HEALING

An account of healing traditions in India would not be complete without a mention of the many faith healers: the *babas*, *fakirs*, *pirs*, and other wandering mendicants who are reputed to have magical healing abilities. There are also many shrines, *mandirs*, and *dargahs*, which, like the famous shrine at Lourdes, are considered to have miraculous healing properties. It should be noted that the belief in faith healing is no more or less in India than in any other country or culture, and that in fact the basis of the healing may be no different than that which is accounted for in the more sophisticated terminology of modern medicine in discussions of the processes of psychoneuroimmunology or the placebo effects. Also, issues of faith, belief, or will toward well-being are stressed in all the systems discussed thus far, even though it may not have been explicitly mentioned in the specific sections. The *Atharva veda*, *Ayurveda Samhita*, and the *Arthashastra* of Kautilya all stress the power of the will and the efficacy of faith and belief in the healing process. Islam, as in the Unani system of treatment, has always given importance to *dua* and *iman*, or faith. Kakar (1982) in his survey of healing traditions of India has presented a psychoanalytic and contextual approach to the understanding of healing in his book; however, many of his discussions about the role of shamans and mystics echo the data and discussions presented in *Mind/Body Medicine* (Goleman & Gurin, 1993), which documents the role that the mind plays in disease and healing.

In India, there are many sacred places, scattered in little villages, towns, and cities or deep in the jungle that are reputed to have mysterious healing powers. Kakar (1982) in his survey makes mention of a number of shamans and sacred places. The temple of Balaji, which is 250 miles south of Delhi, is one such place. This temple, which for many Indians holds the same place of reverence as did the Temple of Ascelpius for the Greeks, holds the promise of relief for many afflictions, including epilepsy, tuberculosis, infertility, and mental illness. *Samadhis* or tombs of great Muslim *sufis* or saints are also considered to have great power, by both Hindus and Muslims.

Causes of Illness

The *Atreya Samhita* divides illnesses into three classes: some diseases are curable easily, some require hard work, and some can only be cured through extraordinary means. Inexplicable illnesses are often attributed to the power of evil forces, spirits (both good and bad), ghosts, sorcery, or the evil eye. The *Ayurveda* makes mention of *bhut*, *pret*, and *chudails*, which are various categories of ghosts, spirits, and witches that may possess the body and produce different kinds of malaise. Divine forces sometimes also may be the cause of ill health. In many parts of India, a goddess called *Sheetla Mata* (the cold mother) is worshipped, so that she may be placated, otherwise people may face an epidemic of smallpox. A common name for smallpox is *chotimata*, or small mother.

Treatment

To treat disorders that are perceived to be of extraordinary origin or to prevent possession by evil spirits, or to ward off the evil eye, many different practices prevail. It is common practice in India to put a black dot on the face or forehead of small children to protect against the evil eye. Tantric shamans employ a variety of rituals to summon the *bhut*, *pret*, or *chudails* possessing the body of the ailing person. The spirit is then asked what their demands are in order to leave the body of the person. Their demands are then fulfilled by providing some special form of food or worship, and sometimes animals are sacrificed to placate the spirit. Amulets are then tied to the arms of the person to protect them against future possession. Many fakirs, swamis, and babas are renowned for their powers of healing, and many of their devotees will undergo long and arduous journeys, just to be in their physical presence. Some of these people who are reputed to have mystical powers are famous both in India and outside of the country, and can lay claim to thousands of devotees: Maharishi Mahesh Yogi, who has popularized Trancendental Meditation, Swami Rajneesh, Satya Sai Baba, Radha Swami Satsang, and Tatbaba, just to name a few. The centers or ashrams established by such spiritual leaders are often considered sacred sites, and many of these centers also impart religious training in matra yoga or other spiritual practices.

India is an ancient land of great geographical, ethnic, linguistic, and cultural diversity. Nowhere, perhaps, is the dizzying fabric of its diversity more visible than in its religious and spiritual traditions. It has been the birthplace of some of the great religions of the world, has exerted great influence, and has, in turn, been influenced by systems developed outside its borders. The confluence of these spiritual traditions, while theoretically distinct, have been absorbed and amalgamated in the actual practices of daily life. Thus it is not unusual to find a Christian woman saying a prayer in front of the sacred *tulsi* tree on her way to church; or a Muslim asking for an amulet for protection for his son from a passing *fakir*; or a childless Hindu woman praying at tomb of the Muslim *fakir* Seikh Baba Salim Chisti, who was reputed to have had great mystical powers and to have saved the life of Prince Humayun, the son of the Moghul Emperor Babur. While Western medicine is firmly established and widely prevalent, traditional healing practices are still a vibrant force in India today.

REFERENCES

Bhattacharya, B. (1949). Ayuvedokt bhautik nadi. *Kalyan: Hindu Sanskrit Ank*, 24, 538–539.

Bhishagratna, K. L. (Trans.) (1981). *Sushruta Samhita*, Vol. I, Varanasi: Chowkhamba Sanskrit Series.

Dixit, P. R. (1988). *Hindu tantra shastra*. Agra: Deep Publications.

Eliade, M. (1969). *Yoga: Immortality and freedom* (2nd ed.). Princeton, NJ: Princeton University Press.

Ghoshal, S. C. (1981). Folk methods of treatment. *Folklore*, August, 160–161.

Goleman, D. & Gurin, J. (1993). *Mind/body medicine*. New York: Consumer Reports Books.

Goyandaka, H. K. (1951). *Patanjali yoga darshan*. Gorakhpur: Gita Press.

Griffiths, W. G. (1946). *The Kols of Central India*. Calcutta.

Hitavada English Daily (1994). January 7, p. 3.

Joshi, K. A. (1993). Dukh Daridriya ke chamatkari yantra. *Rashtriya Sahara Daily*, November 13.

Kakar, S. (1982). *Shamans, mystics, and doctors: A psychological inquiry into India and its healing traditions*. Delhi: Oxford University Press.

Koppers, W. & Jungblur, L. (1976). The bowmen of India. *Acta Ethnologica et Linguistica*, Series Indica, 6, Austria.

Maheshwari, J. K. & Singh, J. P. (1985). Plants used in magico-religious beliefs by the Kols of Uttar Pradesh: A study. *Folklore*, September.

Satyananda, Yogacharya (1980). *Swasthya raksha aur yogasan.* Delhi: Vivek.

Sebastian, M. K. & Bhandari, M. M. (1987). Magico-religious beliefs about plants. *Folklore,* October, 244–247.

Sharma, A. K. (1988). *World famous systems of medicines and therapy.* Delhi: Pustak Mahal.

Shivananda, Swami (1950). *The ten Upanishads: With notes and commentary.* Calcutta: S. P. League.

Shrivastava, R. C. (1993 a). Mahanisha men Shavar mantro ki sadhana. *Nutan Kahaniya,* November, 52–59.

———. (1993 b). Shri Yantra Sadhana. *Nutan Kahaniya,* November, 77–80.

Sushil (1993). Health through meridian exercise. *Jai Jan Jagriti-Hindu Weekly,* December 5.

Vakil, R. J. *Our glorious heritage.* Bombay: The Times of India Press.

Watson, F. (1975). *A concise history of India.* New York: Charles Scribner's Sons.

Woodroffe, J. (1929). *Shakti and shakta.* Madras.

A Study of Curative Options Available in the Southern Province of Sri Lanka

Suneetha S. de Silva and Willie J. Epps

The sun's first rays touch the mountain Adam's Peak. It is the birth of a new day. The silence of a thousand pilgrims who have awaited this moment is broken as the surrounding hills reverberate with the echo of prayer—a melodious mingling of Pali, Latin, Hindu, and Arabic chanting the praises of their individual doctrines.

For over 20 centuries, Buddhists then Muslims and later Christians together have made this pilgrimage of 17 miles by foot up a rough terrain, climbing an altitude of 7,800 feet, often carrying the old and sick, dramatically mingling to share a common place of worship. This is an example of the cultural ability to blend myths, religion, and racial diversity, and the ability to retain a uniqueness within a complexity, thus enhancing the beauty of an island paradise that has caught the imagination of many a writer. "From Seyllan to Paradise is a distance of forty Italian miles; so 'tis said, the sound of waters falling from the paradise is heard there" (Marignolli, cited in Zuber & Bandaranayake n.d.).

Adam's Peak is named after what is believed to be the footprint of Adam when he stepped down from Heaven. According to legend, Ceylon, now Sri Lanka, was God's choice to banish his children to a place of beauty only comparable to the Garden of Eden. The island's Buddhists believe Buddha left his footprint on the mountaintop on his visit to Sri Lanka, while the Christians believe it to be that of St. Thomas, and the Hindus pay homage to the same as the footprint of Shiva.

As the sun rises over the mountaintops, the pilgrims descend peacefully, side by side, carrying the old who have reached inner satisfaction and helping the sick who have been healed by the pilgrimage. Ethnic or religious disharmony momentarily cast aside, these islanders skillfully blend their daily life in the twentieth century with a rich and historic past.

POPULATION

Sri Lanka, an island whose total land area is 24,332 square miles, is occupied by 17 million people of diverse ethnicity, religion, language, and cultural habits.

Sinhalese. The Sinhalese claim to be descendants of a lion (*Sinha*) and with the lion's blood (*le*) coursing through their veins, they speak a language unique to the race: Sinhalese. The Sinhalese pride themselves as either being "low country Sinhalese" of the west, south, and southwest or the "up country Sinhalese" who are from the central province and the hill capital of Sri Lanka.

Tamils. Two-thirds of the Tamils are Sri Lankan Tamils living in the north of the country. They trace their roots to invaders who arrived on the island in the second and third centuries A.D. They speak the Tamil language, which is the same language as the rest of the Tamils living in the central hill country who were brought from India by the British in the early part of this century. Most Tamils are either Hindu or Catholic.

Muslims. The Muslims consist of two groups: descendants of Arab traders who identify themselves as Moors, while the other group affiliates itself with traders from the East, calling themselves Malays.

Burghers. A fraction of the population is made up of descendants of Dutch colonists known as Burghers, differing physically and in social lifestyle from the others. The Burghers of Sri Lanka speak English and follow the Christian faith.

Veddhas. The multiethnic, multireligious Veddha society was preceded by stone-age dwellers dating back to the Balangoda culture 5,000 years B.C. Aboriginal inhabitants of today are remnants of the Yaksa and Naga tribes of *The Mahavamsa.* The Veddhas speak a dialect of Sinhala and "their religion [is] a system of Ancestor worship" (Obesekera, 1987, p. 333) linking the nontheistic religion of Buddhism to a blend of folk cults and beliefs in the supernatural being.

HISTORICAL OVERVIEW

The past of Sri Lanka is far more accessible than that of other South Asian societies because it is recorded in two unique chronicles: *The Mahavamsa* and *The Chulavamsa.* These two volumes together trace events on the island since the sixth century B.C. (Smith, 1979, p. 83).

The southern province of Sri Lanka has held its own against the invasions of foreign settlers. Once a stronghold of Sinhala kings, it is a storekeeper of historical events. The influence of Moorish travelers and spice traders, the Portuguese names, and the fortresses and canals built by the Dutch exist to this day.

The skills of dancing and drumming and the rituals of exorcism pertaining to demonology are exclusive to the southern province. Referred to as low country dancing, the exorcist nature of the dance has earned it the title "Devil Dancing." The successful cohesion of the old and new can be seen best in this southern part of the country. Still a stronghold of a social stratification by caste, skilled craftspeople of dance, drumming, songs, mask making, and jewelry making are seen as nowhere else. The southern women excel in basket weaving, lace making, and cooking. Most marriages are still arranged by elders, and women bring a dowry with them at the time of marriage. A preference toward having sons over daughters still exists.

It is customary at the birth of a Sinhalese Buddhist child that a horoscope—the recorded planetary position at the time of birth—is cast (de Silva, Stiles & Gibbons, 1993). Written on an ola leaf in an ancient script, this is the document that will dictate the individual's life from birth until death. No significant event—entering school, sickness, marriage, or any other change in life—will be carried out without the consultation of an individual's horoscope. No psychologist, educator, or preacher has the power over a horoscope to determine the future of an individual. An astrologer would determine if planetary conjugation were favorable. Any misfortune to an individual or person would be blamed on karma or fate.

A culmination of the historical process from many centuries has given rise to a society in rapid transition, from postfigurative (where elders make decisions and youths grow up into a world modeled after the past) to prefigurative (where the younger members of the clans make decisions for themselves and the present generation moves into an unknown future) (Mead, 1970), living side by side with beliefs spanning from the prehistoric era to the eve of the twenty-first century. However, the society has so far maintained a balance in blending the ancient traditions with the modern trends, creating a transitional epoch. The coexistence of the traditional and modern modes includes fields of dance, music, and folk rituals. This coexistence can be best seen in the field of medicine. The islanders have created an art in the counterpoise of using all "cultural possibilities for the interpretation and alleviation of suffering" (Kapferer, 1983, p. 13).

Sri Lanka, a country that is close in size to the U.S. state of West Virginia, can boast of the existence of over half a dozen medical colleges. While some of them offer training in medicine as practiced in the West, others concentrate on Ayurvedic medicine. The medical profession is highly sought after because of its prestigiousness, parental pressure, and the Buddhist theory of earning merit through one's service to others. Many young men and women, after receiving a general medical degree in Sri Lanka, attend renowned universities in Europe or the United States of America. After training in highly developed techniques, they return to their motherland, where most of them are employed by the government. Thus, the latest methods of treatment in all areas of health care are made available to every citizen. For those who wish to avoid long waits in lines at the free clinics, there are sophisticated private "nursing homes" (as private hospitals are called) with a large price tag attached to the comforts.

Before the introduction of Western medicine, this ancient culture depended on a traditional method to treat sickness and disease. More commonly known as native or Ayurvedic medicine, this treatment is based on the Hindu scriptures of 3,000 years ago. Even today nearly one-fifth of the human race practices Ayurvedic medicine. The lush tropical conditions of Sri Lanka allow the prolific growth of endemic medicinal plants and herbs. In this traditional method of healing, herbs are used in different techniques, taken internally or as applications in the form of oils and/or plasters. Efficiently used, different parts of plants have their own curative properties. The science of Ayurveda was encouraged by kings in keeping with the Buddhist philosophy, which preaches earning merit during a lifetime. Treating the sick was considered a meritous act. This accumulated merit (*Karma*), an eternal investment, pays dividends during successive lifetimes. A knowledge of Ayurveda was expected by nobility, royalty, and Buddhist monks. In a social order divided by caste, gaining merit by honorable trade was the work of the higher castes.

Ayurvedic medicine flourishes today. Many scholars from Europe and other Western countries come to Sri Lanka especially to learn the effective use of natural resources. It is interesting to note, however, that one branch of Ayurveda includes in its cures *bhuta-viya*, those illnesses (*viya*) believed to be caused by demons or ghosts (Parrinder, 1987, p. 230). They include epidemics sent by the gods in response to human offenses, illnesses caused by the unfavorable conjunction of the planets and constellations, and sicknesses caused by the human "evil eye" or "evil talk." This system is less than well defined because the cure is somewhat dependent on the patient's belief in its efficacy. The diagnosis and treatment can be traced to the ancient Sinhala folk region. The cure entails the worship of a pantheon of gods, consultation of astrologers and oracles, and an exotic performance of curative rituals to exorcise the demons and spirits causing the malady. Thus, this branch of Ayurvedic medicine is closely tied in with a form of healing through prayer and faith in one's religion.

Traditional Sinhala religion probably coexisted as it does today with other forms of religious beliefs and practices such as witchcraft, sorcery, and divination. When the great historical religions like Buddhism were introduced into the region, the older religion had to adapt itself to newer circumstances. A clever marriage between folk religion and Buddhism has been achieved by the Sinhala Buddhists. Gods and demons are appeased to help one bear the trials of daily life's traumas, while the devout practice of the philosophy of Buddhism is targeted as an investment for the future, solving the problems of prosperity in life after death, rebirth, and so on until the eventual attainment of Nirvana. In summary, curative options or medical practices could be categorized as the following: (1) medicine as practice in the Western world; (2) Ayurveda, the science of health and healing as practiced by the early Aryans; and (3) using mediators to alleviate sickness through prayers, rituals, or exorcism.

MEDICAL TREATMENT

At the first sign of sickness of a Sinhalese Buddhist individual it is not unusual to initially treat the illness with the usual home medicines. A common cold will be treated with coriander tea. A powdered mixture of roots called a *peyawa*, would treat flu-like symptoms. If the cure takes time, several choices are available.

Western Medical Doctor

A Western medical doctor holds a degree in medicine and practices medicine either at a hospital or at a private clinic.

Ayurvedic Doctor

An Ayurvedic doctor holds a degree in Ayurvedic medicine and practices medicine either in a hospital or private clinic that uses Ayurveda as its method of cure.

Vedamahathaya

A Vedamahathaya (*Veda* [healing] *mahathaya* [gentleman]) is a healer in Ayurvedic method who has no professional training but has gone through an apprenticeship. He (sometimes she) would carry on a trade that has often been handed down from father to son (or daughter). Curative oils, pastes, or mixtures made of indigenous plants would be stored on shelves in his or her home, where patients would visit and be treated.

Bikkhu

A Bikkhu is a Buddhist priest versed in the methods of Ayurvedic medicine who lives in a Buddhist temple. A *Bikkhu* would choose to treat a patient with herbal medicines or by a method of purification called a *pirith* ceremony. One or more Buddhist priests would arrive at the house of the patient. *Gathas* (prayers) from the Buddhist text would be recited, ridding evil influences and bringing about a calm and peace in the household.

Astrologer

An astrologer, or *sastara karaya*, is a soothsayer or reader of horoscopes. This is a trade handed down from father to son. An important member of the community, astrologers are often of the Berawa caste that exorcists belong to. Astrologers visit the homes of their clients to read horoscopes. If the conjugation of planets does not speak in favor of the individual, immediate actions are taken to counteract this "dangerous planetary period (*apele*)" (Kapferer, 1983, p. 13). A simple solution to a period of *apele* could be overcome by the individual wearing a talisman or *yantere*. This scroll-like charm usually prevents the sickness from getting worse (Parrinder, 1987, p. 230). The astrologer being the decision maker of the experts in curative practices would suggest either a Buddhist priest, a kapurala, or an adura, depending on his diagnosis of the malady caused by planetary upheaval.

Kapurala

The Kapurala is a healer who acts as mediator between deities and the patient. A simple ritual consists of giving offerings to deities while intoning prayers and chants appropriate to the circumstances. The Sinhalese place deities in a high cosmic order, below Buddha (Ames, 1966; Obesekera,1966; Gombrich, 1971; Kapferer, 1983), but higher than humans, who are followed by demons. The three worlds of the Sinhalese are *Deva Loka* (Deities World) *Manusa Loka* (Human World) and *Yaksa Loka* (Demon World). Out of fear and respect, some leviathan lords of the malevolent world are viewed as deities, not to be confused with the benevolent deities of the *Deva loka* or God's world. The benevolent deities are served by a person of upper caste, such as a *Kapurala*, and given incense and flowers, which are considered pure offerings (Kapferer, 1983). On occasion, pilgrimages have to be made to specific deities in permanent places of worship. Rituals could be completed by obtaining protective oils to be applied or worn in an ornamental case called a *sure* (talisman), or a thread of protection worn on the patient, or in a lime-cutting ceremony (*Dehi Kapuma*), which expels evil sources or *Dosa*. During a *Dehi Kapuma*, 21 limes are placed at crucial points on a patient's body. These are cut in half and thrown into sizzling oil (Parrinder, 1987, p. 230). The sight and smell along with the sound of boiling oil all add to the mystery of these rituals. As a precaution to the spread of communicable illness a performance of a *kiri Dane* or alms to "milk mothers" is held at the temple. A collection of nursing mothers is treated to a feast of nourishing foods. The merit earned from this deed acts as protection against the spread of disease. Astrologers in their diagnosis do not disregard the possibility of sorcery. "Sinhalese have a cultural belief in eye, mouth and thought evil" (as *Vaha, kata Vaha* and *ho Vaha*, respectively) (Kapferer, 1983, p. 52). It is not uncommon for the Sinhalese people to place responsibility for the illness on another human being as the cause for this momentary grief.

The collectivist nature of the Sri Lankan people would require the consultation of elders during a crisis. The same would apply if a family member was sick. So as not to anger elders or concerned family members, many curative practices would take place simultaneously. If the patient was not cured by the methods mentioned earlier, a *Kattadiya* or exorcist is called as a last resort.

Kattadiya

A *Kattadiya*, or edura or exorcist, is a mediator between the lords of the malevolent world and humans. Unlike the upper-caste *Kapurala* who serves the gods of the benevolent world, the *Kattadiya* is of a lower caste. "Exorcists preserve the ancient folk religious belief in demons, spirits and the occult powers" (Parrinder, 1987, p. 230). It is he who makes offerings to the spirits and demons in persuasion of releasing the person they have taken possession of and returning the patient to a healthy life. Of the multiplicity of medical practices available in a pluralistic medical system, exorcism is by far the most dramatic and exotic ritual to arrest the psyche of patient and perceiver.

THE PSYCHOLOGY OF DEMONOLOGY

Psychology and demonology should not be viewed as subjects separated by centuries of time or geographic boundaries. After the death of his father in 1896, Sigmund Freud, who had plunged into a deep depression, wrote to Wilhelm Fliess, "I have been through some kind of neurotic experience, with odd states of mind not intelligible to consciousness. Cloudy thoughts and veiled doubts with barely here and there a ray of light. . . . I believe I am in a cocoon, and heaven knows what sort of creature will emerge from it (Isbister, 1985, p. 75).

Bruce Kapferer in his study done on demonology in the southern providence of Sri Lanka mentions that "extreme emotional states, fear, anger, attachment to deceased kin, acute sexual longing, either overt or repressed envy and jealousy, are evidence of mental imbalance and are symptomatic of demonic illness" (1983, p. 50). The parallel between the topics was expressed by Freud in his letter to Fliess in January 1897: "Do you remember me always saying that the theory of possessions of the middle ages and the ecclesiastical courts is identical with our theory?" (Isbister, 1985, p. 76). It is the diversity in curative method that brings our attention to the impact of literacy versus religious and ethnic beliefs in a society that creates a cultural uniqueness.

Comparison of Approaches to Treatment

The Western analysis of a patient with disturbed behavior would be based on medical and psychological knowledge of the psychotherapist; the Sri Lankan demonologist (*Yak Adura*) would base his analytical conclusions on cultural knowledge and meaningful explanations. For example, both psychoanalysts and demonologists associate dreams as an interpretation of the subconscious. Whereas a sudden fright, fear, or shock causing a patient to behave in certain ways might be interpreted as a trauma in Western practice, the same behavior to a demonologist would be a demonic attack on the person.

While Western medicine has many fields of expertise practiced by doctors who qualify in specific illnesses, the exorcist has a multitude of skills in rituals he would perform to cure his many patients. In cases such as a barren woman, or someone who attempts to take his or her life, or a young man who has taken to a life of crime, the role of gynecologist, psychiatrist, and the law would be represented by the exorcist as all illnesses of his patients according to the theory of demonology are attributed to the demonic power.

It is not uncommon for the Western patient to be treated by more than one physician for more than one illness at one time. Likewise, the Sri Lankan patient could be receiving medicine from other sources while an exorcist is consulted as an extra precaution. Just as counseling and therapy are not sought after by all, exorcism and the theory of sorcery are not accepted by all Sri Lankans. While therapeutic practices seem to be getting popular and almost a fad in the affluent societies of the West, exorcism that was once held in middle-class homes of the Sinhalese people is shunned as "practice inappropriate to Buddhism and for submitting to superstitions inconsistent with their social standing and education" (Kapferer, 1983, p. 34).

Exorcism today in Sri Lanka is held mostly in the homes and compounds of the lower socioeconomic class. Yet more and more Sinhalese, who can afford to, turn to the Western method of analysis and solutions. The effects of education and modernization are recognizable in events such as this, when old beliefs and modern trends clash.

Just as a complex field of medicine dealing with the mind requires many years of study, skill, and education, *Yaksa-Butha Vidyawa* (demon-ghost/spirit science) is streamlined to specific cultural requirements. The music for the exorcism is provided by drummers. At one time drummers to the kings, the people of the Berawa caste are great preservers of artistic tradition. Members of this caste were the artists who painted religious and historical scenes on temple walls. Experts in dance, folk lore, and drama, they are also talented builders, matchmakers in marriage (*kapuwas*), astrologers, and soothsayers. Today it is not unusual to find other caste members learning and apprenticing in the art of exorcism. A fully fledged exorcist has to have a knowledge of Ayurvedic medicine and of all mantras (chants) and rituals of different exorcisms.

While the methods of psychotherapy would take time to effect a cure, exorcism provides a short-term therapy. A short exorcism would take a few hours; a grand exorcism takes all night.

While the patient does most of the talking under the guidance of the psychologist, the drama of exorcism is the performance of one or many exorcists while the patient plays a relatively passive role.

While the psychologist would encourage problem solving through individual group and/or family therapy, exorcism offers a unique opportunity for self-expression. Sri Lankans have been described as a "society with a highly elaborate system of institutionalized inequality" (Fernando, 1979, p. 29). The culture still turns to astrologers for advice during adolescence, midlife crises, or any major turning point in the life of a human being. There is no guidance offered in child-rearing techniques. Thus a punitive type of pedagogy is maintained and aimed at restraining and deterring evil. Submission and obedience to elders are expected behavior throughout life. The psychological tensions built up in an individual due to a multitude of factors, including subordination, are offered a release during the climax of the exorcism.

Exorcism is an art; the exorcist is an artist who converts his work to a practical purpose. According to demonology, the disturbance of the body is also a disturbance of the mind, treated dualistically. Music, dance, and comedy are used to restore mind and body to a healthy equilibrium. After the initial ritual of enticing the demons through song and offerings during the "evening watch," a climax takes place at midnight. This is the highlight of an exorcism ritual or *thovil*. The exorcist, dressed as a demon, dances to the rapid mesmerizing beat of the drum (*Yak Bera*), inhales demon incense, and goes into a trance. Now he is believed to be under demonic control. Then this demonic role is transferred to the patient, who in turn goes into a trance and dances in step to the beat of the drum. In this altered state of consciousness, cultural inhibitions are abandoned and builtup emotions are released. "The reported lack of consciousness by patients of course absolves them of responsibility for their actions. Some entranced patients abuse and attack their spouses and/or their relatives" (Kapferer, 1983, p. 198).

A cure might not be instant or dramatic in the psychological method, but demonology completes its short-term therapeutic treatment in a fitting finale. In one particular ritual called the *Suniyam Sanniya*, close to the end of the ceremony various offerings are placed around the patient. A live rooster is presented to the demon as a sacrificial equivalent of the human. This is placed at the feet of the patient who is now covered with a white cloth. An ash pumpkin, a kind of gourd, is placed on the stomach of the patient. Amid flaming torches, billowing smoke caused by demon incense (*Dhummala*), the increasing rhythm of drums, and the chant of mantras, the exorcist holds up a gleaming knife. With one downward stroke of this weapon, a practiced hand deftly halves the gourd. (Silva, 1970). The evil forces are released and the exorcism is over.

Western practitioners would be more qualified to diagnose the needs of the patient, whether psychological or medical. But there is a danger of "relying too much on the psychosomatic healers. Some illnesses are obviously more readily treated by psychological means than material means. But when the physical condition is uppermost, it could be unwise to delay too long before getting to the kind of help that modern medicine can provide" (Hoad, 1993).

Unlike Western medicine that opens its doors to both men and women, "exorcists are males and it is the power of their maleness which enables them to control the demonic" (Kapferer, 1983, p. 101).

Female Identity in Exorcism

Demonology exemplifies the cultural attitude toward sex differences and gender identity. The *Yaksa Loka* is dominated by male figures with only one female goddess of malevolence, *Pattini*.

Women, however, are more prone to demonic possessions than men. This could relate more to the cultural construction that men have of women and women have of their own sex. Demons and spirits are identified with pollution and uncleanliness. Women more than men are affiliated with polluting activities. For example, cooking, cleaning, menstruation, and childbearing are considered polluting activities, placing women in a role of subordination. Rituals again demand women in different roles. Funerals, dangerously polluting rituals, are presided over by women who stay inside the house with the body while men stay outside the house.

Due to the superstitions and questionable cleanliness of women, few women professionally take to exorcism, but women astrologers are not uncommon. Often women with psychic powers act as mediators and give offerings to the malevolent goddess *Pattini*, but the flourish and grandiosity of the *Thovil*, or great exorcism ritual, is the privilege of a man.

Even though women are not allowed to take part in exorcism, in the main ritualistic dance male dancers dressed in female attire, their faces made up, betel juice used to redden their lips accentuating femininity, beckon the demon to the ritual grounds. These impersonators seductively act as pawns, moving rhythmically, enticing the demons to be ensnared as prisoners of their own lust. A symbolic representation of women as ornamental objects works to bring about the downfall of the demon.

It is not uncommon for the woman to be blamed in situations of failure of either husband or family. Contradicting this belief, women are treated with great respect in songs, poems, and legends. Traditionally, women are required to be docile. Then again they are expected to be the homemaker, mother, and backbone of the family. A study done in 1988 by de Silva, Stiles, and Gibbons (1992) showed women as self-sacrificing and responsible for others.

Women of Sri Lanka face this antithetic view of themselves. Most women of a society like the Sinhala buddhists of southern Sri Lanka have predetermined values. Parents, religion, caste, social status are but some of the decision makers of their education and marriage.

The women live in what Marcia describes as a state of foreclosure where their goals, aims, and sense of values are determined for them by others. Few reach a state of moratorium, which, according to Marcia, is a period of experimenting different roles thus gaining experiences in becoming more mature (Marcia, cited in Muuss, 1988). Marcia expresses the stage of moratorium as an essential and necessary prerequisite to identity achievement (Marcia, Erikson & Mead cited in Muuss, 1988). The prevalence of women as victims of possession states and other ritualistic means could be a result of this confusion of identity, among a host of other disturbances. "Many women who have exorcism disturbances are young and unmarried or older and past childbearing" (Kapferer, 1983, p. 95).

According to Erik Erikson's theory of identity development, there are transition points of a woman's life. The first stage coincides with "Intimacy versus Isolation" (Erikson, 1968), the second stage of the older woman being "integrity versus despair" (Erikson, 1968; Roazen, 1976). There is also the possibility that these women could be using sympathy to draw attention to the problems of being a woman, driven to exorcist practices to calm an inner turmoil. Living in a culture that has listened to the voices of men over the centuries, women are forced to pursue alternate "voices" to be noticed—"to notice not only the silence of women, but the difficulty in hearing what they say when they speak" (Gilligan, 1982, p. 173).

In a trance state, their voices are heard. For one evening, the invalid experiences an elevation of her status of life—from a mundane existence to being the center of attention of family and its extensions. A whole village witnesses the account in awe as demon and divine forces battle to return the patient to normality.

WHAT THE FUTURE HOLDS

With more young medical doctors returning from Western countries, bringing with them advanced knowledge, the government-extended free health care to the public is even better than it was. Simultaneously, the emphasis on natural foods and healing is turning the Western medical professional toward the East. This widens the future prospects of Ayurvedic medicine in Sri Lanka. Exorcism, on the other hand, is experimenting with new horizons. Seeing better prospects in the booming tourist trade that has taken the island by storm, fear and superstition of the evil spirits have been abandoned. Young men today present shorter versions of the ceremonies on the compounds of local hotels, brandishing flaming torches and carrying on conversations with the devil, while an enthralled crowd of tourists applauds, unaware of the fraudulent mockery of an art of healing, of centuries of belief, craftsmanship, trade secrets handed down from father to son. An extravaganza of talent, unique to a singular caste, has been converted to a new method of amusement.

The charming people of Sri Lanka are an extension of the placid and beautiful island. The close of yet another century finds these serene people straining to maintain old values and cultural norms while acculturating to "global unification" that is being created by the global education to even the most remote village of the island that was until now unaffected by Copernicus, Darwin, or Freud. Enticed by the glamor offered by television programs, village youths leave to seek their fortunes in the world outside that offers these wondrous novelties. Many are lured to garment factories in the city and some do find means to live abroad. Many Sri Lankans have moved to the Middle East in search of jobs, later returning home with foreign currency, which enables them to live a comfortable life. This has more allure than maintaining the skillful mastery of drums, dance, and song.

A society that at one time was highly stratified by kinship and caste is deteriorating. The Sinhalese have always had a respect for a person who wore trousers instead of the sarong that was worn by their ancestors. The ability to speak English and dress in Western attire has taken precedence over pride in ethnicity. "Western attire came to be considered an index of upward mobility" (Fernando, 1979).

The transitional epoch is witnessing the move of a caste-based social system toward the youths being more adventurous in their own professional choices. A musically inclined Govikula entrepreneur might don the masks and study the drums, while an achievement-oriented *Berawa* youth might decide to attend medical college. This is a reversal of the order of "Spirit versus Scalpel." Racial and religious disharmony in recent years has also caused some disparity in maintaining the peace during religious festivals that take place in sites of common worship.

An endless twilight in a tropical paradise elapses to give way to nightfall. Electric switches are replacing the aromatic oil lamps. The tradition of the elderly indoctrinating the young in family history is being replaced by television drama. Still, there might be one familiar rhythm that carries on into the night, that being the dull thud and eerie roll of the *yak bera*. The ominous drama rises to a crescendo as the *yak adura* holds high a gleaming knife. "Spirit faces Scalpel." Time stands still as the balmy night captures thirty centuries in one fleeting moment.

ACKNOWLEDGMENTS

The authors wish to thank Dr. Debbie Stiles of Webster University, Dr. John Hoad of the Ethical Society of St. Louis, and Varsha S. de Silva of the University of Southern California for editing the manuscript; Ellen Eiliceiri, Janice Pallon, and Asouka Situge for helping with research; and Lynn Rucher and Geesia McIntosh for hours of typing.

REFERENCES

Ames, M. (1966). Ritual presentation and structure of the Sinhalese pantheon. In M. Nash (Ed.), *Anthropological studies in Theravada Buddhism* (pp. 27–50). New Haven, CT: Yale University, Southeast Asia Studies.

de Silva, S., Stiles, D. A. & Gibbons, J. L. (1992). Girl's identity information in the changing social structure of Sri Lanka. *Journal of Genetic Psychology, 153,* 211–220.

——— (1996). Gender roles in Sri Lanka. In L. L. Adler (Ed.), *International handbook on gender roles.* Westport, CT: Greenwood Press.

Erikson, E. H. (1968). *Identity: Youth and crisis.* New York: Norton.

Fernando, T. (1979). Aspects of social stratification in modern Sri Lanka. In T. Fernando & R. N. Kearney (Eds.), *Modern Sri Lanka: A society in transition.* (pp. 29–40). Syracuse, NY: Syracuse University.

Gilligan, C. (1982). *In a different voice: Psychological theory and women's development.* Cambridge, MA: Harvard University Press.

Gombrich, R. (1971). *Precept and Practice: Traditional Buddhism in the rural highlands of Ceylon.* Oxford: Clarendon Press.

Hoad, John (1993). Personal interview.

Isbister, J. N. (1985). *Freud: An introduction to his life and work.* Cambridge: Polity Press.

Jayaweera, S. (1979). Aspects of the role and position of women. In T. Fernando & R. N. Kearney (Eds.), *Modern Sri Lanka: A society in transition.* (pp. 163–180). Syracuse, NY: Syracuse University.

Kapferer, B. (1983). *A celebration of demons: Exorcism and the Aesthetics of Healing in Sri Lanka.* Bloomington: Indiana University Press.

Keuneman, H. (1993). Frenzied modes of dance and drama. In J. G. Anderson & R. Anthonis (Eds.), *Sri Lanka* (pp. 255–263). Sri Lanka: Apa Productions.

Mead, M. (1970). *Culture and commitment.* New York: American Museum of Natural History.

Muuss, R. E. (1988). *Theories of adolescence.* New York: Random House.

Obesekera, G. (1966). The Buddhist pantheon in Ceylon and its extensions. In M. Nash (Ed.), *Anthropological studies in Theravada Buddhism* (pp. 1–26). New Haven, CT: Yale University, Southeast Asia Studies.

——— (1979). Popular religions. In T. Fernando & R. N. Kearney (Eds.), *Modern Sri Lanka: A society in transition* (pp. 201–225). Syracuse, NY: Syracuse University.

——— (1987). Sinhala religion. In M. Eliade (Ed.), *The encyclopedia of religion,* Vol 13. New York: Macmillan.

Parrinder, G. (1987). Exorcism. In M. Eliade (Ed.), *The encyclopedia of religion*, Vol 5. New York: Macmillan.

Roazen, P. (1976). *Erik H. Erikson: The power and limits of a vision.* New York: The Free Press.

Silva, S.H.S. (1970). *Suniyam Shantiya.* Colombo: M. D. Gunasena (printed in Sinhalese).

Smith, D. E. (1979). Religion, politics, and the myth of reconquest. In T. Fernando & R. N. Kearney (Eds.), *Modern Sri Lanka: A society in transition* (pp. 83–99). Syracuse, NY: Syracuse University.

Zuber, C. & Bandaranayake, S. (n.d.) *Island civilization* (pp. 333–336). Paris: Editions Delroisse.

Mesa blanca: A Puerto Rican Healing Tradition

Angela Jorge

HISTORY OF *MESA BLANCA*

The Puerto Rican tradition of *Mesa blanca*, which has two major forms—the Kardecian, or scientific, and the eclectic—is one of three major ethno-religious traditions in the Hispanic Caribbean. The other two are Cuban *Santería* and Dominican *Vodú*, which differs in many respects from Haitian voodoo. Although all three ethnoreligious traditions have been transplanted to the United States with the numerous migrations and immigrations of Cubans, Dominicans, and Puerto Ricans, this chapter focuses on the Puerto Rican tradition of *Mesa blanca*. Readers interested in *Santería* and *Vodú* will find *Flash of the Spirit: African and Afro-American Art and Philosophy* by Robert Farris Thompson (1983) and *La otra ciencia: el vodú dominicano como religión y medicina populares* (The other science: Dominican voodoo as religion and folk medicine) by Martha Ellen Davis (1987) excellent resources.

The Puerto Rican tradition of *Mesa blanca* was probably introduced into the United States by some of the intellectuals who formed part of the small Puerto Rican and Cuban community that existed in New York City during the nineteenth century (Andréu Iglesias, 1984, pp. 39–79). The Puerto Rican tradition of *Mesa blanca* serves many different groups within the Puerto Rican community and seems to provide solutions to health problems, to personal and family problems, as well as provides an explanation for the inexplicable. Because it touches the lives of so many people within the community, be they believers or nonbelievers, it is reasonable to assume that this tradition will continue to be one of the unique cultural character-istics of the Puerto Rican community in the twenty-first century.

My professional interest in *Mesa blanca* began in the 1970s; however, my exposure to this tradition began during my childhood, since my family's religious beliefs embrace Catholicism, Protestanism, and *Mesa blanca*. My interest in *Mesa blanca* led to the creation of a liberal arts course on the ethnoreligious traditions of the Hispanic Caribbean at the State University of New York/College at Old Westbury. This course is offered as an elective to students who wish to obtain a Bachelor of Arts degree in Spanish Lan-guage, Hispanic Literature and Culture. It is also one of the courses that nonmajors may take to complete the college's mandatory 40-credit General Education requirement. My personal interest in *Mesa blanca* led to an in-terview with a family member who had been involved in this ethnoreligious tradition for at least six decades. This discussion of the Puerto Rican tra-dition of *Mesa blanca* reports on those interviews as well as on aspects of *Mesa blanca* that seem to be universal to this tradition, according to the information provided by others who were also interviewed.

The Kardecian form of *Mesa blanca* is supposedly based exclusively on the writings of Allan Kardec (pseudonym of Denizard Hippolyte-Léon Rivail), the father of modern spiritism. Modern spiritism promotes a belief in the ex-istence of spirits and in the ability of the living to communicate with the dead (Kardec, 1973, p. 21). The eclectic form of *Mesa blanca* blends the religious traditions of the Amerindian and African peoples who survived the Spanish conquest and colonization of Puerto Rico with Catholicism and the teach-ings of Allan Kardec. In the eclectic form of *Mesa blanca*, unlike the Karde-cian, it is standard practice to use fetishes, religious icons, plaster of Paris images of Amerindians and Africans; to have healing rituals involving cigar smoke, rum, holy water, perfume, incense, and medicinal plants; and to have altars dedicated to the dead or to spirit guides, and food offerings to nature spirits, such as water spirits, and to the dead.

Modern spiritism, called *Espiritismo* or *Mesa blanca* by Puerto Ricans, be-gan in New York State in 1848 with the Fox sisters (Nelson, 1969, p. 1), and reached the shores of Puerto Rico shortly after that. It is generally believed that modern spiritism began in Puerto Rico in 1871, in the city of Mayagüez. It is also believed that by 1889 the opening of the first formal meeting place for believers in the teachings of Allan Kardec had occurred. This formal meeting place, referred to as a *Centro espiritista*, was named *Luz de Pro-greso*, or Light of Progress (Rodríguez Escudero, 1978, pp. 41–42).

The tradition of *Mesa blanca* spread from Mayagüez to the rest of the island, and, in 1903, representatives from the different spiritist centers in Puerto Rico attended a convention at which the *Federación Espiritista de Puerto Rico* (Spiritist Federation of Puerto Rico) was established (Rodrí-guez Escudero, 1978, p. 54). By the early 1920s, Balbino Vázquez San Diego and his wife, María Cruz, residents of Santurce, Puerto Rico, opened their home to the public and through spirit communication helped anyone who came to their door. Unable to accommodate the number of people who came seeking their help with personal and physical problems, in 1922 they constructed a large room that could hold approximately 300 people next to their house. The size of this room suggests that the *Centros espiritistas* and what they stood for were not a passing fad. This added structure served as the foundation of what later became *La Gran Logia Espiritista Núm. 1, Casa de las Almas* (The Grand Spiritist Lodge No. 1, House of Souls), a highly respected spiritist center in Puerto Rico's second largest city (Rodríguez Escudero, 1978, pp. 149–152).

Since the Puerto Rican tradition of *Mesa blanca* spread throughout the island, with *Centros espiritistas* established, it may be assumed that some of the Puerto Ricans who traveled to the United States mainland after 1889, and certainly after 1903, may have been believers in the teachings of Allan Kardec. This assumption is inadvertently corroborated by Bernardo Vega, a Puerto Rican who migrated to New York City in 1916. Vega mentions in his memoirs that *Botánicas* were among the Puerto Rican businesses that existed by 1929 in the Puerto Rican section of New York City's Harlem community. This community, referred to as *El Barrio*, became, according to Vega, "the heart" of the growing Puerto Rican community in New York City by the late 1920s and consisted mainly of cigar-makers and their families (Andréu Iglesias, 1984, p. 155). These cigar-makers constituted a well-educated and politically sophisticated segment of the Puerto Rican community (Flores, 1984, p. x). The presence of *Botánicas* by the late 1920s in a neighborhood in which cigar-makers were the dominant group not only confirms that the tradition of *Mesa blanca* survived the Puerto Rican migration to the United States, it also suggests that the clientele of the *Botánicas* were probably not limited to the uneducated and to the politically unsophisticated, as it is too often assumed.

The Puerto Rican tradition of *Mesa blanca*, whether Kardecian or eclectic, is essentially the tradition of followers of spiritism attending a gathering, or séance, where spirit communication is expected to take place. The séance is presided over by a *Presidente de Mesa blanca* and a number of fully developed spiritist mediums, interchangeably referred to as *Médiums, Mediumnidades*, or *Espiritistas*. The president and the mediums, usually dressed in white, sit at a *Mesa blanca*, or table that is covered in white and on which the following spiritually significant accoutrements have been placed: (a) a clear glass receptacle filled with fresh water, (b) holy water, (c) perfume and/or cologne, (d) and a copy each of *La moral espiritista o El evangelio según el espiritismo* [Spiritist Teachings or The Gospel According to Spiritism] (Kardec, 1950) and *Colección de oraciones escogidas* [Collection of Selected Prayers] (Kardec and other authors, 1966). In addition to these "standards," the following may or may not appear on the "white table": flowers and several small white candles like the ones usually seen on the Jewish menorah, or candelabrum. When the candles are used, one of them will be lit throughout the séance.

The *Botánicas* offer their customers most of these *Mesa blanca* paraphernalia: (a) books by Allan Kardec; (b) colored candles that are dedicated to different spirit guides, such as the African and the Amerindian, or to Catholic saints; (c) prayer sheets and books; (d) paper images of Catholic saints, with their corresponding prayer or invocation; (e) plaster of Paris images of Catholic saints, Africans, and Amerindians; (f) fetishes; (g) perfumed water that is used for healing baths or to change the energy of a room, apartment, house, or business from negative to positive; and (h) herbs and other healing plants or roots flown in from Puerto Rico and the Dominican Republic. *Botánicas*, which sometimes provide the services of practicing mediums to those customers who come seeking help with personal and family problems, can now be found in every major Puerto Rican community throughout the United States.

When modern spiritism arrived in Puerto Rico and spiritist centers were established, my maternal and paternal families embraced the new spiritist philosophy and several members of my family became practicing mediums affiliated with spiritist centers in Santurce during the latter part of the nineteenth and early part of the twentieth centuries. Because of this involvement an interesting family portrait emerged during the family interviews. According to some family members, my great, great grandfather, Agapito Escalera, was a Puerto Rican *Curandero*, or folk healer; my great grandmother, Gabriela Quintana Mora, was an auditive medium, or person who heard voices from the spirit world (Kardec, 1978, p. 207); my grandmother, María Rosario Quintana, was a sensitive, or spiritist, medium who had the ability, or *Un don*, to perceive or "see" spirits (Kardec, 1978, p. 229); and my paternal grandmother's older brother, was a highly respected *Presidente de Mesa blanca*, or president of a *Centro espiritista*, in Santurce. Unfortunately, since all of these people, with the exception of María Rosario Quintana, died before I was born, I was only able to interview my grandmother.

DOÑA MARÍA, "UNA ESPIRITISTA"

María Rosario Quintana, known as Doña María in the Spanish Harlem community where she lived for many years, was born in Puerto Rico circa 1887, and became an *Espiritista* circa 1914. Her mother, Gabriela Quintana Mora, was already a practicing spiritist medium when Doña María was born. In an effort to determine how far back my maternal family had been involved with spiritism, Doña María was asked if her grandparents had also been spiritist mediums. Unable to remember whether they were or not, she proceeded to relate an event that suggests that at least her grandmother respected *Curanderos* (men and women who know how to heal with medicinal plants and folk remedies).

According to Doña María, Alfonsa Mora, her grandmother, became distraught when her granddaughter (Doña María) suddenly lost her sight at the age of 14 and several doctors confirmed that the young girl would be permanently blind. Returning home from the doctors, Alfonsa Mora and her granddaughter met a neighbor. Asked what was wrong, Alfonsa Mora proceeded to relate the doctors' gloomy prognosis. The neighbor offered to help, if Alfonsa Mora accepted two conditions: (a) that there was no guarantee of success, and (b) that her granddaughter would have to move in with the neighbor for seven days. Desperate, Alfonsa Mora accepted the conditions set forth and agreed to the treatment recommended by the neighbor. This treatment, according to Doña María, consisted of (a) being placed in a room devoid of all light, (b) having her eyes bathed daily with the extracts of medicinal plants, and (c) having compresses dampened in water boiled with medicinal plants placed over her eyes and forehead; these compresses were changed periodically during the day. Doña María's eyesight was restored at the end of the sixth day, and she was able to see for the next 70 years.

The success of the *Curandera* in healing the young María Rosario Quintana of her blindness must have served for Alfonsa Mora and her granddaughter as an affirmation that there were gifted healers: men and women who, when Western medicine failed, were able to heal successfully. This success must have also been for them, and for those who came in contact with them, an affirmation of the healing powers of the tradition of *Mesa blanca*, since it is believed that while some *Curanderos* are taught their craft by other, more knowledgeable *Curanderos*, others are guided by the spirit of a deceased person who was a healer when that person lived. This spirit may be the spirit of a former *Curandero*, of an Amerindian or African medicine man or woman, or of a learned medical doctor. Because the eyesight regained lasted nearly a lifetime, Doña María was able to see her 14 children, her grandchildren, her great grandchildren, and her great, great grandchildren before she died in New York City in 1987.

Interviewed when she was nearly 90, Doña María could recall neither the names of the medicinal plants that restored her sight nor the name of the healer. The story she related, nonetheless, suggests that an awareness of and respect for folk healing traditions have existed in my maternal family for at least four generations, beginning with Alfonsa Mora's act of faith circa 1901.

On another occasion, the question posed to Doña María was, how and when did you become a medium? The response was, "It happened one day while I was ironing." Noticing my surprise, she exclaimed that everyone is a medium, that everyone is able to communicate with the spirits of the dead, although not everyone develops as a medium or accepts the responsibility of becoming a practicing medium. Since both her mother and stepfather were mediums and, moreover, her stepfather, Andrés Remigio, was

Presidente de Mesa blanca, Doña María regularly attended the spiritist center in Santurce, where he presided (the *Presidente de Mesa blanca* and the person who actually establishes and runs the *Centro espiritista* do not have to be the same). Consequently, Doña María was not alarmed when, at the age of 27, she was able to see into the future while she ironed. When it happened, she understood immediately that the moment for her to use her spiritual gift to help others had arrived. Doña María was a practicing spiritist medium in Puerto Rico and continued to *Trabajar la obra*, which means to be a practicing spiritist medium in communication with the dead for the benefit of others, when she arrived in New York in the mid 1940s. Doña María, who described herself as *Una mediumnidad consciente*, remained conscious during spirit communication, and it was from a conscious state that she described what she was allowed by God and her spirit guides to physically or mentally perceive or experience.

A third question asked Doña María was, are any of your children mediums? This question reminded her of her son Faustinito, who at the age of seven was an *Espiritista*. When challenged about the youthfulness of the spiritist medium, Doña María explained that chronological age is unimportant in the tradition of *Mesa blanca* because the spirit, or soul, of the individual can be thousands of years old, covering the span of many different lives, or incarnations. She also explained that because of the great energy radiated by the spirits, children are not permitted to experience full spirit possession until they are seven years of age or older and, presumably, can physically tolerate spirit possession.

SPIRIT POSSESSION

The idea of spirit possession has always been mystifying and terrifying to me. Childhood memories include sitting wide-eyed watching mediums in trance possession and wanting to run out of the room and hide somewhere, anywhere, away from the touch of a person who had undergone a transformation that my child's mind could not comprehend. Because of these childhood memories, the subject of spirit possession was broached with a great deal of curiosity, but also with a great deal of wariness. Spirit possession—observed during the past ten years in spiritist centers in New York City and in Santurce—generally effects a voice change, a body language change, and, in some instances, a physical body change such as the crippling of all the extremities. It may even effect a change in lifelong habits. For instance, mediums in trance possession may smoke a cigar or drink overproof rum, although they neither smoke nor drink alcohol in a conscious state.

The first question asked of Doña María about spirit possession was based on some vague memory from childhood. This question was, Why are some people thrown to the floor when the spirit possesses them? Reacting strongly to this question, Doña María responded in a firm voice, *¡Al espíritu, hay que educarlo!* (The spirit has to be educated!). She explained that an individual whose body is to serve as the host for the spirits who communicate during a trance state with the living must communicate to these spirits, often referred to as *Los guías* or *Los guías protectores*, that the body, called *La materia*, is lent willingly on the condition that it neither be thrown to the floor nor physically harmed, nor the individual whose body is possessed be made to grovel like a dog.

This response led to the next question: Why would *Los guías* throw to the floor or physically harm the individual they possess? In response to this question, Doña María explained that the energy levels of the material world and of the spiritual world are different. Asked to be more explicit, she stated that *Los espíritus radian una vibración superior*. This means that the spirits of the dead radiate an energy level that is superior to ours; thus, the sudden infusion of that energy can cause a temporary disorientation, a temporary shock to the host body, and the individual may be thrown to the floor. Doña María also explained that if the individual is not fully possessed, but remains conscious and struggles against spirit possession, the exchange between the host body and the spirit trying to possess it becomes erratic and seemingly violent. This may also cause the individual to be thrown to the floor. She further explained that the loss of balance and the erratic or violent behavior also happen when (a) several spirits try to possess the body simultaneously or (b) an evil spirit possesses the body.

Surprised that more than one spirit would simultaneously attempt to possess the body, she was asked: How and why would this happen? This happens, according to Doña María, when *Los guías* are anxious (a) to initiate the individual's spiritual development, which is one of their primary concerns, and (b) to do good works through the host body that will serve as the temporary *Casilla*, or dwelling place, of the spirits during their visit on earth to help mankind.

When spirit possession is about to take place, by either a good or evil spirit, the role of the *Presidente de Mesa blanca*, which is a role that can be performed by a man or a woman, becomes of paramount importance. A primary responsibility of the *Presidente* is to maintain order and to establish priorities during the spiritist session. Once the spirit possession has taken place, particularly when the possession is by an evil spirit, the *Presidente* must determine if the spirit is accompanied by other spirits and, if so, find out who the other spirits are and why they are present. To exorcise an evil spirit, but not its companion spirits, is to perform an incomplete exorcism.

According to Doña María, when a spirit is about to possess an individual, the *Presidente* must observe carefully to ensure that the possession will not pose any physical harm to the body. If the possession is erratic or violent, the *Presidente* addresses the spirit directly and *demands* that it manifest calmly or disengage itself from the body and postpone possession until another time. The *Presidente* will also request that the individual's own spirit [soul] and spirit guides, since they are observing what is happening and have, with God's permission, allowed it to happen, impose their will on the spirit that causes the traumatic moment or moments.

Establishing priorities, another primary responsibility of the *Presidente*, usually occurs when several spirits are either possessing several mediums at about the same time or when several mediums are simultaneously receiving information from the spirit world that they all want to share with the "patient." The mediums, before they speak, will say, *Con permiso de la mesa*, which literally means, "with the permission of the table." This phrase signals that the medium wants the *Presidente* to grant permission to speak. During a brief exchange between the medium and the *Presidente*, the latter will determine whether or not the information is relevant to the *Causa*, or problem, already under discussion. If the information is relevant, the *Presidente* will consent, and the medium may provide key information that leads to a speedy solution of the problem. If the information is not relevant to the problem under discussion, but is important in order to help someone else, the medium will be asked to wait until later and will be expected, before *El cierre*, or the end of the séance, to share the information.

Another question asked of Doña María was, Why do *Los Guías*, or *Guías protectores*, allow evil spirits to possess the individual they are supposedly protecting or helping to become more spiritually responsive? The response was *Porque hay que trabajar la causa*, which means that the appropriate karmic moment has arrived to exorcise the evil spirit and rid the individual of all the physical, mental, or spiritual negativity that the evil spirit causes in the person's life. After several interviews that addressed this topic, a profile began to emerge of *Los guías* and other spirits.

FOUR TYPES OF SPIRITS AND THEIR EFFECTS

Los guías, or good spirits, seem to cause the least stress to the host body (*Casilla*) during spirit possession. They may manifest (a) in the body of the spiritist medium, (b) in the body of someone who is not fully developed as a medium, or (c) in the body of the individual who has arrived at a spiritist center seeking help. *Los guías* usually manifest (a) to provide information that may help to solve a pressing personal or family problem; (b) to announce future events, good or bad; (c) to announce their presence and mission to be the spirit guides of *Una persona que vino para trabajar la obra*, or a person whose destiny it is to be a spiritist medium; or (d) to *Despojar*, or spiritually strip, the individual of any negative vibrations that may be causing physical, mental, or spiritual harm. The presence of good spirits is considered a blessing and affirms the positive nature of *Mesa blanca*.

Possession by *Un espíritu atrasado*, or evil spirit, also affirms the positive nature of the Puerto Rican tradition of *Mesa blanca*. The information provided by an evil spirit contributes toward the solution of a mental, physical, or spiritual problem that has plagued the individual. When an evil spirit manifests, there seems to be, as observed in the numerous spiritist sessions attended over the years, several uniform key moments that take place after the evil spirit has possessed either the body of the individual who has sought help or the body of the *Espiritista*.

These moments are: (a) the initial reluctance on the part of the evil spirit to acknowledge that it is evil or causes havoc in the life of its victim; (b) the eventual admission of its actual presence and explanation of when and how in the present or previous lifetime the evil spirit was angered or offended by the spirit, or soul, of the victim; (c) the listing of the different ways in which the evil spirit's presence has been experienced by the victim, including physical, mental, and emotional problems, which, when the victim's body is not possessed by the evil spirit, are corroborated by the victim; (d) the eventual admission that the presence of the evil spirit, or of *La causa*, at the spiritist session was dictated by good spirits; and (e) the reconciliation between the evil spirit and the victim, which includes the evil spirit's request, *Perdóname*, or "forgive me," and the victim's response, *Que Dios te perdone*, or "may God forgive you."

In addition to *Los guías* and *Los espíritus atrasados*, there are two other types of spirits. These spirits were never mentioned by Doña María during our interviews, but their existence has been corroborated by several mediums. These spirits are referred to as (a) *Un espíritu que todavía está muy materializado*, and (b) *Un espíritu que está afligido*.

Un espíritu que todavía está muy materializado is a spirit that fails to recognize that it no longer belongs to the material plane, but continues to gravitate toward the material plane and the people it knew and loved when it lived. Moreover, the physical, mental or emotional *Imperfecciones*, or flaws, that were part of the material nature of this spirit when it lived have not been stripped away in the process of transformation from the material to the spiritual world. This spirit may be the spirit of a former relation, such as a spouse, a child, or a parent. Any one of them, or several of them, if still unwilling to accept the reality of death, may make it impossible for the living person to enter into another relationship in which the feelings originally felt for the deceased may be transferred to the new person. Sudden separations or disruptions in what appeared to be new loving relationships are sometimes attributed to some intervention by this spirit. These inexplicable separations may cause feelings of inadequacy, of loneliness, in the living, and these feelings may ultimately become the root of a series of related problems.

This spirit may also, if the person died of a disease, be so close to the living that the survivors may begin to manifest the disease of the deceased.

This "bleed through" from the spirit world can lead to the sudden appearance of a disease or, once this spirit is exorcised by the *Espiritista*, to the miraculous disappearance of the disease.

Un espíritu que está afligido, or a spirit that grieves and is still unwilling to accept its separation from a loved one, may cause sudden, involuntary crying, depression, or hysteria in the living. This emotional *bleed through* from the spirit world may create in the living an inability to function normally and to fulfill whatever responsibilities are required in daily living.

Because of the existence of the aforementioned spirits, an *Espiritista* faced with an individual who is asking for help has to determine which of these spirits, if any, is causing the problem. The *Espiritista* accomplishes this by studying the individual's *Cuadro espiritual*, which literally means spiritual picture. A spiritist medium does this in order to ascertain which spirits, other than the individual's own spirit, or soul, and guardian angel, are part of that spiritual picture. An *Espiritista*, aided by the spiritual guides of his or her own *Cuadro espiritual*, interrogates and studies those spirits that appear in the spiritual picture of the individual who seeks help. The *Espiritista* attempts to determine (a) why those spirits exist in it at all, and (b) what their mission, positive or negative, is in relationship to the individual.

If the individual's imbalance or illness is not due to the presence of any of the aforementioned spirits, the spiritist mediums interviewed unanimously agree that the problem may be caused by the individual's own karmic challenges, since life, according to them, consists of karmic challenges, or *Pruebas*, from which one is to learn before entering the next incarnation, which will have its own *Pruebas*. When this happens the medium will explain that the God-given challenge, or *Prueba*, will persist until the individual decides to see the positive aspect of the challenge and to learn from it.

Finally, unlike the previously mentioned spirits, another spirit may regularly appear during séances or during the monthly meetings held at some *Centros espiritistas* to discuss the works of Kardec and to help mediums who are still developing their particular gift, or *Don espiritual*. This spirit is referred to as *Un espíritu de luz que viene a instruir*. This spirit's mission is to teach, to communicate information about the spirit world or about its own past incarnations for the benefit of the people who regularly attend a particular *Centro espiritista*. This is done to help those attending the séances to have a better understanding of the spirit world and to have an opportunity to discuss with the spirit moral issues that may be particularly challenging. Amalia Domingo Soler compiled the information given through speaking mediums in two excellent books: *Memorias del Padre Germán* (1979) and *¡Te perdono!* (1980).

The Puerto Rican tradition of *Mesa blanca* cuts across gender, race, and economic boundaries. Puerto Rican men and women who are white, black, and mulatto and who are professional and nonprofessional can be observed sitting as spiritist mediums at the same *Mesa blanca*, or attending the same séance. The tradition of *Mesa blanca* has a broad-based following that consists of various groups: (a) the individuals who believe in spiritism because of some proven solution to a problem provided by a spiritist medium; (b) the spiritist mediums who regularly engage in spirit communication and use the information obtained from the spirit world to help others; (c) the believers in spiritism who attend spiritist sessions regularly, although they are unable to communicate directly with spirits and have not been personally helped by a spirit; (d) the nonbelievers who avail themselves of the services provided by a spiritist medium when no other solution to their pressing problem has been found, and, consequently, may become converts; (e) the individuals who have accepted their destiny to be future spiritist mediums and regularly attend spiritist sessions as part of their training; and (f) the individuals who inherited from their ancestors the belief in modern spiritism and pass this tradition on to their children.

Mesa blanca is, for many Puerto Ricans, a way of life, a way of perceiving reality, a way of understanding one's individual mission in life, and a way of solving day-to-day family and health problems. For some, like myself, it's a way of understanding, of connecting to, the worldview of one's ancestors and, consequently, of reaffirming their collective importance in the shaping of who one is.

REFERENCES

Andréu Iglesias, César (Ed.). (1984). *Memoirs of Bernardo Vega: A contribution to the history of the Puerto Rican community in New York* (Juan Flores, Trans.). New York: Monthly Review Press. (Original work published in 1977.)

Davis, Martha Ellen. (1987). La otra cienela: el vodú dominicano como religión y medicina populares. Santo Domingo: Editora Universitaria–UASD.

Domingo Soler, Amalia (Comp.). (1979). *Memorias del Padre Germán*. Buenos Aires: Editorial Kier.

———. (Comp.). (1980). *¡Te perdono! (Memorias de un espíritu)*. Buenos Aires: Editorial Kier.

Flores, Juan. (1984). Translator's preface. In César Andreu Iglesias (Ed.), *Memoirs of Bernardo Vega: A contribution to the history of the Puerto Rican community in New York* (pp. ix–xii). New York: Monthly Review Press.

Harris, Joseph E. (Ed.). (1993). *Global dimensions of the African diaspora*, 2nd ed. Washington, DC: Howard University Press.

Jorge, Angela. (1991). Cuban Santería: A new world African religion. In Kortright Davis and Elias Farajaje-Jones (Eds.), *African creative expressions of the divine*. Washington, DC: Howard University School of Divinity.

———. (1993). La madama francesita: A new world black spirit. In Joseph

Harris (Ed.), *Global dimensions of the African diaspora*. Washington, DC: Howard University Press.

Kardec, Allan. (1950). *La moral espiritista o el evangelio según el espiritismo*. Mexico City: Editorial Orion.

————. (1973). *The Spirits' book: Containing the principles of spiritist doctrine* (Anna Blackwell, Trans.). Mexico City: Amapse Society Mexico. (Original work published in 1857.)

————. (1978). *Book on mediums: or, Guide for mediums and invocators: Containing the special instructions of the spirits* . . . (Emma A. Wood, Trans.). New York: Samuel Weiser.

———— and other authors. (1966). *Colección de oraciones escogidas*. Mexico City: Editora Latino Americana. (Original work published in French under the title *Devotionaire Spiritiste* and anonymously translated into Spanish.)

Nelson, Geoffrey K. (1969). *Spiritualism and society*. New York: Schocken Books.

Rodríguez Escudero, Nestor A. (1978). *Historia del espiritismo en Puerto Rico*. Aguadilla, PR: Nestor A. Rodríguez Escudero.

Rosario Quintana, María. (1984). Personal interviews, January and February.

Thompson, Robert Farris. (1983). *Flash of the spirit: African and Afro-American art and philosophy*. New York: Vintage Books.

The Healing Practices of Mexican Spiritualism

Regina Spires-Robin and Peggy McGarrahan

It is tempting to assume that the experience of pain and illness is constant, that human beings not only suffer similar sensations but will agree on definitions of illness, on appropriate treatment, and successful cures. Common sense would argue that similar assaults should be accorded similar explanations. Yet the fact is that illness and cure are not impersonal concepts. They are intellectual and social constructs based on theories of how the world is organized, by whom, and for what purpose. Thus within any one culture a number of competing explanations, ranging from purely scientific to simply spiritual, are available to explain and treat illness.

Even within advanced industrial societies like our own, alternative therapies exist alongside the socially sanctioned biomedical model with which most Westerners are familiar. In countries not yet fully industrialized, alternative models that do not flow from rationalist, empirical, scientifically based inquiry are far more in evidence and are more freely accepted than would be the case in Europe or America. In Mexico, for example, the sick can consult herbalists, homeopaths, *curanderos*, *cuajos* (women specializing in children's diseases), bone setters, shamans, spiritists, and spiritualists. Each of these folk practitioners offers their patients specific cures and their own special theory of disease.

In this chapter we focus on spiritualism, a Mexican religious sect that incorporates healing rites in its liturgy. Spiritualist healers are particularly interesting, because unlike other folk healers, their healing rituals are part of an organized and hierarchical religious structure. These healing practices, featuring trance and massage along with medicinal teas and some pharmaceuticals, are first and foremost physical experiences. It is our contention that spiritualist healers use bodily processes and reactions to achieve physical, mental, and spiritual effects that in many cases lead to transcendence and transformation. The goal of spiritualist healing is wholeness rather than "cure" in the Western biomedical sense and its success is due to its ability to join what in biomedicine is kept separate: the body and the mind.

The reasons why patients are attracted to spiritual healing practices are less mysterious than the processes and results of their consultations. The distress some patients feel may not be recognized in the biomedical canon as a disease or it may be dismissed as psychosomatic or vaguely psychological. Some illnesses, when treated with antibiotics, simply do not respond. But perhaps most important, there is very little sense in biomedical medical practice of "putting the world to right," of reestablishing order, of reintegrating the person, his or her body, and social reality. For many who believe in the interpenetration of the spiritual and physical worlds, such a reintegration is the essence of healing, and this is what they seek in sects as Mexican spiritualism.

Mexican spiritualism is a dissident religion that appeals to the poor and marginal in Mexican society. The history and practices of this movement have been ably investigated by Kaja Finkler (1983) and the following description draws heavily on her work. Begun in the mid-nineteenth century by a renegade priest who called himself Father Elias, spiritualism boasts an extensive network of temples throughout Mexico as well as a few in the Southwestern United States. These temples are linked hierarchically to each other and to the "mother" temple in Mexico City. In addition, within each temple there is a hierarchy of officeholders. Each temple has a "head," frequently a woman, an "overseer," usually a man, and a "guardian," usually a woman. There are also "pillars" who organize and conduct services, and "clairvoyants" who testify during rituals, a "pen of gold" who transcribes services, and finally "healers" who possess curing powers.

The nineteenth century was a time of considerable religious and political ferment in Mexico. Liberal reform fostered an ideology of social equality and emphasized positivism and materialism. Protestant sects were encouraged to proselytize and one source identifies Mexican spiritualism as a North American Protestant importation (Kelly, 1965). Macklin (1970, 1974), on the other hand, has taken the position that spiritualists and spiritists, such as those she and Harwood (1977) describe, are part of the movement founded by Allan Kardec in nineteenth-century France and later promoted by Joaquin Trincado in Latin and South America.

Allan Kardec (1808–69) was the *nom de plume* of Denizard Hippolyté-Léon Rivail, a Frenchman, who wrote several enormously popular and influential books on spiritism. The best known are *The Spirits' Book* and *The Gospel According to Spiritism.* Kardec believed that living human beings incarnated spirits who could, through spiritual development, rise to the level of pure spirit. He described the search for spiritual enlightenment as a search for "light" and this concept, that spirits are seeking "light," became a cornerstone of the Kardecian tradition. When spirits leave the body, after death, they are released from earthly concerns but they can be contacted by mediums and will provide, when properly approached, direction and advice.

The theology of spiritualism reflects a tolerant eclecticism. It is an amalgam of beliefs about the spirit world, perhaps based on pre-Conquest notions but certainly influenced by Kardecian beliefs about communication between human beings and spirits, and elements drawn from Jewish and Christian theology. Spiritualists call themselves Children of Israel and their pantheon features Jehovah, Moses, Jesus Christ, and the Virgin Mary. Father Elias considered himself the reincarnation of the Holy Ghost.

Spiritualism as a movement is thought to be a response to the increasing differentiation brought on by modern industrialization. Adherents seem to be attracted by the egalitarian yet conservative message of church teachings that encourage the faithful to endure their lot in life and to accept it as God's plan. The church emphasizes socially responsible behavior but does not support social activism and followers do not form a cohesive unit. They come together for rituals but do not interact. During the preaching of God's word they remain motionless and silent. Hymns are sung but at the end of the ceremony the congregation leaves silently and disperses quickly, each going his or her own way. Decorum, dignity, and restraint mark church members' behavior.

The doctrines of spiritualism include 22 commandments that must be strictly followed. These commandments are always recited at spiritualist irradiations (rituals in which God speaks to the faithful through a medium). There are injunctions against drinking alcoholic beverages, taking up arms against one's brother, participating in civil war, abandoning one's children, and believing in witches and idols. Sorcery and witchcraft are vehemently rejected, a posture that promotes social harmony and encourages a more impersonal and less suspicious attitude toward the community. Emotional distance and noninvolvement are cultural ideals within the spiritualist movement.

The emphasis in spiritualism on distance and noninvolvement appears to be a reaction against Catholic ritual and doctrine. In contrast to Catholicism, spiritualism encourages face-to-face contact with the deity. The functionaries in a spiritualist temple are simply the medium by which God speaks to His followers. They do not comprise a special class with special material privileges. Thus spiritualism promotes an egalitarianism and antimaterialism that may comfort people who are experiencing dislocation and stress in their daily lives. People are less likely to be exposed to social differences within a spiritualist temple where social interaction and gossip are specifically inhibited by the structure of the rituals. Spiritualists complain of the lack of order at Catholic ceremonies and accuse Catholics of paying too much attention to money and position. Many adherents and functionaries of spiritualist temples are women who, even more than other groups, are finding it difficult to fulfill their traditional roles, and who find solace and support in the spiritualist movement.

Ceremonies of worship and healing are conducted by functionaries whose fitness for their role is demonstrated by their ability to go into trance and serve as mediums for messages from God and the spirits. A central belief is that God and other spirits speak directly to the faithful through the medium. The rituals wherein God speaks are called irradiations, which vary in length, from a half hour to three hours. They are held on Sundays and Thursdays, and if enough people can be gathered together, on five other days per month.

Irradiations begin with the singing of hymns under the leadership of a temple functionary. While the hymns are sung, from among the temple functionaries who are seated in front of the congregation, the medium who is to convey God's words moves to the throne-like seat facing the audience, closes his or her eyes, and gradually goes into a trance, breathing heavily. The singing stops and the irradiations begin, delivered in rhythmic sentences, with patterned repetitiveness. The message from God usually reminds the faithful of God's goodness and His care for His people. God reminds them that they must be obedient and reproves them for wrongdoing, but He also assures them of His affection and points to their lack of worldly wealth as a sign that they are a chosen people. References to Mexico as the New Jerusalem are usually included and the Mexican flag is displayed on the podium. Every irradiation ends with a blessing for doctors, hospitals, and jails. Then the faithful are asked whether they are satisfied with God's words, to which they respond "yes," but until that moment the congregation has been silent and motionless. The service ends with another hymn or two and then the church members are asked to leave in an orderly manner, those seated at the back rows marching out first. No one leaves before his or her turn. At the door of the temple each is offered a glass of holy water and asked to leave a contribution.

Spiritualist healers encourage those who consult them to attend all ritual activities but especially the irradiation sessions because hearing His word is a part of the curing process. Most patients, however, attend only the healing ceremonies, conducted on Tuesdays and Fridays. These ceremonies begin when the healer arrives at the temple, dons a white robe, listens to a brief prayer recited by the temple head, and then enters the healing room. To summon the spirit protector who will prescribe remedies for patients' ills, the healer sits down, closes his or her eyes, and shakes the upper half of her or his body. The healer stops shaking when the spirit protector takes possession and announces his or her arrival by identifying him- or herself by name and greeting all those present. The healer is now ready to receive patients.

The interaction between patient and healer is quite impersonal. The healer keeps his or her eyes closed and is assisted by a temple functionary. The patient approaches the healer and salutes the spirit protector, saying "In the name of God, all powerful, I salute you brother (or sister, depending on the sex of the spirit protector)." The healer replies, "And I answer you, speak to me." This starts the ritual process. The healer then moves his or her hands up and down the patient's body, massaging it gently while pronouncing a blessing. The patient and healer are either standing face to face or the healer sits and holds the hands of the patient who stands before him. This part of the ritual is called a "cleansing" and is a major component of spiritualist practice. Then the healer asks the patient why he or she has come and the patient states the reason and usually describes his or her symptoms of illness. The healer then authoritatively prescribes a course of treatment. Prescriptions usually include massages, baths, teas made from medicinal plants, and, occasionally, pharmaceuticals. Purgatives are often recommended on patients' first visits to the temple and if the patient complains of intestinal distress, a special food regimen may be prescribed. As the consultation ends, the healer again blesses the patient's body and the patient is expected to thank the healer and leave a small contribution. There is little overt expression of compassion or concern and the time involved in the consultation is quite short. Thus spiritualism's effects cannot be attributed to any strong, personal connection between patient and healer.

As Finkler (1983) shows in the following verbatim accounts of healer-patient encounters, there is little of the personal care and concern that is often considered by Americans to be the hallmark of good medical practice, but there is great certainty conveyed by the healer. Consider these examples:

1. *The patient, an adolescent boy who came with his mother, said nothing.*

Mother: He has had bad luck. He was just released from prison. He was in a car accident and he smashed somebody's car; he has bad luck.

Healer: His *cerebro* is unbalanced. There is no submission and obedience in young people; they are only interested in material things. That's why they become unbalanced—mad.

Prescription

Tea   (Sp.) flor de azares (*Citrus*)

(Sp.) huizaches (*Acacia shaffneri*)

(Sp.) flor de manita (unidentified botanically)

(Sp.) jarilla (*Dodonaea*)

1 bottle of vitamin tonic

Massage	He must do it exactly at noon, made of:
	1 cup mescal
	White wine
	(Sp.) rue (*Ruta chalepneiss L.*)

The healer also instructed the mother to put a cross of rosemary in the house.

2. *The healer is the head of the spiritualist temple. The patient is a middle-aged man from a distant village.*

Patient: I have pain in my stomach.

Healer: How long have you had this pain?

Patient: A year.

Healer: Did you go to the doctor?

Patient: Yes, but I stopped going.

Healer: Did they do an analysis?

Patient: Yes, it was nothing. I wasn't vomiting.

Healer: Nor do you have ulcers?

Patient: No; it only hurts in the morning.

Healer: You are not hungry during those hours?

Patient: No.

Healer: It's an infection of the prostate; you have an upset stomach. I will give you a cleansing.

Prescription	1 bottle of Sal Hepatica in tepid water—to be taken in the afternoon.
	In the morning, take a glass of orange juice.
	1 ampoule of penicillin of 500 mg.
	2 cm in the morning;
	2 cm on Friday; and
	1 cm on Sunday. Return on Tuesday.
Tea	Root of (Sp.) malva (*Malva parviflora*)
	Root of (Sp.) verbena (*Verbena carolina L.*)
	Root of (Sp.) yerba del negro (*Sphaeralcea angustifolia*)

Mexican spiritualism shares with many other religions a belief in a spirit world and a conviction that spirits, both good and bad, act directly in human affairs. Illness is believed to be caused by evil spirits and cure consists, therefore, in the control and manipulation of these spirits. Thus spiritualist healers claim to be able to restore health through their access to the spirit world. The cleansing rituals and herbal potions they prescribe while under the influence of good, protective spirits help the afflicted ward off evil spirits and their noxious intentions and effects. The prescription of herbs and pharmaceuticals is very exact but their true worth, for the believer, comes from the fact that they are ordered by a spirit acting through the medium of the spiritualist healer. There does not seem to be any consistency in prescribing for particular complaints. Pain in the liver, for example, will be treated in a number of ways. Similar complaints will receive dissilimar prescriptions. This is actually quite usual in herbalist and natural medicine, however, and only seems unusual to an observer accustomed to scientific medicine's belief that each ailment has a specific and particular cure. In addition, healers disclaim any particular medicinal knowledge on the grounds that their powers and cures come from their spirit protectors. Healing is thus not a scientific undertaking but an expression of religious belief.

The trance is central to the healing process (Goodman, Henney & Pressel, 1974). It is the vehicle by which the healer establishes contact with the spirit world. From the patient's point of view the trance validates the healer's prescriptions and for the healer the trance establishes his or her authority. The trance is the visible sign of the truth of the cosmology contained in spiritualism; without it the claims of spiritualism would be simply assertions without proof. In addition, the experience of trance can be therapeutic for the patient and in many cases for the healer as well, who is frequently a former patient who demonstrated a talent for trance.

Mexican spiritualism is not alone of course in its reliance on an altered state of consciousness to achieve communion with God. Roman Catholicism, the dominant religion in Mexico, has a long tradition of ecstatic prayer, epitomized by such saints as St. Teresa of Avila and St. John of the Cross. Much as spiritualism contends that it is different from Catholicism, it draws heavily on the region's Catholic heritage, a heritage no less potent because unacknowledged. The fact is that Catholic doctrine and tradition are similar to many of the metaphysical principles underlying healing cult practices and beliefs and it is doubtful that spiritualism would have taken the form it does without this Catholic background.

Catholicism, for example, does not draw any firm line between this world and any other. Angels and saints, even God Himself, are intimately involved with human life and frequently take human form themselves. In reverse, human beings can, through their prayers, touch and influence the spiritual world. Prayers can be and are answered. Furthermore, in common with spiritualism, Catholic teaching has an ethical and moral component. God punishes the bad and rewards the good, but each individual is responsible for his or her behavior. In addition, rituals of the Church, designed to comfort the faithful and present in the symbolic form of mysteries of life and redemption, are undeniably physical: the taking of bread, drinking of wine, washing with water, cleansing with oil. For people brought up within this framework, even if they consciously reject it, the world of everyday and the world of magic, religion, and spirituality are not separate and inviolable. They permeate each other. Borders dissolve. Within very ordinary things can be found the superordinary and the supernatural.

It is thus not surprising that in a region so very Catholic secular healing is frequently attempted within sacred modes or that sacred modes easily incorporate secular healing. Also within this tradition syncretic folk Catholicism is easily aligned with native and Spanish notions of disease etiology, which pay attention to sociopsychological and physiological occurrences: emotions, interpersonal relations, naturalistic processes, and bodily changes (Fabrega, 1970). The Spanish tradition of humoral theories of health and disease emphasizes the need to balance bodily processes; imbalance produces extreme conditions within the body—hot, cold, wet, or dry—and these extremes result in illness. Cure often consists of regaining the hot-cold balance through the administration of purges (hot) and soothing drinks (cool) (Rubel, 1960, 1964; Ingham, 1978). In addition, folk concepts of disease such as *susto* and *mal de ojo* recognize emotions as legitimate causes of illness. Helplessness in the face of disaster, despair, failure to perform one's social role—these are all seen as precipitators of physical malaise (Uzzel, 1974). Furthermore it is common for the magical and the occult to be included in theories of disease. Dreams and portents are given serious consideration (Fabrega, 1973). Spirits are active agents in human lives.

In spiritualism, spirits are categorized according to how well they have followed God's commandments. The highest level, *alta luz*, is composed of exemplary individuals who have completed their mission on earth and only return to earth during consultation rituals. The next group, *media luz*, are still in the process of working themselves up to the highest level. These are the spirits who become protectors of spiritualist healers. They guide and protect them throughout their lives. Some are Aztec heroes, others are Biblical figures or well-known secular doctors or scientists from the recent past. The final category, *seres obscuros*, are dark spirits previously housed in evil people: drunkards, murderers, philanderers, and such. These tormented spirits are being continually reborn, their rebirth signaled by unruly children, other domestic problems, and illness. It is these spirits that spiritualists seek to control. Dark spirits can be released from bondage and move onto the next level of enlightenment if the individual within whom they dwell leads a good and moral life.

Mexican spiritualism is thus a mosaic composed of different elements from a number of different traditions. It seeks to uncover a unity behind the multiplicity of human experience, joining together into one explanatory model what people experience as isolated and disconnected events, especially when the events are tragic and/or defy solution. Spiritualism offers its adherents an explanation that is in tune with their cultural inheritance and accepted ways of thinking, feeling, and behaving.

It also claims to cure them of bodily ills. This is what makes Mexican spiritualism unique and what challenges our notions of medical practice. Patients come to spiritualist healers with a whole range of problems: headaches, joint pains, stomachaches, skin eruptions, diarrhea and vomiting, nausea, chest pains, welts, gynecological complaints, loss of appetite, trembling, apathy, and fatigue. They are treated as described above. Many of them report improvement.

In the only study so far of therapeutic outcomes of spiritualist interventions, Finkler (1983) analyzed 108 cases in which 25.9 percent claimed to be cured, 19.4 percent were inconclusive, 35.3 percent reported failure, and 19.4 percent attributed the status of their health to interventions other than spiritualist therapies. Of the successfully treated cases, the symptoms included: fever, stomach pains, nausea, numbness in hands or feet, loss of weight, itching, vaginal burning and secretions, swollen legs and fingers, white spots on skin, diarrhea, vomiting, fatigue, and paralysis. In Finkler's view spiritualist treatments are effective for four conditions: diarrheas, probably those of nonpathogenic origin; simple gynecological disorders; somatized syndromes; and mild psychiatric disorders. The supposition is that the teas, baths, douches, and laxatives are to some degree effective since Mexicans are plagued with gastrointestinal parasites because of poor water supplies and insufficient sanitary arrangements. The principal causes of death in the State of Hidalgo, where Finkler conducted her study, were enteritis and diarrheas, influenza and pneumonia, the common cold, mange, whooping cough, measles, typhoid, chicken pox, and mumps. Thus in Finkler's view, spiritualist prescriptions, which include herbs known to combat bacteria and viruses, are physiologically beneficial and their efficacy rests on their pharmacological effect, not on the connection between healer and spirit.

The teas, baths, douches, and laxatives that spiritualist healers prescribe use traditional herbs with the occasional addition of an antibiotic, antihistamine, laxatives such as Phillips Milk of Magnesia, mild tranquilizers, vitamins, and antidiarrheals. These medicines are generally available to the public in Latin America without a doctor's prescription. The herbs most frequently prescribed by the healers Finkler observed were rosemary, balm, chamomile, and basil. These have long been staples of herbalists from ancient times in both Europe and Asia and have a well-documented history of effective treatment, although modern scientific medicine has vigorously opposed their use (Mowrey, 1986).

Practitioners of natural and herbal medicine often prescribe rosemary for heart weakness. Chemical analysis of rosemary leaves has determined that they contain many minerals, such as calcium, magnesium, phosphorus, sodium, and potassium, which are needed by cardiac muscles and the nervous system in general for proper functioning (Mowrey, 1986). Rosemary appears to stimulate the circulatory system and often induces a feeling of well being, so a tea of rosemary leaves is considered a tonic for the elderly or convalescents. It also stimulates the digestive tract and soothes cramps (Curtis & Fraser, 1991; Van der Zee, 1982; Meyer, Blum & Cull, 1981).

Balm is a mild, soothing herb that herbalists use to relieve anxiety and calm nervous patients. It has antiviral properties and can be used both as a tea and as a wash for the skin. Combined with rosemary in a tea it is frequently suggested for depression and mental fatigue. Combined with chamomile it is prescribed to relieve nausea and flatulence (Curtis & Fraser, 1991; Van der Zee, 1982; Meyer, Blum & Cull, 1981).

Chamomile is an herb frequently prescribed for women and children in many parts of Europe. It is given for uterine cramps and during labor when pains are excessive and irregular. Colicky babies find it soothing. It is said to relieve coughs and reduces inflammations caused by infections and wounds. It acts against both strep and staph infections and many practitioners recommend it for toothache, or suggest using a chamomile tea as a mouthwash to heal mouth infections and gingivitis. It is also used externally as an eyewash for sore eyes and to heal burns (Curtis & Fraser, 1991; Van der Zee, 1982; Meyer, Blum & Cull, 1981).

Basil is considered an antiseptic herb and is frequently prescribed for intestinal upsets and nervous dyspepsia. It relieves anxiety and depression and has a generally toning effect on the nervous system as a whole. It promotes sweating and so can be used to bring down a fever; and because it is antispasmodic, it is helpful for respiratory ailments such as whooping cough, asthma, and bronchitis (Curtis & Fraser, 1991; Van der Zee, 1982; Meyer, Blum & Cull, 1981).

Other herbs frequently prescribed by spiritualists, such as thyme, garlic, nettles, and nasturtium, have traditionally been used to combat a wide range of pathogens. Thyme is said to act against bacteria, viruses, and funguses, so a tea of thyme will act as a powerful cleanser of a patient's digestive system. It is frequently suggested for respiratory ailments such as asthma, bronchitis, and emphysema. Garlic has long been used for rheumatic complaints and lung infections. It fights infection and can be used for ringworm or athlete's foot and against parasites such as scabies. Nettles are often prescribed for a spring tonic and to cleanse the blood. It is used for diabetes and allergies. The nasturtium prescribed by spiritualists is *nasturtium officinale*, whose common name is watercress. Eaten raw or infused as a tea it is rich in minerals and vitamins and is used for patients suffering from colds and/or anemia. It is also prescribed for swollen lymph glands (Curtis & Fraser, 1991; Van der Zee, 1982; Meyer, Blum & Cull, 1981).

This brief description of the medicinal properties of some of the herbs prescribed by spiritualists is sufficient to indicate that, given the prevalence of infectious agents in the area Finkler studied, prescriptions containing these and other herbs could have a direct, material effect on patients' health. The patients seeking spiritualist remedies are generally poor, probably suffer chronic infections caused by poor living conditions, and the herbal infusions they are directed to use generally contain antiseptic and cleansing ingredients as well as antibiotics deemed effective by Western scientific medicine. According to Finkler, the benefits patients receive should be attributed to the action of these ingredients.

But interestingly a whole other group of patients who reported no physiological change in their symptoms still claimed to feel better. They also acted better, were able to return to normal life, and generally appeared to be healthier. These patients frequently became temple regulars and were encouraged to enroll in "development" courses in which they were taught how to go into trance. One such patient reported on by Finkler was a middle-aged man named Emiliano. His symptoms included insomnia, severe headaches, lack of appetite, and generalized numbness. He also had a large lump behind his ear. He reported nightmares and suicidal thoughts. Prone to anger, he was also easily frightened. Emiliano's wife persuaded him to attend the temple, where the head of the temple invited him to stay at her house for a course of instruction. He described his trance experiences as comparable to a beautiful light that filled him with radiance. He believed it was the light of God that entered him and removed his pain. Following each "development" session he felt happy and experienced a "fresh breeze" passing through his body. After several months Emiliano began to feel better. He regained his appetite and the lump subsided behind his ear.

For this patient the trance state became a therapeutic tool. There is some evidence that physiological changes that occur during trancing affect the autonomic nervous system and result in a reduced heart rate, lower blood pressure and respiratory rate, and increased gastrointestinal motor and secretory functions. Striated muscles relax, decreasing blood lactate levels. Cortical excitation diminishes. Trancers can become either insensible to sensory stimulation or overexcited. Either condition releases trancers from their usual relationship with the world of concrete physical experience (Goodman, Henney & Pressel, 1974). As Wavell (1966, pp. 15–16) comments,

it seems that all men, however primitive or sophisticated, become aware sooner or later of the feeling of being circumscribed, of being chained to their surroundings, their bodies, their feelings and their fate. . . . Each man in his own way tries to get outside himself to escape from the prison of his own senses. They [the trancers] seek to break through the bars of their senses. This exactly, and no less, is the technical object of trance.

Like many other participants in trancing or meditation, Emiliano felt great contentment and elation after the experience, a phenomenon that has been observed in other cultures and other settings. Wavell reported that one of his Balinese friends who had spent a long time in the West complained "with a shade of regret, that until he left for Europe he was able to 'leap into the other world' [of trance] in the space of twenty seconds. 'Now,' he said, 'it takes me at least half an hour and even then I am not always sure of succeeding.' " When Wavell asked him in what way he found the trance state superior to the normal state of consciousness, he said, "Physically, it gives you a sensation of power: spiritually, you feel renewed, recharged."

Entering the trance state has been described as "a little death" (Katz, 1982), and it is not something lightly undertaken. Novice trancers fear letting go. There is always the possibility that they will not be able to return. As one of Wavell's (1966, p. 43) informants said, "A man must die before he becomes a shaman." Not everyone is suited to development training. But for those who are, trancing may provide an experience of death and rebirth in which the most powerful forces in their belief system confer legitimacy on them and give them permission to live.

This kind of experience is not limited to folk medicine. Scientific medicine has long struggled with the fact that some patients get well on sugar pills and some patients feel well even when their physical condition has not changed. A striking example of this occurs in cardiac surgery. There are a substantial number of patients for whom cardiac bypass surgery is not a success; their new arteries quickly close up again. But many of these patients report that their pain has diminished or disappeared and they are able to resume active lives. Medical doctors usually dismiss these results as "the placebo effect."

A different explanation focuses on the spiritual aspects of the operation, particularly on the symbolic death and resurrection that cardiac surgery conveys to the patient. According to Daniel Moerman (1983), cardiac surgery, even more than most surgery, because it involves the heart, is an artificial death. The patient is naked, like a corpse, draped with cloth, like a shroud. In some versions of bypass surgery, the heart is actually stopped for a while. The patient is unconscious for a long time and then is resuscitated through the power of modern science, embodied in the person of the surgeon. Just as the patients of spiritualists feel that the greatest powers in the universe are being brought to bear on their problems, so for cardiac patients, the stainless steel equipment, the drugs, the surgeon in his special garb are indications that they are being helped by the most powerful forces in the world, which are, in the West, the forces controlled by science. All patients are unconsciously affected by these aspects of modern medicine, and for some patients they are sufficient in themselves to enable them to regain normal activity even though their physical condition has not changed.

Describing this phenomenon is easier than understanding how it works and what it means. Seeking to understand how spiritualism heals, Finkler leans toward a materialist and functional explanation. In common with Kleinman (1979, 1983), she considers spiritualist healing that is not specifically physiological to be folk psychoanalysis. In her view spiritualist therapies provide comfort and reassurance for people whose lives are beset with multiple and possibly insoluble problems. She believes that trancing, massage, and "cleansing" rituals, along with the experience of communitas within a group of believers, enable patients to reorder themselves in relation to others and redirect their energies toward productive ends. This kind of analysis, although intuitively reasonable, maintains the distinction between physical and mental ills and between physical and mental cures. But this is exactly the puzzle we need to solve: that patients can recover while still beset with symptoms. In many cases patients who continue to report physiological symptoms of distress feel and act cured.

A first step toward solving this paradox is to make a distinction between curing and healing. Curing means the removal of the cause of the illness and the cessation of physical symptoms. Healing is something else again. It may entail curing but does not require it. Indeed in Mexican spiritualism many of the healers are former patients who find that in curing others they heal themselves. Healing means the return of wholeness, a somewhat existential concept that refers to the patient's sense of self, a self rooted in the experience of the body. Illness can shatter that sense of self and call into question other notions about one's place in society that are related to one's experience of physical life. Displacement from one's place in the world can have an equally shattering effect on one's bodily sense. Illness is thus a dislodgement of the individual in both the physical and social senses from the security of knowing who one is and what one can expect from ones body, family, and community. This disturbance has to be addressed if the patient is to be healed and this is what spiritualism does.

As Nancy Scheper-Hughes and Margaret Lock (1987, p. 9) remind us in a journal article, Western academic analysis has tended to "categorize and treat human afflictions as if they were either wholly organic or wholly psychological in origin: "it" is *in* the body, or "it" is *in* the mind." What the spiritualists remind us is that illness cannot be so neatly dichotomized. In religious healing the two come together. The spiritual and bodily realms are fused. Recovery depends on their interaction.

As long as Western biomedicine neglects the existential aspects of illness and health, relying on a limited reductionist view of sickness and disease, movements such as Mexican spiritualism will be attractive because spiritualism answers the essential questions of "why?" and "why me?" In addition it does so in a manner that emphasizes the unity of human experience. Patients are not relegated to a marginal or stigmatized position. Indeed through their illnesses they establish closer connections with other people and enjoy pleasurable, sensual experiences. As June Macklin (1974,

p. 417) writes, quoting the Mexican poet Octavio Paz, "the dramas of salvation in which they participate repeatedly—like myths and fiestas—'permit man to emerge from his solitude, become one with creation' and find grace." This is a good definition of healing.

For the patient of spiritualist healers, the body becomes the vehicle for recovery through self-induced trance and massage as well as medicinal remedies. The body is no longer the enemy. Indeed through it the patient can obtain both physical and spiritual redemption. This is spiritualism's power. That its power is still mysterious should not prevent us from noting its efficacy.

Understanding how healing operates and what it means will require more information on the physical and psychological effects of trance and the physical and psychological effects of "putting the world to right." These may not be separate. In the person of the healer they frequently come together. The challenge is to develop the vocabulary to describe and analyze the experience of physical and spiritual interaction. Just as most of our thinking is linear, concerned with causation, so is our language. At the moment the best we have for describing what happens to bodies when people begin to recover from illness is poetic description. Images of light and feelings of contentment predominate. People feel at peace and they feel like themselves again.

This is a different kind of knowing, beyond daily, sensory experience, but still intimately connected to bodily sensations. As Katz (1982, p. 53) says of the !Kung shamans during possession trances: "they experience themselves as beyond their ordinary self by becoming more essential, more themselves." For spiritualist healers and patients this enhancement comes through submission to a higher power and the abnegation of individuality and personality. The spirit takes over but the self of the patient is reconstituted and reaffirmed. In submitting to the spirit and following the suggested regimen of medicines, the patient experiences wellness, even though, in many cases, the patient's condition has not materially changed. What this experience is and how it comes about should be the next focus of research.

REFERENCES

Curtis, Susan & Fraser, Romy (1991). *Natural healing*. New York: HarperCollins.

Fabrega, Horacio, Jr. (1970). On the specificity of folk illness. *Southwestern Journal of Anthropology, 26,* 350–313.

Fabrega, Horacio Jr. & Silver, D. (1973). *Illness and shamanistic curing in Zinacantan*. Stanford, CA: Stanford University Press.

Finkler, Kaja (1983). *Spiritualist healers in Mexico*. New York: Praeger.

Goodman, Felicitas D., Henney, Jeannette H. & Pressel, Esther (1974). *Trance, healing and hallucination*. New York: John Wiley.

Harwood, Alan (1977). *RX: Spiritist as needed: A study of a Puerto Rican community mental health resource.* New York: John Wiley.

Ingham, J. (1978). On Mexican folk medicine. *American Anthropologist,* 72, 76–87.

Katz, Richard (1982). *Boiling energy: Community healing among the Kalahari Kung.* Cambridge, MA: Harvard University Press.

Kelly, Isabel (1965). Folk practices in North Mexico. Latin American Monographs, Institute of Latin American Studies, University of Texas at Austin.

Kleinman, Arthur (1983). Indigenous systems of healing. In J. Warren Salmon (Ed.), *Alternative medicines: Popular and policy perspectives.* New York: Tavistock.

———— (1979) Why do indigenous practitioners successfully heal? *Social Science and Medicine,* 13B, 7–26.

Macklin, June (1970). Curanderismo and espiritismo: Complementary approaches to traditional mental health services. In Stanley A. West and June Macklin (Eds.), *The Chicano Experience.* Boulder, CO: Westview Press.

———— (1974). Belief, ritual and healing: New England spiritualism and Mexican-American spiritism compared. In Irving Zaretsky (Ed.), *Religious Movements in Contemporary America.* Princeton, NJ: Princeton University Press.

Meyer, George C., Blum, Kenneth & Cull, John G. (1981). *Folk medicine and herbal healing.* Springfield, IL: Charles C. Thomas.

Moerman, Daniel (1983). *The anthropology of medicine: From culture to method.* New York: Praeger.

Mowrey, Daniel B. (1986). *The scientific validation of herbal medicine.* New Canaan, CT: Keats Publishing.

Rubel, Arthur (1964). The epidemiology of a folk illness: Susto in Hispanic America. *Ethnology,* 3, 268–283.

———— (1960). "Concepts of disease in Mexican-American culture." *American Anthropologist,* 62, 795–815.

Scheper-Hughes, Nancy & Lock, Margaret (1987). The mindful body: A prolegomenon to future work in medical anthropology. *Medical Anthropology Quarterly,* 1(1), 6–41.

Uzzel, D. (1974). Susto revisited. *American Ethnologist,* 1, 369–378.

Van der Zee (Griggs), Barbara (1982). *Green pharmacy.* New York: Viking.

Wavell, Stewart (1966). *Trances.* London: George Allen & Unwin.

10

Shamanism in Alaska

Margaret Fischer

Even as we near the twenty-first century, shamanism is still an alternative method of healing in many Native Alaskan villages despite the technologically advanced practices of medicine and psychology. One of the reasons is logistics. Many villages have less than 200 people. They are in remote locales with no road access, although frequently they have an air strip. In inclement weather they are totally isolated and unreachable by plane or snowmobile. Itinerant doctors and mental health practitioners may serve an isolated community only once or twice a year. During interim periods, in a society where doctoring is the weakest sector of the culture (Spencer, 1976), shamans are viewed by many Natives as fulfilling a needed role. Despite the advent of television, which all villages have, and the acculturation of Native Eskimos and Indians to "white man's ways" as a result of exposure to modern media and more frequent contact with the larger towns and cities of Alaska, old ways die hard among the elders of the villages. Shamanism is part of their heritage, and they preserve the tradition, although some of the youth have identified more closely with Western methods. Indeed, the Bureau of Indian Affairs, which provides free health service to both Eskimos and Indian Natives, has made significant inroads in lowering the infant mortality rate in Alaska, once among the highest in the world, as well as extending the life spans of the Natives. Interestingly, the purported areas of a shaman's expertise were fertility, longevity, and wealth in general (Heinze, 1991).

In a land of mystery, with extremes of climatic conditions that range in the interior from 70 degrees below zero Fahrenheit in the winter to 100 degrees above zero in summer, where celestial phenomena could not be explained by primitive people, the shaman held sway. He offered an explanation for the dancing spectrum of the Northern Lights, the howling sounds of gale-force winds, and the eerie cries of wolves baying at the moon. Animals were personified and became part of the shaman's lore. The early Tlingit and Haida peoples could hear an omen in the hoot of an owl, or a chilling curfew in the croak of a raven. The land otter, as at home in the water as on on land, could conjure in the Tlingit-Haida mind a fearful hybrid being of the spirit world. Chief of all spirits was Raven, the trickster, shape-changer, and transformer who organized the world into its present shape. Changing some inanimate objects into animate beings, endowing men and animals with particular attributes and roles, gaining for all the blessings of water and fire were the modus operandi of the shaman (Beck, 1991).

Real dangers lurk in the omnipresent winter darkness above the Arctic Circle. Hungry wolves and marauding polar bears hunt unwary prey. For months the sun never rises above the horizon. Only the moon and the dancing aurora borealis give light. Then a gradual reversal occurs with the winter solstice. By late spring, the darkness gives way to a sun that never sets. Robert Service (1964), poet of the Yukon, penned:

> The winter! the brightness that blinds you,
> The white land locked tight as a drum;
> The cold fear that follows and finds you,
> The silence that bludgeons you dumb.
> The snows that are older than history,
> The woods where the weird shadows slant;
> The stillness, the moonlight, the mystery,
> I've bade 'em good-by—but I can't.

The cold, dark season was the busiest for the shaman, when the dark skies were set ablaze by the Northern Lights. As fears of displeased gods magnified, the need for the shaman's supernatural powers became imperative for survival. One could call it superstition, yet there are many among us reared in fear of black cats, of raised ladders, of singing before breakfast, of telling dreams before eating, and of the Ouija board who can feel a kinship toward the early peoples of Alaska and their religious beliefs (Loftus, 1965).

Because the extremes of benevolence and malevolence were among his powers, the shaman of the past was often more feared than loved. If successful, he or she (shaman were also women) was viewed as being on a plane above the other villagers and had absolute power over them. Since he or she was thought to be endowed by an unknown and mysterious spirit, the shaman framed the superstition in vogue, interpreted signs and omens, dispelled enchantments by conjuring, practiced bewitchings, predicted future events, and regulated the supply of fish and game (Fienup-Riordan, 1988). The voice of the shaman was the voice of authority. On the other hand, if the shaman was unsuccessful in enlisting supernatural assistance to solve presenting problems, payment for services was more than likely withheld. If the shaman were an inefficient hunter who could not provide food for his own sustenance, he was a pitiful figure indeed, who was met with a shrug of the shoulders and a half-indulgent smile by the villagers (Birket-Smith, 1971). An uncooperative and quarrelsome person, even if a shaman, was considered suspect, was avoided, and often ran the risk of being killed by the relative of some person recently passed, on the ground that this malevolence caused the death (Morris, 1972).

A woman shaman was killed in an Alaskan village in the early part of the century by being clubbed and dismembered, then, each part was soaked in oil and burned. There were also occasions when the people, usually spurred on by another shaman, killed a shaman who was suspected of killing people by witchery (Fienup-Riordan, 1988). Keithahn (1942) reported that in 1894 a shaman named Skun-doo-ooh was arrested for murder, tried, and convicted of manslaughter in Juneau. He had caused the death of many people as witches, but the case that sent him to San Quentin Prison concerned the death of a man at Chilkat. The relatives of the man obtained, for 20 blankets, the services of the noted shaman to determine the cause of the man's death. Skun-doo-ooh went through his drum and rattle act and finally settled on a woman of the tribe. At his orders she was bound and starved for ten days, in an effort to obtain a confession of guilt. However, the unfortunate "witch" died; the news spread, and Skun-doo-ooh fled to the Interior. When he came out of hiding he was arrested and sentenced to three years in San Quentin by U.S. District Judge Warren Truitt. It was generally felt that an "example" was made of a "witch doctor" to stamp out the evils of this occult profession.

Shamanism, however, in bygone years (and today) was not a career choice. It was the result of a selection process. The shaman was chosen because of some unusual physical characteristic, such as red hair, epileptic seizures, physical or mental aberrations, or the belief that discourse with supernatural forces was within his or her purview. It may have been that many were mentally unbalanced, and their susceptibility to influences and possession was symptomatic of psychosis. Misanthropic, hysterical, and aggressive behaviors were frequently observed. Pibloktoq (or Arctic hysteria), in which an individual throws himself on the ground, shouts incomprehensible phrases, and thrashes around oblivious of others and the elements, was a regular part of the shaman's performance.

The shaman's techniques included trances, talking in sentient languages, ventriloquism, and legerdemain (Jorgensen, 1990). The shaman was not a supplicant. Rather he called upon his spirit powers to act. The shaman controlled power, bullyragged spirits, and caused events to happen (Jorgensen, 1990). Birket-Smith (1971, p. 59) described such an event:

Then followed noise and tumult of every kind; rattling, swishing, and flapping sounds, now as of a workshop, now as of locomotives, and then as of large, flying beings. To the accompaniment of the most terrific noise both platform and windowpane shook. Sometimes one heard the Shaman, at the mercy of some great overpowering force groaning, wailing, and shrieking, whining, whispering; at others one heard spirits, some of which had coarse, others tiny, others lisping or shrill voices. Often we heard demoniac grating and mocking laughter. The voices sounded from above, from under the ground, now at one end of the house and now at the other, then outside the house or in the entrance passage. Cries of "hoi, hoi, hoi" died away as if in the most distant abyss. The drum was used with wonderful skill, often moving round the house, and especially hovering over my head. Song often accompanied the drum, sometimes low and subdued as if it came from the underworld. Sweet female singing was sometimes heard from the background. After a deafening, flapping, rattling, and swishing noise, everything suddenly became quiet, and in came the terrible monster, Amortoq. It had black arms, and whoever is touched by it turns black and dies. It went about the house with heavy steps and up on the platform, and roared, "a-mô, a-mô!" Everybody fled to the furthermost corners of the platform for fear that the monster should happen to touch them.

Even in cases such as described, Holm and Petersen (1914) said "one must be cautious about speaking of willful fraud; in ecstasy the Shamans can undoubtedly do a great deal that is not even clear to them."

The Alaska shaman attached great importance to tricks, conjuring performances, sleight of hand, and ventriloquism for the purpose of impressing the audience. There were some shamans who were hanged or burned alive, by their own hands, trusting to their own supernatural powers. Charlatan or not, the shaman sincerely believed in his or her power of divination. It was this confidence in one's own ability that made others place implicit faith in the shaman's help and to seek him or her out when they felt unable to cope with the complexities of life (Loftus, 1965).

Universally, all civilizations have had shamans. Shamanistic characteristics were found not only in the regions where shamanism dominated the religious life of the community (North American, Eskimo, Siberian) but also in regions where it was but one of the constituent phenomena of magicoreligious life (Australia, Oceania, Southeast Asia) (Eliade, 1964). Ecstasy through intoxication by mushrooms was known throughout Siberia and among Indian tribes of America's Southwest. The dervishes of Turkey and the Middle East whirled to the tune of the flute to induce a trancelike, ecstatic state (Brookhiser, 1993). The Paviotso of North America told of old shamans who put burning coals in their mouths and touched red-hot irons unharmed (Park, 1934). In Polynesia, Indonesia, and Fiji, in an apparent state of delirium or hypnotic trance, even today, shamans walk barefoot on a bed of glowing coals, followed by colleagues and, at times, the audience, without burning their feet. In South America the shamans became rich by performing miracles, such as magical flight and swallowing hot coals. The shamans of Polynesia were believed to be able to fly and to traverse vast distances in the twinkling of an eye (Handy, 1927). Ecstatic journeys to the beyond, and especially descents to the underworld, were not only common to Celtic and Germanic legends but to most shamanistic cultures. The rope trick of the fakirs was a variant of the shaman's celestial ascent. The symbolism of the rope, like that of the ladder, implied communication between sky and earth. It was by means of a rope or a ladder (a vine, a bridge, a chain of arrows) that the gods descended to earth and men went up to the sky. These widespread traditions were found both in India and Tibet. The notion that the shaman was different characteristically from others was found in Japan where many female shamans were blind from birth. The concept of "magical heat" was believed by European peoples. The shaman, the master over fire, could incarnate the spirit of fire to the point where, during séances, they emitted flames from their mouths, their noses, and their whole bodies (Propp, 1949). "Magical flight" by Siberian, Eskimo, and North American shamans was a magical power credited to sorcerers and medicine men all over the world. Eliade (1964) concluded from his study of shamanism that the quintessential element of shamanism was not the embodiment of "spirits" by the shaman, but the ecstasy induced by his or her ascent to the sky or descent to the underworld; incarnating spirits and being "possessed" by spirits were universally disseminated phenomena. The symbolism of ascent, with all the rites and myths dependent on it, must be connected with celestial Supreme Beings; we know that "height" was sacred as such, that many supreme gods of archaic peoples were called "He on High," or "He of the Sky." This symbolism of ascent and height retained its value in most religions of the East and West.

Neo-shamans, or New Age enthusiasts, like their traditional shamanic predecessors, believe that a person can journey in alternate reality to gain help and direction from the spirits and other entities that dwell there. Their beliefs are more eclectic than those of the classic shamans. Crystals and other objects in this world are believed to have a spiritual essence and a power that can be used for divination and healing. Spirit guides, spirit teachers, and power animals are critical in dealing with alternate reality. The belief that there is an interconnectedness of all things is fundamental to both traditional shamanism and contemporary beliefs (Doore, 1988).

Interest in the ancient healing techniques of shamanism has enjoyed a recent revival. Krippner (1988) pointed out that shamans were the world's first healers, first diagnosticians, and first psychotherapists, and that they developed sophisticated medical models over the centuries. It is maintained that there are shamanic healing methods that closely parallel contemporary behavior therapy, chemotherapy, dream interpretation, family therapy, hypnotherapy, milieu therapy, and psychodrama, thus indicating that shamans, psychotherapists, and physicians have more in common than is generally suspected.

The environment of shamans in the twentieth century differs considerably from that of paleolithic shamans and so do the needs contemporary shamans have to fulfill. Although urban life is infrequently at the mercy of natural forces, it is dependent on the benevolence of politicians. All citizens have defined responsibilities. Conformity to social and professional norms and control of the antisocial are incumbent upon members of society because we fear loss of our jobs, income, and freedom. Fears of pollution of the Earth and the atmosphere, of losing our health, of sudden accidental death have stayed with us over the millennia. Advances in medicine and new biochemical knowledge have rid the world of the fear of old plagues and epidemics yet new ones replace them. Solutions to fears and anxieties that are not addressed by health professionals lead to the search for holistic cures. Shamans assist in connecting "the inner self"—that is, the mind—with the body (Heinze, 1991). They have developed a psychology of their own similar to that of Abraham Maslow (1962), who say psychology as

a branch of biology, in part a branch of sociology. But it is not only that. It has its own unique jurisdiction as well, that portion of the psyche which is not a reflection of the outer world or a molding to it. There could be such a thing as a psychological psychology.

Shamans can teach social and behavioral scientists ways how individuals as well as societies can regulate their well-being. They can teach psychotherapists the importance of shifting attention, that change is possible by triggering self-healing mechanisms, the capability of which is within oneself; or that by using mental imagery one can stimulate well-being by reconstructing and transforming experience (Heinze, 1991).

In a 1973 interview, Della Keats, a noted Alaskan shaman and medical practitioner who was born in Noatak above the Arctic Circle in 1907, said that for 62 years she used what she called "a gift of God" to help make her people well. "I have no books, nothing for curing; just my hands." Yet she was known throughout the country and in other parts of the world for her healing ability. She received honorary doctorates from the University of Alaska and the San Francisco College of Medicine and a Doctor of Humane Letters from the College of Osteopathic Medicine of the Pacific in Pomona, California. She taught herself anatomy from a book while in school and learned traditional Inupiat ways of healing from her parents and from other Inupiat healers. Learning where the organs are in the body and locating as many as possible in her own abdomen, she became aware of how each organ felt and trained her fingers to note minute changes within the organ. She said she could feel ulcers in the stomach of an inflicted person, if the person relaxed. Making a patient relax was part of her practice. She asked questions, cajoled, teased, and laughed with her patients until they relaxed enough so she could feel or sense the cause of the discomfort. At that point, Keats' fingers went to work, probing, massaging, and exploring. Her tools were herbs, belief in prayer, and her own experience. She made great efforts to train other younger people in the healing arts and shared her knowledge throughout Alaska at the request of doctors, patients, and community health practitioners (Perrigo, 1986).

Della Keats exemplified the new paradigm of shamanism. Hers was a benevolent use of power. The difference between the pathological power that comes from the need to control, use, and demean others and the power that actualizes human potential and produces manifestations of the sacred is critical. Power itself is neutral. In its benevolent form, power provides leadership, protection, and security; such power inspires and nourishes creativity. In its malevolent form, power leads to domination and abuse (Heinze, 1991).

While New Age enthusiasts are right to admire shamanistic tradition, Brown (1989) cautioned that in advancing it as an alternative to our own healing practices, they brush aside stark truths. Shamanism affirms life but also spawns violence and death. The beauty of shamanism is matched by its power—and like all forms of power found in society, it inspires its share of discontent.

REFERENCES

Beck, M. G. (1991). *Shaman and kushtakas*. Bothel, WA: Alaska Northwest Books.

Birket-Smith, K.A.J. (1971). *Eskimos*. New York: Crown Publishers, p. 59.

Brookhiser, R. (1993). Islamic fundamentalism revisited. *National Review*, November 15, p. 63.

Brown, M. F. (1989). Dark side of the shaman. *Natural History*, November, pp. 8 & 10.

Doore, G. (Ed.) (1988). *Shaman's path: Healing, personal growth and empowerment*. Boston: Shambhala.

Eliade, M. (1964). *Shamanism, archaic techniques of ecstasy*. Princeton, NJ: Princeton University Press.

Fienup-Riordan, A. (1988). *The Yup'ik Eskimos*. Kingston, Ont.: The Limestone Press.

Handy, E. S. (1927). *Craighill: Polynesian religion*. Bayard Dominick Expedition Publication No. 12. Honolulu: Bernice P. Bishop Museum, pp. 53, 237–245.

Heinze, R. I. (1991). *Shamans of the 20th century*. New York: Irvington Publishers.

Holm, G. & Petersen, J. (1914). *Legends and tales from Angmagssalik*. Cited in R. A. Morris, Shamanism, common sense and parapsychology, Unpublished paper, University of Alaska, 1972.

Jorgensen, J. G. (1990). *Oil age Eskimos*. Berkeley: University of California Press, pp. 259–262.

Keithahn, E. L. (1942). Gods, demons and ancestral spirits. *Alaskan Sportsman,* January, pp. 91–93.

Krippner, S. (1988). Shamans: The first healers. In G. Doore, (Ed.), *Shaman's path.* Boston: Shambhala, pp. 101–114.

Loftus, A. (1965). *According to grandfather* (the medicine man). Fairbanks: Loftus.

Maslow, A. H. (1962). *Toward a psychology of being.* New York: D. Van Nostrand.

Morris, R. A. (1972). Shamanism, common sense and parapsychology. Unpublished paper, University of Alaska.

Park, W. Z. (1934). Paviotso shamanism. *American Anthropologist, 36,* 98–113.

Perrigo, D. (1986). Della Keats taught herself traditional healing ways. *Anchorage Times,* March 13, p. B-3.

Propp, V. I. (1949). *Le radici storiche dei racconti di fate.* Turin, p. 284.

Service, R. (1964). *The spell of the Yukon.* New York: Dodd, Mead. (Poem written in 1907.)

Spencer, R. F. (1976). *The North Alaskan Eskimo.* New York: Dover Publications, p. 299.

Part III

Treatment and Training

11

Endorsing Irrational Beliefs Cross-Culturally: Clinical Implications

Mitchell W. Robin and Raymond DiGiuseppe

Rational-Emotive Therapy (RET), developed 35 years ago by Albert Ellis as an alternative and more logically rational and pragmatic approach to conventional psychoanalysis, is arguably the origin of the cognitive behavioral therapies. RET's basic premise that emotional disturbance is caused not by events but by the view that people take of them has been documented in numerous studies and outcome reviews (Silverman, McCarthy & McGovern, 1992; McGovern & Silverman, 1984; DiGiuseppe & Miller, 1977). This approach allows the clinician or other mental health professional to intervene more directly and actively in helping clients develop cognitive and behavioral techniques that will allow them to function more effectively in their milieu rather than merely "feeling good."

Central to this approach is the identification and disputation of the clients' "irrational beliefs" (IBs). A belief is irrational if it is illogical, nonempirical, and self-defeating (Ellis, 1962; Walen, DiGiuseppe & Wessler, 1980). Ellis identifies four core irrational beliefs: Demandingness, "Awfulizing"/"Catastrophizing," Global Rating of Self and Others, and Low Frustration Tolerance (Ellis & Dryden, 1988). Demandingness refers to the belief that the world, oneself, and others *must* be as we want them to be. "Awfulizing" or "Catastrophizing" refers to the belief that a specific bad or unpleasant thing that a person encounters is the *worst thing in the world* and will undoubtedly lead to unmeasurably bad consequences from which there is no recovery possible. Global rating of self and others refers to the belief that a single good or bad result marks someone for life and can totally change their worth or self-esteem. Low Frustration Tolerance (LFT) refers to the belief that hassles or discomforts, whether they are physical or social, are intolerable and cannot be withstood if they are encountered. The basic premise of RET holds that the more people tenaciously and rigidly hold onto irrational beliefs, the more likely they are to experience dysfunctional emotions and/or act in dysfunctional and self-defeating ways.

Emotions or behaviors are considered to be dysfunctional if they hinder a person from accomplishing his or her goals. For example, the rigidly held belief "I must always appear perfect and flawless in everyone's eyes; if I ever exposed my fallibility to others it would be terrible and I couldn't ever hold my face up in public again" might lead a person to avoid situations she perceived as "dangerous"—that is, likely to expose her human imperfections and therefore do her in. This particular scenario leads many people to avoid social contact, and to procrastinate about necessary activities such as going to school or asking questions, because almost any situation *might* be dangerous since the goal of total (and even partial) perfection is unattainable and therefore doomed to fail.

Once these beliefs are identified, the therapist examines their flexibility and then disputes their validity and applicability with the client, ultimately teaching the client to dispute them on her own (Walen, DiGiuseppe & Wessler, 1980). Three main forms of disputing are generally employed: empirical, pragmatic, and philosophic or elegant. Empirical disputes take the form of the therapist asking the client to provide "proof" or "evidence" for the beliefs she so tenaciously endorses. Pragmatic disputing asks the client to demonstrate how her particular beliefs benefit her or enable her to reach her personal goals. Philosophic disputation asks the client to consider if she could not be *somewhat* happy, successful or intact even if the world never was as she wants it to be, and even if she routinely encountered hassles and discomforts.

THE ATTITUDES AND BELIEF SCALE II (ABSII)

The Attitudes and Belief Scale II is a measure of Ellis's Irrational/Rational Beliefs (DiGiuseppe, Leaf, Exner & Robin, 1988). It consists of 72 items, carefully worded so that three items fit into a $4 \times 3 \times 2$ matrix. The first factor for Cognitive Process has four levels representing the irrational beliefs processes of Demandingness, Self-Worth, Low Frustration Tolerance, and Awfulizing. The second factor, Content/Context has three levels: beliefs about Affiliation, Achievement, and Comfort. The third factor has two levels: irrationally worded items and rationally worded items. For example, an irrationally worded Global Rating item about Comfort might be, "When I experience discomfort or hassles in my life, I tend to think that I am not a good person." A rationally worded item for the same area might be, "Even when I feel tense, nervous, or uncomfortable, I know that I am just as worthwhile as other people." There are three items in each of these 24 cells.

Definitions were written for each of the 24 cells and items were selected for use in the scale only if there was unanimous agreement among 13 judges who were therapists at the Institute for Rational-Emotive Therapy (IRET) in New York and had studied under Dr. Ellis. In previous studies the scale has shown adequate internal consistency (DiGiuseppe, Leaf, Robin & Exner, 1988) and correlated with such measures of emotional upset as the 13-item version of the Beck Depression Inventory (Beck & Beck, 1972), the General Psychological Well-Being Scale (Dupue, 1984), the Goldberg General Health Questionnaire (GHQ—a measure of mental disturbance) (Goldberg, 1972), the Satisfaction with Life Scale (Diener, Emmons, Larsen & Griffen, 1985), and Spielberger's Trait Anxiety and Trait Anger Scales (Spielberger, Jacobs, Russell & Crane, 1983; Spielberger, Johnson, Russell, Crane, Jacobs & Worden, 1985; Robin & Eckhardt, 1993). The ABSII was also able to discriminate between inpatients at a residential treatment center for substance abuse, outpatients at the IRET, and college students (DiGiuseppe, Robin, Leaf & Gorman, 1989), and has also been found to correlate well with personality disorders as measured by the Millon Clinical Multiaxial Inventory–II (MCMI–II) (Robin, DiGiuseppe & Naimark, 1990), and to discriminate between various forms of narcissism (DiGiuseppe, Robin & Primavera, 1991). Interest in using this test as a way of measuring cross-cultural/cross-ethnic emotional disturbability dates back to its inception (Robin & DiGiuseppe, 1987).

CROSS-CULTURAL/CROSS-ETHNIC ENDORSEMENTS OF THE ABSII

This chapter examines the responses of 1,220 participants who were attending undergraduate psychology classes at three different colleges in the Connecticut, New Jersey, New York area. The participants represented five diverse ethnic or cultural groups: White (n=934), Black (n=140), Hispanic (n=89), Asian (n=31), American Indian (n=9), plus a catchall category called Other (n=17). When a significant difference in the "Other" category was found the authors went back to their students and asked if those who checked off "Other" on the ethnic ID question would be willing to provide further information about their ethnicity if their identity could remain anonymous. The students agreed to hand in a slip of paper with the name of their ethnicity and/or religion written down. When the slips were examined it was discovered that they tended to identify with the Middle Eastern community. Informed consent slips were obtained for all participants and only those questionnaires that were complete were analyzed statistically. Analyses of variance were calculated and if significant between group means were obtained then Least Significant Difference Test (LSDT) T-tests were conducted.

RESULTS

Tables 11.1–11.7 present the data on cross-cultural/cross-ethnic endorsement of the ABSII. For ease in reading, only the means, standard deviations, and significance for each group are reported. As can be seen from an inspection of Table 11.1, there is a significant difference in endorsement of the entire ABSII between the White and Black participants. While other ethnic differences are suggestive, they failed to reach significance.

Table 11.2 reports the ethnic differences in endorsement of the four core irrational belief subscales: Awfulizing, Demandingness, Global Self-Rating, and Low Frustration Tolerance. As can be seen, Blacks score significantly higher than Whites on the Awfulizing, Demandingness, and LFT subscales; while Asians scored significantly higher than Whites on the LFT subscale alone.

Table 11.3 reports the differences in endorsement of the three context area subscales: Comfort, Approval, and Achievement. As can be seen there was a significant difference obtained between Black and White participants, with Blacks having a greater rate of endorsement. Again, other group differences failed to achieve significance.

Tables 11.4–11.7 report the differences in endorsement of the four core irrational beliefs within the three context areas. Table 11.4 specifically reports the data for the Awfulizing subscale. Again the only significant difference is between the Black and White participants. Table 11.5 examines

Table 11.1
Ethnic Differences in Endorsement of the Total ABSII

Ethnicity	n	Mean	SD
White	934	81.06	36.71
Black	140	*97.25	33.79
Hispanic	89	92.53	34.31
Asian	31	102.26	41.31
Am. Indian	9	68.60	32.35
Other	17	97.28	34.26

* The difference between the Black and White sample is significant at the .05 level

the data for the Demandingness subscale. Significant differences are again observed between Black and White participants as well as between Other and White participants. Table 11.6 presents the data for the Global Self-Rating Subscale. Again the only difference that achieved significance was between the Black and White participants and then only on the Comfort items. Table 11.7 presents the data for the Low Frustration subscale. Significant differences can be observed between the Black and White participants on the Comfort and Achievement items. However, Asians scored significantly higher than Whites on all three context categories: Comfort, Approval, and Achievement.

Similar results to the above have been reported since these data were first examined in 1990 (Robin, DiGiuseppe & Alvarez, 1991a; Robin & DiGiuseppe, 1992; Robin, DiGiuseppe & Kopec, 1993b).

DISCUSSION

The use of the ABSII clearly seems to provide the practitioner with a useful tool for the identification of a client's most commonly endorsed irrational beliefs. Since RET tends to be an hypothesis-based system of therapy[1] (Walen, DiGiuseppe & Wessler, R. L, 1980; Burgess, 1986), any tool that provides the therapist the means to formulate hypotheses to be tested within the therapeutic situation is to be valued. Previously cited studies have clearly demonstrated the usefulness of the ABSII as both a clinical and a research tool and have provided additional support for Ellis' hypothesis that people who endorse irrational beliefs have a greater tendency to suffer from both emotional and personality disturbance.

This study attempted to extend the use of the ABSII as a tool for the delivery of mental health services to cross-cultural clients. The current data are suggestive of that potential usefulness. They clearly show that there are cross-cultural/cross-ethnic differences in endorsement between the Black and White samples as well as between the Asian and White samples. Other differences, while visible, did not reach statistical significance. We feel that this was an artifact of the small sample sizes of the other groups studied and that it will disappear when large enough samples can be gathered. This study, and the other cross-cultural data previously cited, constituted a preliminary investigation of the hypothesis that participants from other cultures would have no trouble with the task and could find the questions personally relevant.

When we debriefed the cross-cultural participants we asked them about the questions' phraseology and content. We were pleased to note that none of the participants thought that the questions addressed unusual themes or content areas, and indeed most participants could identify themes that they had thought were unique to their culture. In fact one of the by-products of the debriefing was the participants' surprise that "Americans" thought like

Table 11.2
Ethnic Differences in Endorsement of Four Core Irrational Beliefs: Awfulizing, Demandingness, Global Self-Rating, and Low Frustration Tolerance

Ethnicity	Awfulizing		Demandingness		Self-Rating		L. F. T.	
	Mean	SD	Mean	SD	Mean	SD	Mean	SD
White	19.96	10.85	23.44	9.88	12.31	10.45	25.83	10.87
Black	*25.50	10.67	*27.20	9.60	14.95	11.45	*30.63	9.41
Hispanic	23.27	9.66	26.22	9.24	14.20	10.66	27.83	9.84
Asian	26.15	10.50	25.50	11.08	16.61	13.03	**33.54	11.23
American Indian	18.67	14.53	26.67	6.53	8.60	12.52	20.67	10.48
Other	24.43	7.18	30.21	6.47	13.21	15.06	28.42	12.48

* The difference between the Black and White sample is significant at the .05 level.
** The Difference bewteen the Asian and the White sample is significant at the .05 level.

Table 11.3
Ethnic Differences in Endorsement of Three Context Areas: Comfort, Approval, and Achievement

Ethnicity	Comfort		Approval		Achievement	
	Mean	SD	Mean	SD	Mean	SD
White	27.33	12.92	21.56	13.86	33.33	14.36
Black	*34.43	13.87	24.90	14.03	*39.43	11.37
Hispanic	31.87	12.88	24.14	13.18	36.52	12.40
Asian	34.58	13.22	28.60	15.68	39.70	15.00
American Indian	21.60	9.94	23.00	16.32	32.17	12.88
Other	28.21	11.97	26.79	17.83	42.29	12.64

* The differences between the Black and White sample are significant at the .05 level

Table 11.4
Ethnic Differences of Endorsement of the Four Core Irrational Beliefs within the Three Context Areas of Comfort, Approval, and Achievement—Awfulizing

Ethnicity	Awfulizing					
	Comfort		Approval		Achievement	
	Mean	SD	Mean	SD	Mean	SD
White	6.48	4.11	7.29	4.21	6.25	4.45
Black	*8.72	4.52	*8.72	4.49	*8.20	4.16
Hispanic	7.88	3.86	8.23	3.86	7.47	4.04
Asian	8.54	4.34	9.36	3.92	8.50	4.57
American Indian	5.17	5.98	7.83	4.83	5.67	5.12
Other	7.07	3.38	9.50	4.07	7.86	3.39

* The differences between the Black and White samples are significant at the .05 level.

Table 11.5
Ethnic Differences of Endorsement of the Four Core Irrational Beliefs within the Three Context Areas of
Comfort, Approval, and Achievement—Demandingness

| Ethnicity | Demandingness | | | | | |
| | Comfort | | Approval | | Achievement | |
	Mean	SD	Mean	SD	Mean	SD
White	7.33	4.05	4.49	3.71	11.48	4.41
Black	*8.90	4.51	4.98	4.27	*12.92	4.43
Hispanic	8.49	4.28	5.24	3.91	12.68	3.82
Asian	8.08	4.01	5.04	4.29	12.92	4.12
American Indian	7.67	3.08	5.00	4.77	16.28	2.52
Other	8.00	3.64	5.57	4.14	**16.29	2.52

* The differences between the Black and White sample are significant at the .05 level.
** The difference between the Other and White sample are significant at the .05 level.

Table 11.6
Ethnic Differences of Endorsement of the Four Core Irrational Beliefs within the Three Context Areas of Comfort, Approval, and Achievement—Global Self-Rating

Ethnicity	Global Self-Rating					
	Comfort		Approval		Achievement	
	Mean	SD	Mean	SD	Mean	SD
White	3.38	3.72	3.51	3.99	5.48	4.19
Black	*4.74	4.71	4.42	4.62	5.95	4.10
Hispanic	4.05	3.75	4.09	4.27	6.14	4.21
Asian	5.37	4.42	4.96	5.07	6.58	4.35
American Indian	2.00	3.94	5.00	4.82	3.83	5.08
Other	3.00	4.52	4.43	6.08	5.79	5.33

* The difference between the Black and White sample is significant at the .05 level.

Table 11.7
Ethnic Differences of Endorsement of the Four Core Irrational Beliefs within the Three Context Areas of Comfort, Approval, and Achievement—Low Frustration Tolerance

	Low Frustration Tolerance					
	Comfort		Approval		Achievement	
Ethnicity	Mean	SD	Mean	SD	Mean	SD
White	9.60	4.23	6.45	4.47	9.89	4.42
Black	*11.39	4.27	7.10	4.49	*12.08	3.95
Hispanic	10.61	3.88	6.83	4.02	10.42	3.63
Asian	**12.20	3.75	**9.24	5.05	**12.40	4.57
American Indian	6.83	2.23	5.17	4.49	8.67	5.05
Other	9.14	4.35	7.28	5.91	12.00	5.60

* The differences between the Black and White samples are significant at the .05 level.
** The differences between the Asian and White samples are significant at the .05 level.

they did. This outcome was not as surprising as it might appear. The senior author has conducted professional workshops on the use of RET in a cross-cultural context in many international venues (Robin, DiGiuseppe & Alvarez, 1991b; Robin, DiGiuseppe & Kopec, 1993a) and the typical response of the mental health professionals in attendance is "Oh, these ideas of yours [RET or cognitive behavioral] are highly compatible with our culture. In fact I didn't know that we thought so much like you in the United States."

This similarity provides a springboard for clinical interventions by therapists who are not only culturally identical to the populations they serve but, more importantly, are culturally *dissimilar* to the populations they serve. In a world where cultural diversity is increasingly the norm rather than the exception, therapists not only need to develop cultural sensitivity to diverse populations but also to develop tools that are appropriate within those populations. The former issue is being addressed by the growing body of literature about the unique issues of culturally diverse clients (Sue & Sue, 1990; Sue, Bernier, Durran, Feinberg, Pedersen, Smith & Vasquez-Nuttall, 1982; Atkinson, Morten & Sue, 1989; Pedersen, 1985). The latter issue, unfortunately, is less well addressed.

Content Versus Process Approaches to Psychotherapy

Therapists who treat culturally diverse clients, either as a matter of necessity or inclination, are told that sensitivity alone is sufficient retooling or that their toolbox is inadequate to the task at hand because culturally diverse clients do not relate to or respond to Western cultural interventions. In contrast, we maintain the position that sensitivity alone is useless without appropriate interventions regardless of the culture that developed those interventions. By and large we agree that many interventions developed by Western therapists might be inappropriate for use within a cross-cultural context because they attempt to force all cultures into the same theoretical framework. Such therapies (e.g., psychoanalytic psychotherapy) can be referred to as content therapies—that is, they assume that all people, regardless of culture, have the same underlying psychic content and that the job of the therapist is to make the latent content manifest over time. We agree with Sue and Sue (1990) that this form of therapy is not appropriate for use with non-Western clients and may be inappropriate for use even with ethnic minorities raised within Western cultures, because it ignores the very real differences that culture imposes on the way one sees his or her reality.

Another kind of psychotherapy (e.g., cognitive behavioral, or RET) can be called process therapy. Process therapy assumes no universal underlying reality and therefore does not attempt to force the client to fit the assumed underlying content. Process therapy further assumes that people largely construct their reality via their behaviors and cognitions and that the vital job of the therapist is to intervene when and if those constructions are dysfunctional—that is, when they interfere with the person attaining their goals. It is the process of challenging the client's dysfunctional cognitions and behaviors either within his or her own culture or within the culture that he or she is currently living that is at the heart of process approaches to therapy. While cognitive and behavioral interventions also have their critics, we maintain that these interventions are probably more adaptive to cross-cultural use than those that are content based, largely because they tend to be more pragmatic and adaptive.

When someone is referred to psychotherapy it is typically because they are "hurting." Western clients assume and expect that their therapists will know how to treat them and, depending on the therapeutic modality they select, know roughly how long it will take. Many choose psychoanalytically oriented psychotherapy precisely because it takes a long time and presumably uncovers latent content. Non-Western clients and many cultural minorities, if they come into psychotherapy at all, have differing expectations. They assume that the therapy will target their current problem and offer practical, and hopefully immediate, results. Their less-than-accepting response for many of the current forms of psychotherapy is often misconstrued as resistance but might be more appropriately termed impatience or mistrust. They are impatient with the time frame and mistrustful that the therapist is actually listening to them and taking their problem in.

They are particularly mistrustful of the outcome. As one Islamic client said to me, "Am I going to have to be like you in order to get better?" This concern is not a trivial one. Content-oriented psychotherapy with its claims of universal latent substrates has a tendency to homogenize cultures and thereby may serve to heighten the diverse client's anxiety that the gaining of mental health requires the loss of cultural identity. RET and other cognitive behavioral therapies work toward changing the client's thoughts and behaviors *only when they are dysfunctional*—that is, when they stop the client from achieving his or her own goals. Process therapy, since it does not assume a universal underlying reality, latent or otherwise, encourages the client to maintain his or her own culture at all times. The process-oriented therapist assumes that the client is an "expert" about his or her own reality and asks to be let in on the client's thought processes, actively listening and hypothesis testing throughout the session. This active listening not only builds rapport but also helps establish one of the central components of the therapeutic alliance: a mutually agreed upon therapeutic goal. In RET, for example, the client is asked if he or she is willing to work to a specific outcome and the process of potentially achieving that outcome is presented. Misunderstandings as to outcome, such as those of my Islamic client, can be cleared up, since the outcome is overtly stated and agreed upon before the process begins.

Since RET and other cognitive therapies assume that people largely disturb themselves by the thoughts they have about the world, themselves, and others, then demonstrating that different cultural groups endorse irrational beliefs at different rates is a valuable one. If the endorsement rates reported here are trustworthy, then the therapist has a powerful tool for use with his or her culturally diverse clients. While use of such data may have the drawback of generating yet another set of stereotypes with which minority groups may be stigmatized, it can also act as a heuristic for the generation of testable hypotheses both in therapy and in research.

Culturally Congruent, Culturally Incongruent, and "Superethnic"

As the previous data show, while the endorsement of irrational beliefs is positively correlated with emotional and personality disorders, we can now see that specific cultural/ethnic groups endorse specific irrational statements differently and therefore may have different cognitive experiences underlying their disturbance. If we can trust the Black/White differences in endorsement and it is true that while both groups strongly desire success, Afro-Americans are less likely to equate failure with personal failure or ego failure as frequently as their Caucasian counterparts do, then we should be able to anticipate that Afro-Americans might not experience the same level of depression over failure as their Caucasian counterparts, nor might they experience the same degree of panic when contemplating the implications of failure. This response, while "healthier," offers considerable opportunities for intercultural as well as intracultural conflict. The dominant middle-class Caucasian community drives itself "crazy" with its demands for success and equates failure at a task with blows to esteem and worth, and therefore may have trouble understanding the apparently more laid-back lack of caring of its Afro-American neighbors. Dominant culture therapists may be tempted to cure these clients by helping them care about success and thereby encourage the endorsement of appropriate dominant culture "craziness" while missing the boat entirely as to the logical emotional consequences of this laid-back response. If it is true that Afro-Americans expect success and are intolerant of discomfort, then one might more appropriately expect anger rather than depression at its lack of easy attainment. Instead of assuming depression as a given, it is fitting to work toward overcoming the resistance about that diagnosis. However, the process of hypothesis testing could be appropriately used cross-ethnically in either scenario. The cross-culturally appropriate therapist might therefore ask, "Since you seem to believe that you should be effortlessly successful, are you experiencing any anger over your current situation?" If the client responds in the negative, then an alternative hypothesis could be tested via gathering more information.

Intracultural conflict is also possible as a result of these cognitions. It is more likely that Afro-Americans are more diverse in their endorsements than this current study demonstrates. The Black sample was largely comprised of three different groups: lower socioeconomic inner-city youths, working class adults, and some recent immigrants from the West Indies and Africa. This study does not treat them separately and therefore misses areas of diversity that undoubtedly exist, since their cultural realities are so different. However, if we assume for the point of argument that some segment of the Black population is represented by this endorsement, then what about other segments within the culture that might have differing viewpoints? One potential source of intracultural conflict arises as a result of people within the same community not sharing the same cognitive assumptions. If we assume for a moment that some of the Black or Afro-American sample share the reality of the dominant culture, what happens when they meet someone from their same ethnic group who shares a different cognitive reality? It is our position that such people might experience intracultural conflict and that this conflict might be a reason to seek out counseling or therapy.

Some of my Afro-American clients indeed are experiencing this conflict as are clients from other cultural/ethnic minorities. We are also seeing this form of conflict in women and men within our own community as they grapple with changing sexual roles brought on by the feminist movement, the men's movement, and the post-Stonewall homosexual community. The issue seems to be one of cultural congruence versus cultural incongruence. As long as the client sees him- or herself as behaving congruently within the culture, then they do not experience conflict. However, who "defines" the cultural experience and what does it mean to be congruent within the culture? *If* you don't see yourself as being represented by that definition, what is the consequence for you? What does it mean to be Black, Jewish, Islamic, or White for that matter? Rational-Emotive Therapy suggests that the therapists dispute the rigidly held "musts" and "shoulds" and not the preferences as long as the preferences, if achieved, do not result in illegalities for the person living within the culture. The competent cross-cultural therapist is not the role model of normality, even when he or she acts appropriately within his or her culture. She or he can only identify the sources of conflict as they arise from the endorsement of rigidly held irrational beliefs. For example, a client who suffers as a result of cultural incongruence may be assuming that a spokesperson for a segment of the culture (subculture, minority) represents the entire culture and that she or he *must* think, act, and feel like the cultural spokesperson recommends or else lose his or her ethnic identity. As one of my Afro-American clients put it, "If I don't act like a gangsta rapper then I am not Black." The cross-culturally competent therapist helps the client understand that there are many ways of appropriately acting as a male, an Afro-American male, or American (i.e., dominant culture) male. The therapist then goes on to show that one source of the client's emotional disturbance is the rigidly held belief that there is a universal standard for Afro-American male behavior. Additionally the therapist helps the client see what the emotional and behavioral consequences would be for any of the choices available. Typically these choices are threefold:

1. Opt to try to be congruent with the dominant culture and run the risk of being considered deviant by the subculture, and possibly by the dominant culture as well—"Gee, you don't act like the rest of them, but we sure as hell know you are not us."
2. Opt to try to be congruent with the cultural "spokesperson" and run the risk of being considered deviant by the dominant community—"All of those people are alike."
3. Opt to try to behave, think, and feel in ways that work for you and too bad what other people (even "important" people) think.

Each of these choices provides additional opportunities for both rational and irrational thinking and the therapist is well advised to pursue them.

Another source of cultural conflict that may arise in therapy we have taken the liberty of calling the "superethnic." Superethnic is defined as someone who is experiencing difficulty within his or her own culture as a result of too rigidly endorsing the mainstream values and as a consequence is more American than the Americans, or more Islamic than the Islamics, and so on. Superethnics assume that by rigidly following the rules of their community they will always be emotionally stable, functionally behavioral, and politically correct. However, when this perfection fails to occur, superethnics experience increasing disturbance because they have behaved as they are "supposed" to and still are not getting their due, as they "must." By challenging these and other irrationalities cross-culturally competent cognitive therapists aid their clients in developing more flexible philosophies that may prove to be more personally satisfying and adaptive than the ones they previously held.

Space does not permit a fuller discussion of these issues, but we hope we have outlined some of the reasons why the ABSII and RET are potentially useful sources of identifying and disputing the irrational beliefs that underlie emotional disturbance for all clients regardless of culture. We are currently collecting data for a much larger study, which we hope will address the issues of sample size and intracultural diversity in order to more fully investigate the relationship between cross-cultural/cross-ethnic endorsement of irrational beliefs, within "normal," clinical, and inmate populations; and their correlation with specific mental health issues such as depression, satisfaction with life, and anger.

NOTES

Versions of this paper were presented as part of *The Spirit or the Scalpel*, a Conference on Issues in Health Care Delivery cosponsored by the State University of New York, College at Old Westbury and The Institute for Cross-Cultural and Cross-Ethnic Studies at Molloy College, on February 10, 1990; and as part of a panel on New Developments in Rational-Emotive Assessment Techniques, at the World Congress on Mental Health Counseling, Keystone, Colorado, June 15, 1990.

1. In actual practice the RET therapist typically uses active listening to ascertain the client's core irrational beliefs. Once these beliefs are identified, RET therapists will typically intervene by testing out a series of hypotheses about the behavioral and emotional consequences of holding such a belief. Alternatively, after initially ascertaining the client's emotional state or behavioral problem, RET therapists might intervene by testing out hypotheses about the irrational beliefs that the client might be endorsing.

REFERENCES

Atkinson, D. R., Morten, G. & Sue, D. W. (1989). *Counseling American minorities: A cross-cultural perspective* (3rd ed.). Dubuque, IA: William C. Brown.

Beck, A. T. & Beck, R. W. (1972). Screening depressed patients in family practice: a rapid technique. *Postgraduate Medicine, 52* (December), 81–85.

Burgess, P. M. (1986). *Belief systems and emotional disturbance: An evaluation of the Rational-Emotive Model.* Doctoral Dissertation, University of Melbourne.

Diener, E., Emmons, R. A., Larsen, R. J. & Griffen, S. (1985). The satisfaction with life scale. *Journal of Personality Assessment, 49,* 71–75.

DiGiuseppe, R., Leaf, R., Robin, M. W. & Exner, T. (1988). The development of a measure of irrational/rational thinking. Presented at the World Congress on Behavior Therapy. Edinburgh, September 6.

DiGiuseppe, R. & Miller, N. J. (1977). A review of outcome studies on rational-emotive therapy. In A. Ellis & R. Grieger (Eds.), *Handbook of Rational Emotive Therapy.* New York: Springer.

DiGiuseppe, R., Robin, M. W. & Dryden, W. (1990). Rational-emotive therapy and the Judeo-Christian tradition: A focus on clinical strategies. *Journal of Cognitive Psychotherapy: An International Quarterly, 4* (4), 355–368.

DiGiuseppe, R., Robin, M. W., Leaf, R. & Gorman, A. (1989). A cross-validation and factor analysis of a measure of irrational beliefs. Presented at World Congress of Cognitive Therapy, Oxford, England, June 29.

DiGiuseppe, R., Robin, M. W. & Primavera, L. (1991). Cluster Analysis of Narcisstic Personality Scores on the MCM12. Presented at the Ninety-Ninth Annual Convention of the American Psychological Association, San Francisco, August.

Dupue, H. (1984). The general psychological well-being scale. In N. K. Wanger, M. E. Mattson, C. D. Fienberg & J. Elenson (Eds.), *Assessment of quality of life* (pp. 353–356). New York: Lejacq Publishing.

Ellis, A. (1962). *Reason and emotion in psychotherapy.* Secaucus, NJ: Citadel.

Ellis, A. & Dryden, W. (1988). *The practice of Rational-Emotive Therapy.* New York: Springer.

Goldberg, D. P. (1972). *The Detection of psychiatric illness by questionnaire: A technique for the identification and assessment of the non-psychotic psychiatric illness.* Oxford: Oxford University Press.

McGovern, T. & Silverman, M. (1984). A review of outcome studies on rational-emotive therapy. *Journal of Rational-Emotive Therapy,* 2, 7–18.

Pedersen, P. (Ed.) (1985). *Handbook of cross-cultural counseling and therapy.* Westport, CT: Greenwood Press.

Robin, M. W. & DiGiuseppe, R. (1987). Toward the development of a cross-culturally valid measurement of irrationality. The featured presentation sponsored by the Institute for Cross-Cultural and Cross-Ethnic Studies of Molloy College, hosted by the Psychology Program of Fordham University (Lincoln Center Campus) August 27.

Robin, M. W. & DiGiuseppe, R. (1992). Endorsement of irrational/rational beliefs: Cross-cultural & cross-ethnic implications for mental & emotional health (part 2). Presented at the World Congress of Cognitive Therapy '92, Toronto, June 18.

Robin, M. W., DiGiuseppe, R. & Alvarez, F. (1991a). Endorsement of irrational/rational beliefs: Cross-cultural & cross-ethnic implications for mental & emotional health. Presented at the XXIII Interamerican Congress of Psychology, San Jose, Costa Rica, July 9.

Robin, M. W., DiGiuseppe, R. & Alvarez, F. (1991b). Using Rational-Emotive Therapy with culturally diverse clients. A workshop presented at the XXIII Interamerican Congress of Psychology, San Jose, Costa Rica, July 9.

Robin, M. W., DiGiuseppe, R. & Kopec, A. M. (1993a). Using Rational-Emotive Therapy with culturally diverse clients. A workshop presented at the Third Annual European Congress of Psychology, Tampere, Finland, July 4–9.

Robin, M. W., DiGiuseppe, R. & Kopec, A. M. (1993b). Measuring irrational beliefs: Cross-cultural implications. A poster session presented at the Third Annual European Congress of Psychology, Tampere, Finland, July 4–9.

Robin, M. W., DiGiuseppe, R., & Naimark, H. (1990). Irrational beliefs and MCMI–2 personality disorder scores. Presented at a Division 12 Poster Session on Assessment and Diagnosis of Personality Disorders, Eating Disorders and Alcohol Abuse at the 98th Annual Convention of the American Psychological Association, Boston, August 13.

Robin, M. W. & Eckhardt, C. (1993). Clinical assessment of anger/hostility disorder. Part of the symposium Assessment, Diagnosis, and Treatment of Clients with Anger Problems presented at the 101st Annual Convention of the American Psychological Association, Toronto, August 23.

Silverman, M. S., McCarthy, M. & McGovern, T. (1992). A review of outcome studies of Rational-Emotive Therapy from 1982–1989. *Journal of Rational Emotive & Cognitive Behavior Therapy,* 10(3), 109–186.

Smith, T. W. (1989). Assessment in rational-emotive therapy: Empirical access to the ABCD model. In M. Bernard & R. DiGiuseppe (Eds.), *Inside Rational-Emotive Therapy: A critical appraisal of the theory and therapy of Albert Ellis.* Orlando, FL: Academic Press.

Spielberger, C. C. Jacobs, G. A., Russell, S. F. & Crane, R. S. (1983). Assessment of anger: The State-Trait Anger Scale. In J. N. Butcher & C. D. Spielberger (Eds.), *Advances in personality assessment* (Vol. 2). Hillsdale, NJ: LEA.

Spielberger, C. D., Johnson, E. H., Russell, S. F., Crane, R. S., Jacobs, G. A. & Worden, T. J. (1985). The experience and expression of anger: Construction and validation of an anger expression scale. In M. A. Chesney & R. H. Rosenman (Eds.), *Anger and hostility in cardio-vascular and behavioral disorders* (pp. 5–30). New York: Hemisphere/McGraw-Hill.

Sue, D. W., Bernier, J. E., Durran, A., Feinberg, L., Pedersen, P., Smith, E. J. & Vasquez-Nuttall, E. (1982). A position paper: Cross-cultural counseling competencies, Education and training committee, Division 17, A.P.A. *The Counseling Psychologist, 10*(2), 45–52.

Sue, D. W. & Sue, D. (1990). *Counseling the culturally different: Theory & Practice* (2nd ed.). New York: John Wiley.

Walen, S. R., DiGiuseppe, R. & Wessler, R. L. (1980). *A practitioner's guide to Rational-Emotive Therapy.* New York: Oxford University Press.

12

Religion Versus Medicine Versus Clinical Psychoanalysis or "Spirit" Versus "Scalpel" Versus "Castration" in a Case of Recovering Alcoholism

C. Edward Robins

In this chapter I will present some excerpts from the case itself, and then offer some Theoretical Reflections. In the following excerpts from sessions, I have enclosed my speech in brackets.

THE TREATMENT

A pale-looking and overweight 60-year-old executive came to see me for the first time a little over a year ago. He walked in, sat down heavily, and immediately said: "I am a recovering alcoholic." Then he told me that recently a woman at work had sharply confronted him, and, as a result, he was now in what he called an "agitated depression." He explained that his heart was troubling him, and he feared a total heart failure. His cardiologist had recommended a complicated bypass operation to alleviate his distress. After a few initial sessions, we decided to begin working together to see if his depression would lift.

Mr. H (as I will refer to him here) spent the whole first month of his treatment telling me the story of his mother's death when he was 11. That very day his grandmother had asked him to run to the drugstore for some medication for his mother, but he had said no because his friends were waiting to take him target practicing. When he returned home he saw the ambulance in front of his house. He would never see his mother alive again.

During these sessions of the first month, he reported two dreams of "sitting alone in a little hut." He explained that right after his mother's death, he began "creating little huts" in the fields near his house. "What *fun!*"

he exclaimed, "it was to build them." Some weeks later, he spoke about what happened when he was alone and quiet in a hut: He would be filled with the most exciting fantasies of being a great hero—the kind of hero he knew *his mother* loved. (Actually, his first name was chosen by his mother because it was that of "one of her heroes." And so he carries her desire forever in his name.) After a few months more he spoke about what else he did in the hut. He masturbated. His voice stumbled and faltered as he spoke about it, and about how guilty he has continually felt. He went on to tell me that in his early 20s, he married the first girl he was intimate with, and that the marriage ended in divorce when their children reached adolescence.

Several months into his treatment, Mr. H began to speak about his father. "My father was full of fears . . . he was always depressed, always holding back. His voice was *so* loud: 'Don't get into trouble! Don't make a mess!' That's the voice I hear inside myself all these years, even now. I always answer 'No!' and then do just the opposite of what he says! It's a goddamn game where I just hurt myself. I should tell you that *he* ran away from home when he was 14—just after an argument with *his* father."

About five months into his treatment, Mr. H started to speak about how he became an alcoholic. He so hated that inner, criticizing voice of his father yelling at him: "Do the right thing!" "Don't get drunk!" that he did just the opposite. "Getting high" and "impulsively having fun" meant shutting up that voice within. And, what was delightful, it signaled a wonderful, harmonious feeling of "being-with-Mom."

His professional and personal life began to collapse. After repeated attempts to stop drinking on his own, he finally sought treatment from Alcoholics Anonymous (AA). Now he could finally give up his drinking. Why? He explained that it was because of the "Higher Power." (For those not acquainted with the "Higher Power," let me briefly cite the first three of AA's Twelve Steps: First, admit one is powerless over drink; second, acknowledge there is a Higher Power; third, commit your problem to the Higher Power.)

He said "The Higher Power did it, the Higher Power bailed me out. . . . We're powerless over alcohol. . . . We pray to God to restore us to sanity. . . . and I got sober." That was when he first joined AA. "It really worked for me," he said. It has been 15 years since Mr. H joined AA, and he has never returned to drinking since. But now something has shifted. Whereas at first he felt that the Higher Power was "bailing me out," he now feels that the Higher Power is *refusing* to "bail me out" unless, he, Mr. H, does it for himself. "The Higher Power told me: stop playing the enabling game!"

"But now I'm still waiting. For the light to come. To be relieved from my inner fight, that constant critical voice inside. Whatever was supposed to come from the outside never really came. Once I stayed in bed for 48 hours waiting for the voice to come. Finally what I heard was: "Get off your ass." ["Who was speaking?"] "I was. I was the voice. I have to do it myself" he said sadly.

"I had some thoughts. The Higher Power, God, is telling me that I can do it because others have done it, too. But why do I still have to overcome this inertia I feel within myself? Why won't God help me to do it? Say, to get out of bed? I still keep waiting for the right voice. . . . And then for *some unknown reason* I start to think: my mother's dead, my father's dead.

"My grandmother and mother did everything for me when I was small. That is what I wanted the Higher Power to do. I want the Higher Power to say: 'I'll make it easy for you.' But it's not true! *I* still have to do it. It pisses me off because *I* have to exert myself!

"I looked for the 'easy way' for more than 40 years. I read all the self-help books, did all the programs like EST, and so on. Mother, grand-mother, Higher Power: all of them won't do it. *I* have to do it."

Now, from a session a few months later: "I realize now, that, as a child, I really talked only to my dog. It's painful to tell you this. Because my mother mostly ignored me too. Then her death. And the only fun was building huts and playing the fantasies. Funny. When I was drinking I never had fantasies! I guess the alcohol took the place of the fantasy. . . . I made the fantasies to cover my hurt feelings about my mother."

Mr. H reported this dream just two months ago. "I was in a hotel room. There was a pounding on the door. And then shooting. And then people running through the hotel killing people. I decided to hide, and crawled up into the ceiling of the closet, unscrewed the lightbulb, put my feet and back up against the wall so they couldn't find me."

Then he said: "Well, that was the dream. The people didn't find me, they left." ["Unscrewed"?] He said "Yes, the light bulb, and then I pulled the cord up so nobody'd yank on it." ["Hiding . . . unscrewed."] He said: "I'm afraid to get close to a woman, like this last week when I told you about the younger woman in that group who seemed to like me. What would the other people think if they knew I had screwing on my mind? And what if I actually could be with her? My wife told me that, sexually, I could never do the right thing for her, so I don't want to go through all that again." ["I wonder if you'll be killed if you screw?"] "I just feel like I'll be over-whelmed." ["You don't want anyone 'yanking on the cord'?"] He said: "It's the masturbation. It's really the masturbation that makes me so iso-lated; it always has, ever since I've been a boy. So I yank on my own cord. In the dream if I try to screw in the thread—hey, "thread" just sounded like "threat" and that's what it really is, a threat. Well, if I screw in the bulb, then *I can be seen*. The others can really *see* me then. I feel very vulnerable just now. . . . If I screw, then it'd start all over again, people'll make demands on me, and I'll have to please them all over again!

"That's always the way it's been with sex: I have to make the woman happy, and if I can't, then I'm unhappy. . . . I keep thinking that all this has to do with my trying to do something so that the woman won't leave me. You know, like my mother. But it never seems to work, it all just keeps repeating itself. And I keep losing. So I end up not screwing—just screwing myself over. . . . I kept losing with alcohol, and now it's the same with food: I won't let myself succeed, but keep repeating some kind of failure, never letting myself lose the weight I really want."

The next session he came in and said: "I was thinking about the dream and how I didn't want *anyone else* to 'yank on the cord.' Do you recall my telling you about that man who tried to touch my penis? That's probably it. And to think that just because of that experience I've never let myself show any affection for men, like putting my arm around them, even patting them on the back when I wanted to!"

Now from a session one month ago. "That critical voice inside whips me, makes my life unbearable. I have to shut it up! Before, I just got numb on alcohol! I'd say screw it! I'm not going to listen to you, and then I'd drink. . . . I still have that voice. I could stop it when I drank, or when I was filling my mind with what AA said—you know, all the slogans. Then when I stopped AA and started dating that woman, the voice came back."

Just the week before last, after telling of the return of "deep down feelings of rejection," he began speaking about what he calls "my religion." "That God loves *me* is what's important. Because I know I don't love myself, I can't. I don't accept myself. Only if God loves me can I then love myself, accept myself. And then maybe I can love others too."

Finally, here is what he said at a session just last week. "I awoke at 3 AM. I realize there's a wall between what I want and what others want. I'm always looking for somebody to tell me what to do—so I'm always looking *over* the wall. If I don't have the wall, if I do what *I* want, then I get argued with, and put down. I can't do what I want, there are always obstacles. . . . I was thinking this: religion tells me: 'do *God's* will'—so I kept looking *out there* to get some direction from God's will—instead of what's *in here* (he points to his breast), waiting for something to happen from the other side! Waiting for the voice! A 'no win' situation. When I do get direction from out there, like at work, then they don't know what they want either, they aren't sure, so why should *I* do it? They criticize me when I do what I want, and even when it works out well, even then they don't take back their criticism."

["You were looking out there for God's will?"] He said: "I realize now he's in here (points to his breast). It only works if *I* do what *I* want to do! Yet why do I resist it so much?" ["What do you want?"] "A never ending puzzle to figure that out. I don't know. Mainly, I'm fearful I won't be accepted. The times I've exerted myself I get disagreement. Then my perception gets distorted. I take everything so personally. . . . Ha! (laughs to himself). I'm *alone* if I do what I want, that's it! But I also feel alone if I do what the crowd wants! If I give people what I think they want, it's still not what they want! Why do I have to keep doing this? *They don't need me. I don't need them.* When they ask me 'what do you want?' I ask them 'what do *you* want?' It's a game. . . . I always try to foresee what the woman wants to hear rather than giving her what *I* want to say! That's when I hide behind the wall. Then nobody can pick on me. But I can't get any satisfaction either because I'm not doing what I want. So I'm split inside, like two different voices, two different people. . . . " After a long silence he continued speaking: "I'll always be in conflict. I wish that God, me—the voices—could all have a smooth joint control over me, but it just doesn't seem to work. I'll always have some kind of void, no matter how I try to overcome it."

THEORETICAL REFLECTIONS

I want to clarify the essential difference between Mr. H's treatment in Alcoholics Anonymous and his treatment in psychoanalysis—as conceived by Freud and Lacan. What is at stake is who Mr. H is in his human subjectivity: Is he anyone—a subject—beyond his "mother addiction" (alcohol), and beyond his "father addiction" (the Higher Power of AA)? How can he discover that for himself? Freud and Lacan suggest a pretty horrible solution: Mr. H's "castration." Here, "castration" means that Mr. H is *utterly* unable to recover the lost paradise with his mother or recreate a new one with a Higher Power; that the promise of fulfillment is false; that he is "thrown" broken, limited, limping—basically lacking. And that it is only from this position of lack that Mr. H's true desire—and sexuality— will speak, and that he will be more revealed to himself.

Mr. H clearly describes what happened in his treatment in Alcoholics Anonymous: how it was only when he could admit that he was completely powerless before alcohol and, as a result, could place his faith in a "Higher Power," that he achieved sobriety. As clinicians we admit how difficult it is to successfully treat alcoholism, and many of us give Alcoholics Anonymous high marks for their successful work. But why, psychologically, does the AA model work?

From a clinical point of view, we can reconstruct Mr. H's dilemma in the following way: his addiction is (in his own words) a "love affair" with his mother, to the exclusion of the interdiction of his father, who forbade the ongoing symbiosis between the two. Mr. H was caught, addicted to this dyadic symbiosis, and it could be broken only when a "third term," what Lacan (1977) calls the "paternal metaphor" (or what AA calls the "Higher Power") entered his life. In Alcoholics Anonymous, then, God becomes the "paternal metaphor" who "allows" the addict to be incorporated into a triangulation that "works"—that is, one where the mother does not stop existing (note the alcoholic's credo: "I am always an alcoholic") but where, with the help of the "father," the child can give her up. Mr. H is always facing her—every day—and gives her up continually at the insistence of the father's interdiction. Now Mr. H's position is that of one term not in a dyad but in a triangulation: with alcohol (mother), God (father), and himself (see Figure 12.1). Since addiction is the love affair with his mother, then his father becomes the "third term," the "no" that ruptures the mother-child couple. Threatened by this triangulation, the addict—who deeply desires to remain an addict—is in the position of constantly saying his own "No!" to the "No!" of the father, as Mr. H tells us he does.

Let us now briefly reconsider Freud's view of religion. I am going to quote at length from his work (1957) on Leonardo da Vinci, originally published in 1910.

Psycho-analysis has made us familiar with the intimate connection between the father-complex and belief in God; it has shown us that a personal God is, psychologically, nothing other than an exalted father. . . . Thus we recognize that the roots of the need for religion are in the parental complex; the almighty and just God, and kindly Nature, appear to us as grand sublimations of father and mother, or rather as revivals and restorations of the young child's ideas of them. . . . [W]hen at a later date he perceives how truly forlorn and weak he is when confronted with the great forces of life, he feels his condition as he did in childhood, and attempts to deny his own dependency by a regressive revival of the forces which protected his infancy. The protection against neurotic illness, which religion vouchsafes to those who believe in it, is easily explained: it removes their parental complex, on which the sense of guilt in individuals as well as in the whole human race depends, and disposes of it, while the unbeliever has to grapple with the problem on his own (p. 123).

In *Totem and Taboo* (1955) Freud speaks about the "slain father" who has become the "God" of his guilty sons; and in *The Future of an Illusion* (1961), he says that the perception of our own helplessness and the longing for a protective father is decisive in the individual's construction of the illusion "God." From Freud's Leonardo quote, we see that although religion exorcises the terrors of nature, it nonetheless founds a system of denial against grief, mourning, loss, and tragedy. Freud's words are: "religion protects against neurotic illness." Freud maintained this position to the end, as we see in *Civilization and Its Discontents* in 1930 (Freud, 1961, p. 85). There he further writes that he can find in himself no "oceanic feeling" like Romain Rolland describes, but that for him—Freud—the "longing for father is the *incontrovertible* source of religion" (emphasis added) (p. 72).

Lacan differs somewhat from Freud. He writes that religion "covers the traumatic" in life (Lacan, 1974). Rather than facing the trauma of the "absolute lack" in life's response to him (namely, the deprivation of his mother's presence), Mr. H fabricated a "cover" for his lack: alcohol, and

Figure 12.1
The Triangulated Relationship

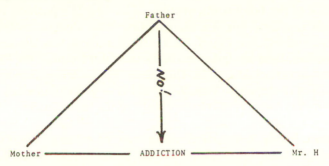

then, in AA, another cover, the Higher Power. Mr. H told us clearly that his alcohol addiction substituted for his *imagining*—his fantasies—that his mother was unconditionally present, available to him; then, the Higher Power took its place, and in that wake, he refound his self-respect inside himself, and in the AA fellowship where others continually resurface the triangulation of mother (as addiction), father (as interdiction), and self.

Here God = unconditional love, the kind of love he *fantasied* his mother had for him. We recall Mr. H's words: "God loves and accepts me unconditionally; therefore, I can love and accept myself." Now, in saying that God loves him unconditionally, Mr. H is trying to grasp himself as somehow fulfilled, whole, at peace, with no gaps, no loss: "I'm totally loved and now I can love!" he had hoped.

I want to emphasize the importance of what Lacan (1977) calls "the paternal metaphor"—that is, the need for any human to have a "third term" that comes between himself and his mother or addiction. We know of the beginnings of human life, when the infant is "immersed" in its mother. The theoretical role of the father is to make a cut, to rupture that symbiotic bond between the mother and child, to put, as Lacan says, the mother "under the law." Under what law? The law that forbids incest: that she cannot reincorporate her child into her, that she cannot "keep" her child to herself: if she does, the child will be forever crippled or, in clinical terms, psychotic. But the lure of "staying with the mother" is so often irresistible: witness the epidemic of severe addictions, and listen to addicts speak of their "highs" in the same blissful terms that describe the early mother-infant symbiosis. This is especially true of hard core addicts who are often multiply-addicted to heroin and cocaine. I personally have interviewed and tested over 1,000 homeless people for a jobs program in Manhattan, and I am continually struck by the coincidence of severe addiction and the lack of a father: at least 90 percent of all severe addicts had no viable connection to a father (which is especially calamitous for the black male population).

To return to my argument: what is essential, then, is an intact tripartite structure—what Freud called the Oedipus complex—to pull someone out of the depths of psychosis and addiction. The father's role was so primary for Freud that, as we read, "God" for Freud could *only* be a projection of the wished-for father who protects us, never a projection of the wished-for mother, as, for example, Carl Jung held (see Milanesi & Aletti, 1973, p. 58).

Lacan (1974) further specifies that religion "covers the Real." What he means by "Real" is the absolute core of reality, which is basically impenetrable, basically tragic, and basically *Unheimlich* (uncanny). Religion for Lacan covers death, tragedy, and unspeakable chaos that lie under our conscious level of existence. Remember Mr. H saying that "I still keep waiting for the right voice. . . . And then for *some unknown reason* I start to think: my mother's dead, my father's dead." Like in a tale of Edgar Allen Poe, it is death itself who dogs the tracks of Mr. H, and gives the lie to Mr. H's fantasies of reunion with mother, perfection, and fulfillment. Religion covers up our limits, Lacan argues, and promises instead immortality, bliss, and a community of brotherly love. (We see that in AA the Higher Power is the "glue" that holds the fellowship together.) Without religion, the tragic is exposed: you may have heard people say: "Without my religion I would surely kill myself."

Psychoanalysis, in the eyes of Freud and Lacan (but certainly not in the eyes of many American psychoanalysts) directs people to live the loss, to accept the basic alienation from self and other, the lack of fulfillment, to live with the abyss—as Mr. H says "the void I'll always have with me." So, in Mr. H's treatment, the question remains: to face his loss or to cover it up?

The human subject, Lacan (1977) emphasizes, is constituted originally by a loss—a split that occurs in the person's separation from the mother. And so the human subject is doomed to live a "basic alienation without end." This, and not the humanistic conception of an always more perfectible happiness, an actualization of a "true self," is the fate of man according to Lacan and Freud.

If psychoanalytic treatment means retrieving one's subjectivity, then Mr. H is on the road to recovering his own human subjectivity when he stops hiding his from sexuality and lets his true desire speak. Because for both Freud and Lacan, the unconscious subject arises in the field of sexuality.

While we are on the topic of sexuality, let us go back to Mr. H's dream. "I am in a hotel room." Is the "h" in hotel like the "h" in hut—where he fantasied about his mother and masturbated? Listen again to his words: "There is a *pounding* . . . " "And then *shooting* . . . " "And then people running and *killing* people." "Pounding" is a word often used to describe masturbation; "shooting" could signal ejaculation. If so, then all this sexuality has something to do with *death*—the "killing." Death again. This time a familiar mixture: sex and death. We may further say that his position on the closet shelf (with feet and back up *against* the wall), plus the very fact of his being in "a *closet*" suggest he is protecting himself against homosexual fears or wishes. We remember he begins the very next session by bringing up this topic (about the man who wanted to touch his penis). I probably don't have to remind you, that for Freud and Lacan in particular, everyone has homosexual conflicts.

CONCLUSION

There are many different types of cures or treatments for people like Mr. H: medical, religious, and psychoanalytic, to mention only a few. Remember that one surgeon strongly advised Mr. H to undergo a complicated bypass operation. We have reviewed the Alcoholics Anonymous approach: the religion of the Higher Power. The psychoanalytic approach of Freud and Lacan would aim at something different: what they call "castration." I have pointed out that although religion may be able to "cover up" the traumatic, it cannot cure it; psychoanalysis can uncover it—not cure it— can help release the subject trapped repeatedly in his symptoms, which symptoms are the body's way of "speaking."

At this date, now that Mr. H has been coming to therapy for over a year, his body is "speaking" differently: he appears to be less trapped. Having been convinced in the last five months that he will not suffer heart failure, he has, with his physician's consent, successfully discontinued his heart and blood pressure medications, has lost some excess weight, and as he reports it, "for the first time in years I've got sexual feelings."

REFERENCES

Freud, S. (1955). Totem and taboo. In J. Strachey (Ed. and Trans.), *The standard edition of the complete psychological works of Sigmund Freud*, vol. 13. London: Hogarth Press (original work published in 1913).

———— (1957). Leonardo da Vinci and a memory of his childhood. In Strachey, *The standard edition*, vol. 11 (pp. 63–139). London: Hogarth Press (original work published in 1910).

———— (1961). Civilization and its discontents. In Strachey, *The standard edition*, vol. 21 (pp. 59–149). London: Hogarth Press (original work published in 1930).

———— (1961). The future of an illusion. In Strachey, *The standard edition*, vol. 21. London: Hogarth Press (original work published in 1927).

Lacan, J. (1974). Conference du press du Dr. Lacan (October 29). Paris: Centre Culturel Francais.

———— (1977). *Ecrits: A selection* (A. Sheridan, Trans.). New York: Norton (original work published in 1966).

———— (1988). *The seminar of Jacques Lacan*, vol. 1 (J.-A. Miller, Ed., & J. Forrester, Trans.). New York: Cambridge University Press (original work published in 1975).

Milanesi, G. and Aletti, M. (1973). *Psicologia della religione*. Torino: Leumann Elle di ci.

13

The Role of the Referral Agent in Treatment Selection and Treatment Efficacy: A Cultural Perspective

Charles V. Callahan

The problems encountered by modern medical practitioners in achieving acceptance of their treatment methods by traditional societies and by isolated subcultures within modern nations has received considerable attention in the literature. Yet there has been very little mention of the role of referral agents in determining the uptake of health services by these Third World cultures. In much of this research, referral activity is typically ignored or viewed as incidental to the more important accommodations that must be made by practitioners of modern medical wisdom. The problem of developing a network of referral agents or patching into existing networks is not addressed directly. Instead, anecdotal experiences and some practical wisdom are presented incidental to accounts of successes and failures of attempts to establish a health service in a traditional society.

As a psychologist in private practice dealing with other health professionals in the modern context, I have come to appreciate the value and purpose of referral agents. Having frequently functioned as a referral agent to other providers of health services over 17 years of practice, I have gleaned insights and impressions that form part of the basis of this chapter.

This chapter will attempt to compare and elucidate the process and problems of referral in modern and traditional cultures more explicitly. It will also propose that careful attention to developing networks of referral agents, or integrating with existing referral networks, will greatly facilitate the uptake of modern medical methodologies. Considering the sensitivity that may be required to accomplish this objective, this chapter might appropriately be subtitled, "Please don't squeeze the Shaman!", after a toilet tissue commercial on television a few years ago.

ROLE OF THE REFERRAL AGENT

The act of referring a person for medical treatment arises as a particular instance of the growing division of labor and knowledge within a developing society. Credible referral sources are often held in high esteem in their communities as gatekeepers to an array of services offered by various practitioners of the healing arts. Their function helps insure adequate service delivery in areas critical to the well-being of society.

All successful practitioners, in this culture or elsewhere, have a network of referral agents—individuals of varying degrees of familiarity with the practitioners' services who, collectively or individually, channel prospective patients to them for treatment. The best of these referrals are "qualified"— that is, initiated by agents who are familiar with the type of service provided by the health practitioners, their areas of specialization, the segment of the population they service, and their track records with problems similar to those referred for treatment. "Blind" referrals, made in relative ignorance of these characteristics, tend to result in less favorable treatment outcomes.

It is proposed that the referral agent optimizes treatment outcomes for the practitioner. In so doing, the referral agent may fulfill several roles to varying degrees, as follows:

1. The referral agent improves the goodness of fit between patient and practitioner in matching presenting problems with appropriate treatment tactics. This selectivity implies an assortment of practitioners from which to choose and/or specific knowledge of the practitioner's skills as the basis for the match.

2. The referral agent actively shapes a definition of the patient's presenting problems that qualifies the patient for the type of treatment suggested. In some respects, this amounts to a preliminary diagnosis of the complaint and becomes the basis for the referral. A defective definition of a presenting problem at this stage could actually obscure effective treatment.

3. The referral agent encourages realistic expectations on the patient's part with respect to the practitioner's approach and the likelihood of successful treatment and cure. Inflated expectancies resulting in a disappointing response to treatment would only serve to discredit the referral agent.

4. The referral agent encourages compliance with the treatment tactics prescribed, and in some instances may actually share responsibility for applying those treatments.

5. The referral agent encourages continuation of the treatment to its conclusion, thereby enhancing treatment outcomes.

6. The referral agent ensures that successful outcomes and cures are properly attributed to the treatments rendered by the practitioner.

7. The referral agent coordinates the delivery of services, especially when the services of more than one practitioner are required. In effect, a referral agent may act as a case manager for the patient and practitioners.

8. The referral agent functions as mediator and arbitrator between patient and practitioner when confusion or disputes about treatment arise.

9. The referral agent holds the practitioner accountable for treatment outcomes, and in some instances may participate in the development and implementation of the treatment plan.

10. The referral agent must maintain some passing familiarity with presenting problems, effective treatments, and available practitioners in order to optimize his or her own effectiveness and maintain credibility.

11. The referral agent helps maintain the practitioner's status, credibility, and well-being in maintaining a reliable flow of referrals for treatment, publicizing past accomplishments and cures, and answering inquiries about the practitioner's services.

12. The referral agent helps to bridge the gaps between patient and practitioner regarding differences in modes of comprehension of the problem and its treatment. Modern and traditional perspectives are often incompatible and require reconciliation and translation from one perspective into the other.

13. The referral agent serves as a contractor between patient and practitioner, implicitly or explicitly setting the rules and expectations for treatment. He or she may even negotiate the fee for the practitioner's services, arrange appointments, provide transportation and other incidentals required to initiate the treatment.

14. The referral agent serves as a guide to the practitioner in regard to the local beliefs and customs of the patient population.

15. The referral agent serves as cotherapist in treatment, collaborating with patient and practitioner to ensure optimal outcomes.

Any or all of the above functions may be descriptive of the role of referral agents in both modern and traditional cultural contexts. For those of us who aspire to deliver the benefits of modern health services to traditional cultures, an awareness of these functions will certainly enhance our effectiveness. Clearly, the absence of a network of referral agents that meaningfully links a segment of society with providers of service results in little or no uptake or integration of those services and their presumed health benefits.

It seems quite sensible, then, that establishing productive liaisons with referral agents should be an integral part of any plan to achieve the successful delivery of health services, in this or any other culture. Let us consider some of the means by which this is achieved.

ESTABLISHING A NETWORK OF REFERRAL AGENTS

In modern societies there are numerous (and some fairly obvious) ways to develop or patch into a network of referral agents, with many parallels to "traditional" societies:

1. The practitioner must first establish a location for the delivery of services. This place of operation must be accessible to the patient population that will be served and to the referral agents controlling access to that population. As in business, location is critically important, and should be chosen with great care as well as sensitivity to the community served.

2. It is customary to inform the public of the availability of one's services, as well as one's credentials and qualifications to provide services. In modern societies, a fair degree of propriety exists in these regards. Formal announcements, notices, introductions, and solicitations are common practice, as are phone calls to prospective referral agents in the same and related disciplines. Public speaking engagements, workshops, volunteered services, follow-up contacts acknowledging referrals and reporting progress thereupon are also commonplace. In traditional societies these methods may require considerable modification so as to accommodate the expectancies and physical realities of the culture.

3. It is important to establish a presence in the community independent of one's professional role. Contributing to the common good of the people via volunteer work, advocating popular causes, participating in community functions, and the like greatly reduces the suspicion with which outsiders are viewed and facilitates the integration of the provider and his or services into the community.

4. Patients who are successfully treated by the practitioner often become an important source of referrals, especially for problems similar to their own. Handling the patient with sensitivity and respect maximizes the likelihood of subsequent referrals.

5. In order to facilitate referrals, the provider of service should attempt to reduce the perception of differences between her- or himself and the patients that would discourage the uptake of her or his services (e.g., language, dress, manner, lifestyle, espoused beliefs, etc.). Conversely, the practitioner should attempt to enhance the perception of critical differences that may relate to positive expectations for treatment (e.g., knowledge, training, status, power, etc.).

6. The modern practitioner should undertake a careful study of the traditional culture one intends to service and its dynamics. The practitioner should attempt to forge alliances with indigenous providers of treatment in traditional cultures and embrace and be accepted by them as colleagues rather than competitors. He or she should share responsibility with them in providing treatment, and divide the labors of treatment according to the likelihood of successful outcome. Improvements in treatment outcomes

should be allowed to enhance the status of the indigenous provider, the practitioner, and the referral agent alike. This is preferable to the alienation, disenfranchisement, and culture shock that so frequently accompany dramatic changes in societies.

7. It is often quite possible to actively develop referral agents through training programs in which potential agents are prepared to function in some paraprofessional capacity. In providing lower level health services and recognizing conditions beyond their expertise, these agents are encouraged to make referrals with the assurance of cooperation by the practitioner, and are rewarded for their services. In many underdeveloped countries, where modern practitioners are scarce, the use of indigenous paraprofessionals has greatly facilitated the uptake and distribution of modern medical services. Such arrangements work nicely in isolated subcultures of developed nations as well.

8. The publication of research and clinical work in professional journals and books, informative articles, and personal profiles or interviews in magazines and newspapers are also effective, though less frequent, methods of announcing the availability of services. Such opportunities may be far more limited in traditional cultures, where word of mouth may be the local equivalent of a newspaper.

9. In this age of mass communication, we now encounter newspaper, radio, and television advertisements for health services that may encourage referrals for treatment and sidestep the usual referral channels. Some providers have even achieved celebrity status by virtue of their appearances on television talk shows and in movies. Unfortunately, many of these celebrities may not represent the best that a profession has to offer. But fortunately, many of these options are not available in traditional cultures. It may also be inadvisable to go direct in offering services to traditional cultures, as such tactics may be poorly received.

10. Many health services have preferred provider arrangements or may actually employ health professionals to service their subscribers. These services effectively constrain referrals to the participating providers by reducing the cost to the patient in using their approved physicians. Analogous situations may exist in traditional cultures, where a powerful or prestigious individual or organization controls the referral process.

11. Many community service and religious organizations, by virtue of their mission, regularly make referrals to independent professionals. In modern societies, many organizations run telephone hotlines and outreach programs that target specific health service needs and facilitate the recognition and treatment of various types of problems (e.g., alcohol, drug abuse). These vital services offer suggestions on where to go for help and frequently make direct referrals to participating practitioners.

12. Clinics and agencies often serve as training programs for beginning professionals who have not yet established an independent network of re-

ferral agents (allowing them to establish a name, reputation, and contacts that follow into independent practice). A similar apprenticeship arrangement may be feasible in traditional cultural contexts.

13. With the high level of specialization and division of labor so prevalent in the modern medical establishment, a careful match of treatment methodology with symptomatology often requires collaboration of two or more professionals or paraprofessionals and the referral source. Such collaborative ventures often develop new sources of referrals for the practitioner, and may be quite workable options in traditional cultures.

14. The practice of paying a fee to a referring agent for making a referral has been commonplace in the legal profession in this country for quite some time. Though such fee splitting has been frowned upon as unprofessional in health care circles, recent actions by the Federal Trade Commission have opposed the use of ethical codes by professional associations to condemn the practice, so it is likely to become more commonplace in the future. In some traditional cultures, a fee or token of appreciation may be expected in acknowledgement of a referral.

There are certainly plenty of places to plug in to the system of health care delivery in any culture. Yet accounts of the failures of modern medicine to achieve acceptance persist in the recent literature. There is clearly a demonstrable need for systematic research on referral practices in traditional cultures.

OVERCOMING RESISTANCE

Perhaps the greatest obstacle to the uptake of modern health services is our own narrow, scientific perspective on what we do.

As a graduate student back in the 1960s, I attended a series of case conferences at a local state mental hospital, and most of the patients presented were chronic schizophrenics or intractable depressives. I was impressed with the cognitive and emotional states of the patients reviewed and their seeming inaccessibility to the rational methods of psychotherapy. At the conclusion of the meeting, I half-jokingly suggested to the chief psychologist that what this place really needed was a good faith healer. He was clearly not amused by the remark, and, needless to say, a healer was never hired by the hospital. Yet it's entirely possible that some of these patients would have fared better with an alternative practitioner of the healing arts.

It seems as though a certain inflexibility has crept into modern medicine, such that its practitioners regard what they do as having an aura of absolute truth or objective reality to it, whereas shamans, which we insist on squeezing out of the health service arena, are derogated as witch doctors and perceived as relying on superstitious rituals and beliefs that presumably have no basis in fact. Of course, objective verification procedures and standards of evidence are the choice of those advocating their own versions of reality, so it should come as no surprise that these measures often support their claim to superiority. The arrogance of this posture encourages non-cooperation with these strange modern methodologies by indigenous practitioners.

It would appear that the dissociation of modern medicine from religious and spiritual modes of comprehension has been an obstacle to its acceptance in traditional cultures where religion and medicine are not clearly differentiated. Attributions of cause and effect are frequently incompatible for modern and traditional practitioners, and the anticipated uptake of our services is not forthcoming. Perhaps this has been somewhat less of a problem for mental health services because the spiritual aspects of treatment are retained to a greater degree in modern practice and perceived differences in approach are less dramatic.

Healing must be viewed in the broader cultural context as both a physical and a spiritual phenomenon. The modern health practitioner is heir to a legacy of healing arts that extends back to antiquity. Rather than deny and resist the wealth of insight into the nature of humankind and its spirit inherent in this tradition, we should embrace it and learn from it. We must accommodate traditional medical approaches and collaborate with their practitioners if we are to achieve success in integrating modern medicine and its benefits with traditional cultures.

14

Cultural and Psychological Influences on Mental Health Issues for Chinese Americans

Diana Chen

Cultural background plays an important role in the shaping of one's world-views, personality traits, manifestation of problems, and adaptation style. In the United States, sensitivity toward cultural influences on mental health issues flourished in the 1960s and 1970s. Along with this development, attention has been placed on how classical models of treatments can be modified to better serve the needs of minority groups, counteracting prior bias toward minority members as poor candidates for psychotherapy.

The trend of cross-cultural research on mental health supports the notion of cultural relativism. Berk and Hirata (1973) refer to cultural relativism as a group's conception of normality; whether a person gets labeled as "ill" or "abnormal" will be a function of that group's standard or conception of normality. In addition, groups differ in their tolerance of and response to deviance. The current state of research supports a relativistic perspective in studying mental disorders and treatment modalities within the client's cultural context.

In America, the principle of cultural relativity is an outgrowth of the ideology of cultural pluralism, which fosters acceptance and respect of cultural diversity in the society at large (Sue & Moore, 1984). Rappaport (1977) extols the need to respect cultural differences as sources of strength rather than weakness. Cultural pluralism contradicts the assimilation policy of making each cultural group adopt the culture of the mainstream. These polar ideologies have great political ramifications and it is beyond the scope of this chapter to discuss them in detail. Nevertheless, it is important for researchers and practitioners in the field of psychiatry to be aware of how their own outlooks influence their work.

This chapter looks at mental health issues for Chinese Americans from the perspective of cultural relativity. First, it will explore how mental disorders and healing practices are culturally and psychologically defined in the Chinese context, for Chinese Americans brought with them their traditions and beliefs when they immigrated to America. Implications of culturally relevant psychiatric practices will also be discussed, with specific interest on learning how native healing practices can be combined with mainstream psychiatric practices.

The development of psychology and psychiatry in mainland China and Taiwan is a fairly new phenomenon, existing only in the past 25 years. Prior to this, no separate attention was paid to the study of mental illness. Instead, it was fully integrated with physiological problems and treated under the auspices of the traditional medical system. In Chinese culture, the concept of mental illness refers to the more severe pathology such as psychotic behaviors in addition to mental retardation (Kleinman, 1980). Tremendous stigma is attached to mental illness; thus minor psychiatric problems are viewed and treated as medical ailments.

ETIOLOGY OF MENTAL ILLNESS

The Chinese view of the etiology of mental illness comes from two major traditions: the medical approach and folk beliefs and practices.

Medical Approach

Under the traditional medical approach, the most basic conceptualizations of diseases are the polar yin-yang principles (Tan, 1981). Diseases are thought to result from an imbalance of the yin-yang principles in the body. In a wider context, the concept of balance or harmony is the fundamental principle governing both the macrocosm and microcosm in the Taoist tradition (Lin, 1981).

As described by Lin (1981), yin and yang are a pair of polar terms used to describe qualitatively contrasting aspects inherent in the universe. Yin is thought of as the female, the cold, the negative aspect of nature; whereas yang represents the male, the hot, and the positive components. These two polar elements exist in each person and disease arises when the proportions of the two elements become imbalanced. For example, the condition of impotence may be considered to be due to an excess of the yin principle, whereas a headache or a rash may be thought of as due to an excess of the yang principle (Tan, 1981). In addition to delineating the nature of diseases, the yin-yang principles are also applied to categorize food and diet, and medication and herbal medicine. Special diet and herbal medicines are considered to be remedies aimed primarily at the restoration of balance in the body. Significantly, somatic symptoms have been treated under this Chinese medical tradition for centuries.

Mental illness is believed to be caused by five harmful emanations of yin and yang. According to the *Nei-ching* (The Classics of Internal Medicine) (Veith, 1966), the five disturbances are numbness, wildness, insanity, disturbance of speech, and anger. It is believed that excess or deficiency of physiological functions—for example, breathing, eating, bowel movement, sexual activities, physical exercise or exhaustion—can upset the yin-yang balance, thus rendering the person susceptible to mental illness.

Another medical influence is the view that considers internal organs as centers for both physiological and psychological functions. Lin (1981) points out five important centers: heart, kidney, lung, liver, and gallbladder. The heart is regarded as the organ harboring *shen* (spirit or mind), which is the integration center of all psychological functions. Kidney is considered the reservoir of *ching* (essence or energy). When the terms are combined, *ching-shen* denotes mental functioning. The Chinese term for the study of psychiatry is *ching-shen ko*, which if taken literally refers to the study of the functions of heart and kidney. In addition, lung is susceptible to worries and sadness; similarly, stomach and spleen are related to thinking too much. Liver and gallbladder are believed to be especially predisposed to anger.

This medical view inevitably affects Chinese concepts of psychological problems. According to Lin (1981), when a person suffers from psychological difficulties and is aware of his or her emotional state, his or her attention is diverted from affect and channeled to preoccupation with the physiological function of the related body organ. It is important to note that somatization has its roots in the traditional Chinese medical system. Lin further asserts that, contrary to popular assumption, Chinese do not appear to lack psychological awareness; they deal with it differently.

Emotional expression is not totally denied in the Chinese culture, but it does not share the European psychological tradition that extols emotional catharsis as a hallmark of therapeutic cure. Instead, Chinese people follow two main indigenous philosophical traditions of Confucianism and Taoism, whose teachings emphasize maintaining harmony in the social orders and one's relationship with nature. Under these teachings, Chinese people make an effort to avoid excesses of emotions. They value moderation and adjust their emotional states to their social and natural milieus (Lin, 1981). The philosophical teachings of Confucianism and Taoism jointly reinforce the quality of equanimity among Chinese and legitimize suppression as a psychoculturally adaptive coping mechanism (Lin, 1981).

Folk Beliefs

The other major influence on the Chinese view of the origin of mental illness is folk beliefs. Folk beliefs show elements from the indigenous animistic tradition, Buddhism, and Taoism and are based mostly on supernatural causes (Lin, 1981).

Spirit possession is often used to account for the more bizarre symptoms of mental illness when the yin-yang explanation fails. In terms of psychiatric phenomenology, spirit possession states may range from severe hypochondriasis or histrionic overbreathing in hysteria to the psychotic or catatonic states of schizophrenia (Tan, 1981). Treatments can include prayers and offerings at Buddhist temples performed by the family of the mentally ill person, or the afflicted person visiting mediums in the Taoist temple for exorcism (Lin & Lin, 1981; Tseng, 1972). The theory of spirit possession has the beneficial consequence of attaching no blame to the patient, thereby reducing the stigma attached to mental illness (Sidel, 1973).

Other folk beliefs on the causes of mental illness come from moralistic and religious standpoints. Mental illness may be regarded as a punishment for neglecting filial piety or respect owed to ancestors, or regarded as the wrath incurred from gods and ancestors by the patient or family members for wrongdoings done in either present or former lives (Lin & Lin, 1981). One of the most popular folk healing practices in Taiwan is shamanism, which is still available in most of the rural areas. A shaman is called a *tang-ki*, who enters into trance states in which he is possessed by a supernatural power (Lin, 1981). Utilizing the shaman as a medium, the client can consult with supernatural forces such as a god, ghost, or ancestor for instructions in dealing with life problems (Kleinman, 1980). The shaman can also prescribe praying, worshipping ancestors, or changing the location of an ancestor's tomb to restore the proper family functions.

Another common folk practice is *chou-chien*, which literally means "drawing a divine stick" (Tseng, 1975). *Chou-chien* resembles fortune-telling but divine instruction is implied. One goes to the Buddhist temple to worship and then randomly draws one bamboo stick from a container to seek answers to one's questions. Many kinds of questions can be asked, about business, marriage, childbirth, wealth, health, and disease. Upon drawing a stick, the worshiper then gets a divine paper that contains a Chinese poem providing an answer to various problems. In general, the divine papers are characterized by suggestions to be conservative, to be patient, to cultivate oneself, and not to do things that are inappropriate for one's social role and status (Hsu, 1974). From a psychotherapeutic point of view, the interpretations given through this practice provide hope for the worshiper and eliminate anxiety about the future (Tseng, 1975). In addition, this practice reinforces culturally appropriate and adaptive social behaviors.

Tseng (1975) views each of these common practices as having a specialized function. *Chou-chien* or fortune-telling is a form of counseling, advising clients on daily life problems. Traditional herbal medicine treats primarily somatic complaints. These practices have existed for centuries and have proven to be helpful for minor psychological problems. However, for major psychiatric disorders, traditional treatments have not been found as effective.

SHAME

The Chinese family has long represented a microcosm in which its members enjoy social and emotional closeness, stability, and a shared sense of identity and responsibility. A member's triumphs and failures reflect on the family. Thus, within the Chinese family context, the burden of the stigma of mental illness tends to fall more on the family than the afflicted individual (Lin, 1981). In addition, rooted in the cultural views of the etiology of mental disorder, the family may feel ashamed for failing to guide or protect the afflicted individual, or for failing to perform proper ancestral worship (Lin & Lin, 1981). The stigma attached to mental illness originates in the Chinese family's fear of exposing its shame to outsiders (Lin & Lin, 1981). Furthermore, the act of having brought shame upon the family name would also induce a sense of guilt in the head of the household, because such an act violates filial piety, the most essential virtue required in every Chinese family. It is no wonder that families with mentally ill members attempt to deny the existence of mental illness or minimize the problem under a more socially acceptable label such as eccentricity or physical illness. As a result, shame plays an important role in the symptom formation of somatization.

SOMATIZATION

Somatization is the most prevalent form of symptom manifestation in Chinese patients (Lin, Kleinman, & Lin, 1981). The substitution of psychological and emotional concerns in the form of a physical complaint is more culturally acceptable. It removes the blame from the family; at the same time it relieves the associated psychological burden of shame and guilt, and the fear of the stigma of a mental disorder. The most popular term for somatization used in mainland China and Taiwan is "neurasthenia." According to Lin et al. (1981), the term originated with European psychiatrists in the late nineteenth century to label neurotic conditions associated with weakness, lack of energy, sleep disturbance, vague physical symptoms in the absence of organic etiology. The Chinese term for it is *shen-ching shuai-jo*, which literally means "neurological weakness," and it conveys a vague physical malaise. Kleinman (1980) views neurasthenia as the most commonly used label in Taiwan for sanctioning a medical sick role for psychoneurosis and interpersonal problems. The somatic complaint is treated as the primary problem. Usually the diagnosis of neurasthenia is accompanied by a referral to traditional Chinese herbal medicine for treatment.

DEPRESSION

Kleinman (1980) investigated specifically the somatization of dysphoric affect in Taiwan. His work promotes a deeper understanding of the important role culture plays in specific patterning of symptoms and behaviors. In his study of depression, Kleinman notes that Chinese patients rarely complain of depression, anxiety, and related psychological concerns. Instead, Chinese patients go to medical doctors for treatment of the biological concomitants of depression such as insomnia, weight loss, dry mouth, constipation, or loss of energy. There is no Chinese word that describes the dysphoric affect correlated to the Western description of depression. The common Chinese character for depression is *men* which pictorially includes the heart radical enclosed within a doorway radical. The character infers a heart being locked in or suffocating behind a door. Thus in the Chinese experience, depression is communicated with a physical image. Kleinman further notes that in the Chinese language, many words for affective states express emotions in terms of bodily organs, particularly the heart and kidney. A corollary is that there is a relatively impoverished vocabulary for psychological concerns in the Chinese language. Kleinman ventures to suggest that depressive feelings are not simply suppressed and masked with somatization by Chinese and expressed by Americans, but rather they may be experienced as different feelings. The distinctive manifestation of depression in terms of physical symptoms may result in underdiagnosing depression as a clinical entity and improper treatment (Kleinman, 1980; Lin & Lin, 1981).

COPING MECHANISMS

Besides somatization, Kleinman (1980) proposes minimization or denial, dissociation, and displacement as other dominant cognitive coping mechanisms or defenses for managing affective experiences in Chinese culture. Through minimization and displacement, Chinese patients tend to reduce the intensity of dysphoric affect by keeping them undifferentiated and to shift concern from the affect to describing in detail the external situation that generated it. Kleinman also frequently finds denial among Chinese clients. The denial usually involves conscious suppression, as in minimization; sometimes denial appears to be unconscious.

The mechanism of dissociation is frequently associated with unconscious denial. Kleinman (1980) describes dissociation as a range of coping practices by which affect is separated from consciousness, cognition, behavior, or the specific stimuli provoking it. An example of dissociation is found in hysterical behaviors, including hysterical psychosis. Kleinman observes that some Chinese clients, without prior major psychopathology, exhibit strong affect only during a trance at the shamans' shrines. Kleinman concludes that trance behaviors are culturally sanctioned mechanisms that permit the release of otherwise strong, unacceptable, and deeply disturbing affects that cannot simply be suppressed or displaced.

Kleinman postulates that the above-mentioned coping mechanisms used by the Chinese all function to reduce or block introspection as well as direct expression of dysphoric affects. Instead, affects are channeled into somatic, situational, or dissociated behaviors.

CHINESE AMERICANS

The aforementioned Chinese cultural and psychological influences on mental health issues continue to be a pervasive force that affect the pattern of help-seeking behaviors of Chinese living in the United States. Researchers (Ho, 1976; Tsai, Teng & Sue, 1981) continue to find that traditional belief systems about mental health and cultural influences regarding shame and stigma play an important role in Chinese underutilization of mental health services in America. Tsai et al. (1981) cite several other reasons for the underutilization of services: availability of alternative resources such as reliance on family, kinship, and herbalists; cost of mental health services; and lack of proximate bilingual services.

Among the small proportion of individuals who seek psychiatric help, there is also evidence supporting the notions that Chinese Americans exhibit greater somatic complaints and higher severity in disorders than non-Asians (Sue & McKinney, 1975; Sue & Sue, 1972). The finding of a higher severity in disorders among Chinese Americans does not necessarily refer to a higher incidence of psychopathology among this particular cultural group. Instead, it may reflect a cultural stigma toward mental illness and a subsequent pattern of help-seeking that only the most severely disturbed Chinese individuals seek psychiatric services.

PATTERN OF HELP-SEEKING BEHAVIOR

The only available study on the pattern of Chinese help-seeking behavior is the Vancouver study (Lin, Tardiff, Donetz & Goresky, 1978), which shows how Chinese families handle a mentally sick member of the family. Five phases of help-seeking behaviors are outlined: (1) exclusive intrafamilial coping; (2) inclusion of certain trusted outsiders in the intrafamilial attempt at coping; (3) consultation with outside helping agencies, physicians, and finally a psychiatrist while keeping the patient at home; (4) the labeling of mental illness and a subsequent series of hospitalizations; and (5) scapegoating and rejection (Lin & Lin, 1981). The pattern shows the extreme delay of a Chinese family in seeking psychiatric help for the mentally afflicted member. The Chinese family would utilize all alternative resources before consulting a psychiatrist or other mental health professional. It is no wonder that by the time the patients reach a psychiatric service, they show severe symptomology and a protracted course of illness. Serious mental disorders often represent the majority of cases seen in psychiatric hospitals and clinics.

Other types of mental problems such as depression, neurosis, and psychosomatic diseases are underrepresented in mental health services because either these are not regarded as mental illness, or they are considered as physical illnesses treated by other physicians (Lin & Lin, 1981). There are other underrepresented psychological problems confronted by Chinese Americans that pertain to their unique experience of being an immigrant group transplanted in the American culture. The new and recent immigrants first face economic, linguistic, and social problems. Then as acculturation progresses, other problems become prominent: cultural, value, and identity conflicts; erosion of the close-knit extended family; intergenerational conflict marked by a cultural gap between traditional grandparents and parents, and Americanized English-speaking children; as well as changes in the traditional male-female role relationship. Societal racism and prejudice that restrict the availability of social services, economic resources, and advancement can further create stress and mental health problems (Cheung & De Rios, 1982).

TREATMENT

In the past 15 years, the focus on service delivery has been on establishing independent bilingual and bicultural mental health facilities for Chinese Americans. These are clinics that are located within communities with concentrated Chinese populations. To meet the need for inpatient admission, two hospitals, San Francisco General Hospital and Elmhurst Hospital in New York City, have separate psychiatric wards specifically for Asian Americans.

At present, community clinics fall into two service models: a multiservice center model and the community mental health clinic model. A multiservice center usually provides bilingual mental health as well as medical, social, recreational, and legal services. One advantage of the comprehensive care system is that less stigma may be attached to mental health treatment when it is an integral part of total care. This type of facility is particularly helpful to the recent Chinese immigrants. The other model, the community mental health clinic, although not comprehensive in nature, provides referral resources to other community programs (Cheung & De Rios, 1982).

There is a growing interest in developing a new model of combining native healing methods with mainstream psychiatric practices. On a small scale, acupuncture has been tried with some success and added into the Western treatment model for alcoholism and drug addiction. However, no model exists yet in integrating traditional Chinese methods and Western services as complementary treatments for other mental disorders. The alignment between traditional and modern treatments can be beneficial in lessening the stigma toward mental disorders.

Traditional and Western practices have coexisted in Chinese American communities. However, the lack of understanding of each other's practices among the different types of providers results in problems of misdiagnoses, lack of appropriate referral, and inadequate care for Chinese Americans. The responsibility would lie with the collective effort of providers to implement more effective services for the community. Sue and Morishima (1982) suggest an idea of a community network composed of community leaders, academicians, researchers, practitioners, administrators, folk healers, and consumers to collaborate in forming and improving community mental health services.

Since information on a Chinese integrative model is deficient, it is important to learn from existing integrative models utilized by other cultural groups. Ruiz and Langrod (1976) describe an interesting liaison program at the Lincoln Community Mental Health Center in New York City, where psychiatrists and spiritual healers can work together to provide more effective services to an Hispanic community. As part of the liaison program, a number of the locally well-known mediums were hired as community mental health workers. At the same time a preservice training program was designed to familiarize the clinical staff at the center with the approaches utilized by folk healers, as well as cultural values and traditions of Puerto Ricans and blacks in the United States. In turn, the spiritualists attended seminars about psychiatric diagnostic techniques and medical resources for referral and backup. This type of mutual sharing and learning can enhance and improve the collaborative efforts to unify treatments.

Also worth studying are the changes in the treatment of mental illness in other Chinese cultures. Mainland China and Taiwan are coming up with innovative ideas of incorporating Western techniques with their traditional medicine. For example, in mainland China acupuncture has been used along with Western drug therapy to relieve associated symptoms of schizophrenia, such as of excitement, catatonia, and depression (Sidel, 1973). Acupuncture has been considered as a major method of treatment in lowering the relapse rate. In a study of 157 cases of schizophrenia for one year at the Shanghai Mental Hospital, 74.5 percent of the patients were cured or much improved with acupuncture (Sidel, 1973). Without acupuncture treatment, there was a 70 percent relapse rate. In addition, the milieu of the inpatient environment, which stresses self-reliance and mutual help among patients, occupational therapy, community and family support, and the teachings of Mao Tse-Tung, help motivate patients to fight their diseases (Sidel, 1973).

Another example is the use of Chinese herbal medicine along with Western medicine. The latter is considered useful for critical conditions but often has debilitating side effects; thus one can benefit from the use of herbal medicine, which is considered to revitalize and strengthen a person's constitution (Topley, 1976).

In terms of psychotherapy treatment, a system of psychotherapy indigenous to the Chinese has yet to be developed. The psychoanalytic, insight- or feeling-oriented therapies have not been found to be effective with Chinese Americans (Sue & Morishima, 1982; Sue, Wagner, Ja, Margullis & Lew, 1976). Techniques of asking questions of a highly personal nature, asking the patients to reflect on feelings, and making interpretations may induce a great deal of discomfort and shame and may result in the premature termination of treatment (Sue & Morishima, 1982). These techniques contradict a culture that values self-control, restraint over strong emotions and morbid thoughts, conformity, and respect for parental or authority figures.

Some writers suggest the need to devise modified techniques that are consistent with the client's culture and experiences in order to facilitate psychotherapy. Therapy that utilizes strategies that are more structured, supportive, directive, and geared toward problem solving are more effective than insight-oriented techniques (Kleinman, 1980; Sue & Morishima, 1982).

For those clients who have no previous experience with psychotherapy, a pretherapy orientation is advised to reduce client's anxiety and resistance toward treatment (Ho, 1976; Sue & Morishima, 1982). A pretherapy orientation would include information about the therapy process, expectations, and nature of the therapeutic relationship.

The establishment of trust is paramount in the therapeutic relationship with Chinese clients. Trust is needed to overcome strong cultural barriers to psychotherapy such as shame, somatization, and lack of disclosure. Ho (1976) suggests that setting only short-term goals with attainable, concrete results during the beginning of treatment can help a client establish trust and confidence in the process. Once trust is developed, the client can work on long-term goals or more dynamic issues.

Sue and Morishima (1982) suggest three attributes in therapists that are important on working with Asian Americans: knowledge of client's culture, experience in working with these individuals, and the ability to apply one's knowledge and experience. The emphasis here is that knowledge of the client's culture alone is inadequate; the therapist has to be able to apply it in a clinical setting. For instance, in working with family conflicts, it is important for the therapist to understand and respect culturally prescribed roles and relationships. The Chinese response to parental authority is traditionally expected to be obedient and compliant. Thus, if a client suffers a conflict regarding parental demand, guiding the client toward behavior rebelliously toward parental authority may be countertherapeutic. It may increase rather than resolve the client's problem (Tseng, 1972).

CONCLUSION

The movement toward improving mental health care for Chinese Americans is still in its infancy. Much work lies ahead in increasing and improving areas of service delivery, treatment modalities, practical and theoretical research, and training, as well as meeting the diverse needs within the Chinese American population. Since available manpower is still small, special recruitment is needed to attract more bilingual people into the various professional paths in the mental health field.

REFERENCES

Berk, B. B. & Hirata, L. C. (1973). Mental illness among the Chinese: Myth or reality? *Journal of Social Issues*, 29(2), 149–166.

Cheung, F. & De Rios, M. D. (1982). Recent trends in the study of the mental health of Chinese immigrants to the United States. *Research in Race and Ethnic Relations*, 3, 145–163.

Ho, M. K. (1976). Social work with Asian Americans. *Social Casework*, March, 195–201.

Hsu, J. (1974). Counseling in the Chinese temple: Psychological study of divination by "chien" drawing. In W. Lebra (Ed.), *Culture and mental health research in Asia and the Pacific*. Honolulu: University of Hawaii Press.

Kleinman, A. (1980). *Patients and healers in the context of culture*. Berkeley: University of California Press.

Lin, K. M. (1981). Traditional Chinese medical beliefs and their relevance for mental illness and psychiatry. In A. Kleinman & T. Y. Lin (Eds.), *Normal and abnormal behavior in Chinese culture*. Holland: D. Reidel.

Lin, K. M., Kleinman, A. & Lin, T. Y. (1981). Overview of mental disorders in Chinese cultures: Review of epidemiological and clinical studies. In A. Kleinman & T.TY. Lin (Eds.), *Normal and abnormal behavior in Chinese culture*. Holland: D. Reidel.

Lin, T. Y. & Lin, M. C. (1981). Love, denial, and rejection: Responses of Chinese families to mental illness. In A. Kleinman & T. Y. Lin (Eds.), *Normal and abnormal behavior in Chinese culture*. Holland: D. Reidel.

Lin, T. Y., Tardiff, K., Donnetz, G. & Goresky, W. (1978). Ethnicity and patterns of help-seeking. *Culture, Medicine and Psychiatry*, 2, 3–13.

Rappaport, J. (1977). *Community psychology: Values, research, and action*. San Francisco: Holt, Rinehart and Winston.

Ruiz, P. & Langrod, J. (1976). Psychiatrists and spiritual healers: Partners in community mental health. In J. Westermeyer (Ed.), *Anthropology and mental health: Setting a new course*. Chicago: Mouton.

Sidel, R. (1973). Mental diseases and their treatment. In J. R. Quinn (Ed.), *Medicine and public health in the People's Republic of China* (DHEW Publication No. NIH 73–67). Washington, DC: U.S. Government Printing Office.

Sue, S. & Mckinney, H. (1975). Asian-Americans in the community mental health care system. *American Journal of Orthopsychiatry, 45*, 111–118.

Sue, S. & Moore, T. (Eds.) (1984). *The pluralistic society: A community mental health perspective*. New York: Human Sciences Press.

Sue, S. & Morishima, J. K. (1982). *The mental health of Asian Americans*. San Francisco: Jossey-Bass.

Sue, D. W. & Sue, S. (1972). Counseling Chinese-Americans. *Personnel and Guidance Journal, 50*(8), 637–644.

Sue, S., Wagner, N., Ja, D., Margullis, C. & Lew, L. (1976). Conceptions of mental illness among Asian and Caucasian-American students. *Psychological Reports, 38*, 703–708.

Tan, E. S. (1981). Culture-bound syndromes among overseas Chinese. In A. Kleinman & T. Y. Lin (Eds.), *Normal and abnormal behavior in Chinese culture*. Holland: D. Reidel.

Topley, M. (1976). Chinese traditional etiology and methods of cure in Hong Kong. In C. Leslie (Ed.), *Asian medical systems: A comparative study*. Berkeley: University of California Press.

Tsai, M., Teng, N. & Sue, S. (1981). Mental health status of Chinese in the United States. In A. Kleinman & T. Y. Lin (Eds.), *Normal and abnormal behavior in Chinese culture*. Holland: D. Reidel.

Tseng, W. S. (1972). Psychiatric study of shamanism in Taiwan. *Archives of General Psychiatry, 26*, 561–565.

───── (1975). Traditional and modern psychiatric care in Taiwan. In A. Kleinman, P. Kunstadter, E. R. Alexander & J. L. Gale (Eds.), *Medicine in Chinese cultures: Comparative studies of health care in Chinese and other societies*. (DHEW Publication No. NIH 75–653). Washington, DC: U.S. Government Printing Office.

Veith, I. (1966). *The Yellow Emperor's classic of internal medicine*. Berkeley: University of California Press.

15

Culture and Health Care: A Review of the Literature and Suggestions for Curriculum Development and Implementation

Lisa Whitten

Although there have been numerous books and articles on the role of culture in health and illness (Conner & Higgenbotham, 1986; Dressler, 1985; Fandetti & Goldmeier, 1988; Hutchinson, 1992; Payne & Ugarte, 1989; Wright, Daleebey, Watts & Lecea, 1983), traditional health beliefs (Kleinman, Eisenberg & Good, 1978), and differences in health care utilization by various racial and ethnic groups (Green, 1988; Pedersen & Paruffati, 1985), research on the knowledge of medical students regarding these topics is limited, as is literature on strategies for teaching and developing curriculum about these concerns. This chapter will focus on the practical application of cultural information to a particular group of health care practitioners: medical students. The relationship between medical training on physical and mental health will be discussed. A review of the literature on teaching and curriculum relevant to the role of culture in health care will be presented, and suggestions regarding strategies for curriculum development and implementation will be offered. Strategies for managing faculty and student resistance to these issues will be addressed.

The relationship between mental health and physical health is well documented. In some cases, emotional disorders are misdiagnosed as physical illness (Stewart, 1990). Further, there is evidence that individuals with mental illness may be more susceptible to physical disorders (Fink, 1990). Many patients present with both physical and psychiatric problems, and physicians must be prepared to treat and diagnose both (Misiaszek, Crago & Potter, 1987). Yet, in the literature, health and mental health are more frequently treated as separate entities. This is beginning to diminish with the trend toward interdisciplinary treatment teams and holistic treatment strategies.

According to Mechanic (1992, p. 1345), "health is a product of culture and social structure, and derives from the belief systems and patterned activities reinforced by the ways of life of particular cultural communities." Mull and Mull (1981, p. 520) assert that "good cross-cultural communication is essential . . . as it forms a basis for both high quality care and optimal learning experiences." It is important for physicians to be more aware of cultural issues because this will enable them to establish rapport and to recognize psychological concerns in their patients. Successful referral to mental health practitioners can be facilitated when physicians have good rapport with their patients.

The other important reason for focusing on health issues and the training of physicians is that mental health practitioners are often responsible for the unit(s) on culture, race, and ethnicity in medical school curricula. It is important for these instructors to be cognizant of the current state of knowledge in medical education in order to impart useful information to these health care providers about culture and mental health.

The following brief examples are illustrative of the need for additional attention to the role of cultural issues in diagnosis, treatment, and prevention:

A third year African-American medical student traveled to Liberia for a two month training session in a rural hospital. After several weeks, she learned that when she asked patients "are you feeling better?" they said no, but if she asked "is it coming down small, small?" they responded in more detail. It appears that this information should have been provided to the student prior to her arrival (Sims, 1987).

Anthropologist Sonia Patten . . . cites the case of a woman from Southeast Asia who complained about pain in her abdomen. The doctor checked the woman for appendicitis. The woman actually was suffering from a genital infection—but she had been taught to refer to the abdomen when having such problems. . . . The doctor was unfamiliar with this aspect of the woman's background (American Association of Family Physicians, 1984).

With regard to the prevention of AIDS in the Dominican Republic, health care workers found limited compliance regarding condom use when they warned men that they might contract an illness. This was probably in conflict with their need to feel strong and powerful. However, when they appealed to the culturally determined importance of the man as protector of his family by stating that he should protect his wife from contamination, condom use increased tremendously (Kreniske, 1990).

RATIONALE FOR CURRICULUM REVISION

It is important for health care providers to obtain training on how to enhance the personhood (Proctor, 1988) and increase the self-worth of their patients. This should occur along with the provision of health care information in order to enhance compliance, and to encourage a healthy doctor-patient relationship. One cannot provide adequate care without knowledge of the individual's attitudes about health and illness, about relationships between caregivers and patients, and about other issues relevant to health care. Given the racial distribution in the United States, people of color are often treated by white physicians, nurses and others. There can be a lack of communication between the patient and the caregiver, which can have serious consequences. Berlin and Fowkes (1983) note that patients who have beliefs that are different from their physicians are often reluctant to discuss their ideas for fear of criticism or ridicule. Training of medical students in cultural issues and communication across cultures can help bridge this gap.

REVIEW OF THE LITERATURE

Although the literature on teaching about culture and health is limited, there are a number of useful articles. Wyatt, Bass, and Powell (1978) conducted a survey of the inclusion by medical schools in the United States of material on culture, and found that there was a serious lack of such curricula. They assert that "the invisibility of the ethnic and sociocultural aspects of medical care in the curricula of health care professional schools creates barriers to an effective health care delivery system for minority group people" (p. 632). Similarly, Poulton, Rylance, and Johnson (1986) found that information on practicing in a multiracial and multicultural society is missing from medical education in Great Britain. Only 11 of 23 schools surveyed included curriculum on the cultural aspects of ethnic minority groups, and it was their opinion that the information that was available to students has been poorly publicized and disseminated. They contend that medical education must play a role in combating racism.

Glastra and Kats (1992) found that some educational films on health care and interethnic relations emphasize the patients' traditional culture as the primary reason for setbacks the patient experiences. They contend that these films should pay more attention to institutional constraints.

According to Kleinman, Eisenberg, and Good (1978), health care practitioners can be ethnocentric and "medicocentric" in their views of health. They assert that health practitioners must free themselves from these views in order to recognize other important issues that have been ignored in the past. They assert that "changes in the interrelation between professional and popular care have the potential for far greater effects on cost, access and satisfaction than changes in professional care alone" (p. 251).

Mull and Mull (1981) found that residents were unfamiliar with the traditional health beliefs of Mexican patients they cared for in a Southern California clinic. The students in the sample saw at least 250 Mexican patient visits each during the year they spent at the clinic. Beliefs that were demonstrated to be held by a large proportion of the Mexican clients were not known by a large proportion of the 30 residents in the sample. Furthermore, the residents' knowledge did not increase as they received more training, and even the Mexicans and other Spanish-speaking residents showed no greater awareness of these beliefs. Mull and Mull assert that medical school faculty often assume that these beliefs will be "picked up" by students during training, and that this is a false belief. They advocate formal curricular material on traditional health beliefs.

Although this study was based on a small sample of residents in a particular location, it demonstrates the need for additional training in this area. One must note that Mexican or Spanish-speaking students might deny knowledge of traditional beliefs for fear of being labeled backward or ignorant. They might have felt that as medical residents, they should only espouse the beliefs of Western medicine.

Berlin and Fowkes (1983) present a cogent model of training in cross-cultural health care based on the acronym LEARN (Listen, Explain, Acknowledge, Recommend, Negotiate). They train residents in what they call a process-oriented model "by which the cultural, social and personal information relevant to a given illness episode can be elicited, discussed and negotiated or incorporated" (p. 938). They state that this is a good approach because it is difficult if not impossible for health care providers to obtain in-depth knowledge about the health beliefs of every population they serve.

Wells, Benson, and Hoff (1985) noted that many medical schools may not include materials on sociocultural aspects because the curriculum is already so full. They designed a workshop for first-year medical students that helps them anticipate the role of these factors in medicine. It is included as part of a six-month required course on human behavior. The topics covered are: a definition of culture and ethnicity; cultural variation in patients' preferences for health care; cultural differences among patients in health, access to care, and use of health services; the formation of prejudice and other social attitudes in both physicians and patients; the impact of the cultural background of the physician and the patient on their relationship (p. 493). Students are encouraged to share information about their own cultural background and health care experiences.

Gonzalez-Lee and Simon (1987) outlined a comprehensive program for preparing second-year medical students for work with Latino populations that includes instruction in Spanish and in overcoming cultural barriers. They operate on the assumption that "effective communication encompasses both linguistic and cultural perceptions of verbal and nonverbal behaviors" (p. 502). The program emphasizes within-group as well as between-group diversity, and assists students in the development of skills that will facilitate understanding of their patients' concerns.

The training programs cited here all emphasize the importance of communication, a thorough knowledge of the culture and history of the people being served, particularly with regard to concepts of health and illness, and the importance of accurate interpretation of the patient's concerns. There are differences regarding the importance of language acquisition and of negotiation with the patient regarding treatment strategies.

CURRICULUM

Curriculum on culture should not be limited to one or two lectures, but should be infused throughout the curriculum. Kleinman, Eisenberg, and Good (1978) are very clear about the fact that cross-cultural studies should be integrated into clinical teaching of medical students. They assert that medical anthropology "enables the student and practitioner to step out of an ethnocentric professional framework and to recognize clinical reality as culturally constructed and pluralistic" (p. 257). They discuss the importance of institutional support for units on culture and health care.

To accomplish curricular reform, clinical social science requires administrative support, curriculum time, and budget allocations for both teaching faculty and research. To be effective, programs must be integrated with departments of internal medicine and surgery as well as psychiatry. . . . The danger of pedagogic isolation remains, however. Medical practice will benefit from social science only to the extent that social science becomes a clinical discipline and is taught in the context of patient care (p. 257).

Kleinman et al. also assert that house officers and students should routinely be reviewed on their ability to assess the patient's model of the illness, which is a core clinical function (p. 256). Students should be taught to differentiate and distinguish between the beliefs and value systems of the patient and the doctor, and should be taught to communicate the medical model to students.

Medical trainees should also be exposed to a wide range of other issues with regard to the social and cultural context of health and illness, including the following:

1. An understanding of racism (individual and institutional) and its impact on treatment decisions and on the lives of patients and students and people in general.

2. A review of the history, sociology, and psychology of the groups treated in the hospital/clinics students will work in during their training.

3. A review of some of the notions of the populations being treated about health and illness and how these can be compared to the views of the students. It is important to keep in mind that value judgments should be avoided. Students

should be taught the distinction between cultural difference and cultural deviance, and the notion of victim blaming (Ryan, 1976).

4. A review and correction of some of the destructive myths regarding the populations being served.

5. Techniques for establishing rapport with culturally different patients.

6. A recognition that while certain patterns exist, generalizations and assumptions should be avoided.

7. Encouragement to continue to examine their own and their clients' beliefs.

Students and faculty must be taught to be wary of broad generalizations regarding the patients they treat. For example, there is tremendous intragroup variation among African Americans regarding the degree to which they identify as black or African. This can influence the degree to which their attitudes and behavior conform to some cultural expectations. The processes of acculturation and accommodation in many ethnic groups and in immigrant populations can have an effect on the adherence to folk beliefs and other beliefs about health and illness. Students must recognize that while certain trends exist, they will encounter departures from or variations on these patterns within groups in addition to many similarities between groups. This overlap does not mean that differences between groups are unimportant or insignificant.

PEDAGOGY

Pedagogy related to culture and health care should move beyond the traditional lecture format. Students can benefit from participation in role-playing exercises, collaborative learning exercises, and other structured and semi-structured activities to facilitate learning. Ideally, groups will be multicultural, and instructors will come from a broad range of cultural/racial/ethnic backgrounds. Ongoing supervision must continually address these issues. A multidisciplinary approach will be needed in order to accomplish this task.

SMALL GROUP EXERCISES

Small group exercises can be useful to encourage students to think critically about culture and health. Possible exercises involve having students:

1. Generate a variety of questions that will elicit patients' beliefs about health and illness.

2. Discuss the traditional health beliefs of their own cultural/racial/ethnic/religious group.

3. Role-play an interaction with a patient from a different cultural group. Video-

tape and analyze the interaction with special attention to both verbal and non-verbal communication.

4. Generate ways of negotiating with patients' medical treatments that integrate traditional health beliefs.

5. Analyze folklore and/or autobiographies (Griffith, 1981) to understand the importance of culture in human development and to analyze attitudes about health and illness.

USEFUL JOURNALS FOR PRACTITIONERS INTERESTED IN CULTURE AND HEALTH/MENTAL HEALTH

American Journal of Orthopsychiatry

American Psychologist

Cross-Cultural Research

Culture, Medicine and Psychiatry

Ethnicity and Disease

Journal of Behavioral Medicine

Journal of Black Psychology

Journal of Cross-Cultural Psychology

Journal of Medical Education

Medical Anthropology Quarterly

Medical Education

Psychological Medicine

Radical Teacher

Social Science and Medicine

Social Work

Sociology of Health and Illness

Western Journal of Medicine

Women and Health Care International

World Psychology

SUGGESTED STEPS TOWARD IMPLEMENTATION

In order to move the curriculum toward greater sensitivity to cultural issues, there are a number of stages a program should consider:

1. Review the current curriculum for inclusion of materials relevant to race, culture, and ethnicity.

2. Assess the ethnic and racial characteristics of the patients with whom students come in contact during their training. Training on culture should focus on this group while providing guiding principles that can be applied to understanding the role of culture for all people.

3. Survey patients about their experiences with same race/ethnicity and different race/ethnicity caregivers. This can be useful even if it is only a pilot study.

4. Survey students about what they would like to learn and about situations in which they felt that cultural differences influenced their interaction with and/or feelings about the patient, and/or the care a patient received.

5. Infuse material relevant to the populations being served into the curriculum.

6. Clearly state the emphasis on culture and other issues of diversity in the school's mission statement and in the catalog. This could potentially aid the recruitment

of students and faculty who are people of color or from other diverse or underrepresented groups.

7. Evaluate the cultural component of the curriculum on an ongoing basis.

8. Encourage in students respect for professionals from a wide range of disciplines.

CHALLENGES RELATED TO IMPLEMENTATION OF CURRICULAR CHANGE

Administrators can expect resistance to these kinds of curricular revisions. Berlin (1969, p. 115) notes that mental health professionals resist change because "such change may reduce their status, financial return, sense of personal satisfaction and feeling of competency." These issues must be addressed with faculty in order for curriculum implementation to be effective. Faculty might complain that they already have too much content to cover, that the issues are unimportant, and that they are irrelevant to the work of physicians—that is, psychologists or social workers should deal with these concerns. These beliefs often grow out of lack of knowledge regarding the impact of culture on health and health care, and anxiety about lack of skill regarding teaching in these areas. To manage faculty resistance to curricular revision, administrators can publicly reward students and faculty who conduct research on and attend or present at conferences on these topics. In addition, training can be provided on how to teach about race and culture.

Faculty development workshops can be planned within previously scheduled faculty, department, and/or grand rounds presentations in order to facilitate attendance. Guest speakers can be invited to explore these issues and to provide concrete information, ideas, and materials that can be incorporated into existing curriculum. Ongoing evaluation of the extent to which faculty are integrating notions about culture into their lectures, and the effectiveness of their presentations, should be conducted. Gessner, Katz, and Schimpfhauser (1981) outline a useful institutional strategy for curricular change that involved the appointment of a dean of multidisciplinary education.

Another form of resistance occurs in departments that are more homogeneous culturally. Faculty might argue that everyone is the same in their service, therefore culture is not a factor. Faculty and students should be assisted in recognizing the variations between individuals regarding their conceptions of health, illness, and help-seeking, even if the group is racially homogenous. Ideas and values might vary along religious, ethnic, gender, sexual preference, or class lines.

The presentation and discussion of this material can result in some strong emotional reactions that must be managed in order for learning to take place. Often, victim blaming can occur and this must be explained as counterproductive to the helping process. Students and faculty can sabotage efforts to introduce new ideas and concepts into the curriculum. Whitten (1993) outlines a number of emotional reactions that students and faculty might have to discussions of race and culture, as well as many useful strategies for constructively handling these reactions.

CONCLUSIONS

The strategies outlined here in relation to race and culture can be applied to the curricular and pedagogical issues related to diversity, such as age, class, disability, sexual preference, and gender. Depending on the particular population being treated, these concerns should receive more or less attention. Instituting curricular change of this type is not easy. Convincing some students and faculty that it is crucial to cover material of this type can be a tedious process. It can be helpful if administrators and faculty view curricular/institutional change as an ongoing process that will require time. In the long run, sensitive attention to cultural issues and a stronger linkage between mental health practitioners and physicians could facilitate the enhancement of medical training and health care for all people.

REFERENCES

American Association of Family Physicians (1984). Family doctors use extra skills to treat cross-cultural patients. *AAFP Reporter, 11*(9), 1–4.

Berlin, E. A. & Fowkes, W. C. (1983). A teaching framework for cross-cultural health care, application in family practice. *Western Journal of Medicine, 139*, 934–938.

Berlin, I. N. (1969). Resistance to change in mental health professionals. *American Journal of Orthopsychiatry, 39*, 109–115.

Connor, L. H. and Higginbotham, N. (1986). An integrated sociocultural curriculum for community medicine in Bali, Indonesia. *Social Science and Medicine, 23*, 673–682.

Dressler, W. W. (1985). The social and cultural context of coping: Action, gender and symptoms in a southern Black community. *Social Science and Medicine, 21*, 499–506.

Fandetti, D. V. & Goldmeier, J. (1988). Social workers as culture mediators in health care settings. *Health and Social Work, 13*, 171–179.

Fink, Per (1990). Physical disorders associated with mental illness: A register investigation. *Psychological Medicine, 20*(4), 829–834.

Gessner, P. K., Katz, L. A. & Schimpfhauser, F. T. (1981). Sociomedical issues in the curriculum: A model for institutional change. *Journal of Medical Education, 56*, 987–993.

Glastra, F. J. & Kats, E. (1992). Culturalizing the ethnic patient: Educational films and images of interethnic relations in health care. *Health Education Research*, Special issue on qualitative research. 7(1), 187–186.

Gonzalez-Lee, T. & Simon, H. J. (1987). Teaching Spanish and cross-cultural sensitivity to medical students. *Western Journal of Medicine, 146,* 502–504.

Green, E. C. (1988). Can collaborative programs between biomedical and African indigenous health practitioners succeed? *Social Science and Medicine, 27,* 1125–1130.

Griffith, E. E. (1981). The black autobiography as a teaching tool in psychiatry. *Journal of Medical Education, 56,* 404–408.

Hutchinson, J. (1992). AIDS and racism in America. *Journal of the National Medical Association, 84*(2), 119–124.

Kleinman, A., Eisenberg, L. & Good, B. (1978). Culture, illness, and health care: Clinical lessons from anthropologic and cross-cultural research. *Annals of Internal Medicine, 88*(2), 251–258.

Kreniske, J. (1990). Social and political factors affecting AIDS transmission in the Third World: Focus on the Dominican Republic. Presentation at the May 1990 Faculty Development Symposium, SUNY/College at Old Westbury.

Mechanic, David. (1992). Health and Illness behavior and patient-practitioner relationships. *Social Science and Medicine. 34*(12), 1345–1350.

Misiaszek, John, Crago, Marjorie & Potter, Rebecca (1987). Patients with combined physical and psychiatric problems. *Psychosomatics, 28*(12), 622–631.

Mull, J. D. & Mull, D. S. (1981). Residents' awareness of folk medicine beliefs of their Mexican patients. *Journal of Medical Education, 56,* 520–522.

Payne, K. W. & Ugarte, C. A. (1989). The office of minority health resource center: Impacting on health related disparities among minority populations. *Health Education, 20,* 6–8.

Pedersen, D. & V. Paruffati (1985). Health and traditional medicine cultures in Latin America and the Caribbean. *Social Science and Medicine, 21,* 5–12.

Poulton, J., Rylance, G. W. & Johnson, M. R. (1986). Medical teaching of the cultural aspects of ethnic minorities; Does it exist? *Medical Education, 20,* 492–497.

Proctor, Samuel (1988). Keynote speech at the National Conference on Black Student Retention in Higher Education, New York, November.

Ryan, W. (1976). *Blaming the victim* (rev. ed.). New York: Vintage.

Sims, L. (1987). Personal communication, October.

Stewart, Donna (1990). Emotional disorders misdiagnosed as physical illness: Environmental hypersensitivity, candidiasis hypersensitivity, and chronic fatigue syndrome. *International Journal of Mental Health, 19*(30), 55–68.

Wells, K., Benson, M. C. & Hoff, P. (1985). Teaching cultural aspects of medicine. *Journal of Medical Education, 60,* 493–495.

Whitten, L. (1993). Managing student reactions to controversial topics in the college classroom. *Transformations, 4*(1), 30–44.

Wright, R., Daleebey, D., Watts, T. & Lecea, P. (1983). *Transcultural perspectives in the human services.* Springfield, IL: Charles C. Thomas.

Wyatt, G. E., Bass, B. A. & Powell, G. J. (1978). A survey of ethnic and sociocultural issues in medical school education. *Journal of Medical Education, 53,* 627–632.

Index

About the Contributors

HELMUT E. ADLER is Professor Emeritus at Yeshiva University. He is the translator of *Elements of Psychophysics*, Volume 1 by Gustav Theodor Fechner; is co-editor (with Robert Rieber) of *Aspects of the History of Psychology in America, 1892–1992* (copublished by The New York Academy of Sciences and the American Psychological Association, 1994); and has participated in many national and international conferences and symposia as presenter, organizer, or chairman.

LEONORE LOEB ADLER is the Director of the Institute for Cross-Cultural and Cross-Ethnic Studies and Professor Emerita in the Department of Psychology at Molloy College, Rockville Centre, New York. She was recently elected to the American Psychological Association's Committee on International Relations in Psychology. She conducts cross-cultural research and has organized meetings and presented papers both nationally and internationally. Dr. Adler has published over 70 professional papers and chapters and is the author, editor, or coeditor of 14 books, most recently *Women in Cross-Cultural Perspective* (Praeger, 1991); *The International Handbook on Gender Roles* (Greenwood Press, 1993); *Cross-Cultural Topics in Psychology* (with Uwe P. Gielen) (Praeger, 1994); and *Violence and the Prevention of Violence* (with Florence L. Denmark) (Praeger, 1995).

JOHN BEATTY is a Professor of Anthropology at Brooklyn College of the City University of New York. He has held Invited Professorships at the

Universität des Saarlandes in Saarbrücken, Germany, and at Ohu University in Koriyama, Japan. Dr. Beatty is the author of six books and has contributed chapters to many edited works.

EDWARD H. BENDIX is a professor at the City University of New York. He has done fieldwork in Nepal, the Caribbean, and New York. His most recent publications are "The Grammaticalization of Responsibility and Evidence," in *Responsibility and Evidence in Oral Discourse* (edited by J. Hill and J. Irvine) and *The Uses of Linguistics*, an edited Annal of The New York Academy of Sciences.

CHARLES V. CALLAHAN is Professor of Psychology at Molloy College, Rockville Centre, New York, where he has developed (with Leonore Loeb Adler) one of the first graduate programs in cross-cultural psychology. He recently coauthored a chapter (with Sergei V. Tsytsarev) for *Violence and the Prevention of Violence* (coedited by Leonore Loeb Adler and Florence L. Denmark) (Praeger, 1995).

DIANA CHEN is a New York State licensed psychologist, at present working as a Senior Psychologist in the Adult Outpatient Psychiatry Services at Woodhull Medical and Mental Health Center. Her research and publications have included areas of political socialization in Communist China, political attitudes of Chinese and Puerto Rican women, Chinese interracial marriage, and mental health issues for Chinese Americans.

SUNEETHA S. de SILVA is a doctoral candidate at Southern Illinois University (SIU) at Carbondale. She works for SIU at Edwardsville, St. Clair County Head Start as Program Development Specialist. She is coauthor of a chapter on Sri Lanka for the *International Handbook on Gender Roles* (edited by Leonore Loeb Adler) (Greenwood Press, 1993).

RAYMOND DiGIUSEPPE is Associate Professor of Psychology and Director of the School Psychology Program at St. John's University, and Director of Professional Education at The Institute for Rational-Emotive Therapy. He holds the Diplomate in Clinical Psychology and the Diplomate in Behavioral Psychology, is a Fellow of the American Psychological Association, and a Member of the Executive Board of the American Board of Behavioral Psychology. Dr. DiGiuseppe is on the editorial boards of three academic journals and is the author of five books and over 40 professional articles and book chapters.

WILLIE J. EPPS, a renowned author and educator, is Director of the East St. Louis Campus of Southern Illinois University at Edwardsville.

MARGARET FISCHER (Ph.D. and J.D.) has been a clinical psychologist in private practice in Alaska since 1978 and is affiliated with the Alaska Psychological Services. She is a member of the Board of Psychologists and Psychological Associates Examiners, and is a recent past president of the International Council of Psychologists. Dr. Fischer is the editor of *Who's Who in International Psychology.*

UWE P. GIELEN is Professor of Psychology at St. Francis College. He is President (1994–95) of the International Council of Psychologists. Dr. Gielen is coeditor (with Leonore Loeb Adler) of *Cross-Cultural Topics in Psychology* (Praeger, 1994) (with L. L. Adler and N. Milgram) of *Psychology in International Perspective* (1992), and coauthor (with L. Kuhmerker and R. Hayes) of *The Kohlberg Legacy for the Helping Professions* (1991). He is the Founding Editor of the journal *World Psychology.*

ELAN GOLOMB is a psychotherapist for individuals and groups and is President of the Division of Social Issues and Cross-Cultural Psychology and Secretary of the Independent Practice Division, both of the New York State Psychological Association. She is the author of *Trapped in the Mirror: Adult Children of Narcissists in Their Struggle for Self*, and is working on a film about "The Oracles of Ladakh."

ANGELA JORGE is an Associate Professor of Spanish language, Hispanic literature, and culture at the State University of New York/College at Old Westbury, where she introduced a course on the ethnoreligious traditions of U.S. Hispanics. She has lectured worldwide on *Espiritismo (Mesa blanca)* and *Santería.* She has recently contributed chapters to Joseph Harris (ed.), *Global Dimensions of the African Diaspora* (1993) and to Kortright Davis and Elias Farajaje-Jones (eds.), *African Creative Expressions of the Divine* (1991).

DAP A. LOUW is Head of the Centre for Behavioural Sciences and Professor in the Department of Psychology at the University of the Orange Free State. He is the author of 12 books that are widely used in South African universities, and serves on the Advisory Board of the Institute for Cross-Cultural and Cross-Ethnic Studies at Molloy College.

PEGGY McGARRAHAN is a medical anthropologist. She has taught at Hunter College, New York City Technical College, Fordham College, and the State University of New York at Purchase. Dr. McGarrahan is the author of *Transcending AIDS.*

NIHAR RANJAN MRINAL is on the faculty of the Department of Psychology at Nagpur University, India. He is a Fellow of the Indian Association of Clinical Psychologists, a Life Member of the Indian Science Congress Association, a Member of the Advisory Board of the Institute for Cross-Cultural and Cross-Ethnic Studies (at Molloy College), and a Member of the International Council of Psychologists. Dr. Mrinal is the post-doctoral recipient of Distinction in Clinical Psychology from the Institute of Psychiatry, Ranchi, India. He is the coauthor (with Uma Singhal Mrinal) of "Tribal Women of India: The Tharu Women," in Leonore Loeb Adler, ed., *Women in Cross-Cultural Perspective* (Praeger, 1991).

UMA SINGHAL MRINAL is Chair of the Department of Psychology at Bhagwandin Arya Kanya Post-Graduate College in India. She is a member of the Advisory Board of the Institute for Cross-Cultural and Cross-Ethnic Studies (at Molloy College), and is the author or coauthor of several articles and book chapters. Dr. Uma S. Mrinal and Dr. Nihar R. Mrinal are both involved in cross-cultural research.

B. RUNI MUKHERJI is Associate Professor of Psychology at the State University of New York College at Old Westbury, where she teaches research methodology, cognitive psychology, and clinical neurophysiology. She has a broad variety of interests, which are reflected in her publications in the areas of cognitive, clinical, and cross-cultural psychology, and in gerontology. She has presented papers in national and international forums, and has served as consultant to a number of projects in the design, development, and implementation of multicultural curriculum for elementary schools.

ALBERT PEPITONE has taught graduates and undergraduates, directed Ph.D. dissertations, and carried out programs of research at the University of Pennsylvania for over four decades. He has published numerous articles, book chapters, and a book. His special interest in the last two decades has been in the specification of the cultural determinants of social cognition and particularly of how beliefs affect the explanation of life events. He has been President of the Division of Personality and Social Psychology of the American Psychological Association, the Society for the Psychological Study of Social Issues, the Society for Cross-Cultural Research, the Society for the Advancement of Field Theory, and Vice President for North America of the Interamerican Society of Psychology.

ENGELA PRETORIUS is a Lecturer in the Department of Sociology at the University of the Orange Free State. She is the coauthor of a monograph and a book on traditional health care in South Africa. She is involved in research on traditional health care in Africa cross-nationally.

MITCHELL W. ROBIN is a licensed New York State Psychologist, an

Associate Professor of Psychology at New York City Technical College, and a Staff Psychotherapist and Fellow of the Institute for Rational-Emotive Therapy (RET). He is the coauthor (with Raymond DiGiuseppe) of the ABSII, a measure of endorsement of irrational beliefs (IBs). His recent research, at the cross-cultural and cross-national levels, deals with RET and IB issues.

C. EDWARD ROBINS practices psychoanalysis and psychotherapy in New York City and is on the faculties of the Institute for Contemporary Psychotherapy, Long Island Institute of Psychoanalysis, and Fordham University. He is an active presenter of Lacan's Theory in New York, Seattle, Buenos Aires, and Italy.

REGINA SPIRES-ROBIN is a Professor of Anthropology at New York City Technical College and is on the faculty at The New School for Social Research. For the past 30 years Prof. Spires-Robin has been engaged in cross-cultural research, with emphasis on indigenous groups in Mexico. The history of healing, the alternative methods of healing, and the efficacy of folklore are subjects of particular concern to her.

LISA WHITTEN is an Associate Professor in the Psychology Program at the State University of New York/College at Old Westbury. She has conducted workshops on curriculum and teaching in the multicultural context. Dr. Whitten served as Eastern Regional Representative for the Association of Black Psychologists and is a Past President of the New York Chapter.